THE
LITURGICAL
YEAR

THE
LITURGICAL
YEAR

its history & its meaning
after the reform of the liturgy

Adolf Adam
translated by Matthew J. O'Connell

A PUEBLO BOOK

The Liturgical Press   Collegeville, Minnesota

Design:
Br. Aelred Seton Shanley

Originally published in Germany
as *Das Kirchenjahr mitfeiern: Seine
Geschichte und seine Bedeutung
nach der Liturgieerneuerung*
© 1979 Verlag Herder
Freiburg im Breisgau.

English translation
© 1981 Pueblo Publishing Company, Inc.,
© 1990 by The Order of St. Benedict, Inc.,
Collegeville, Minnesota.
Published by The Liturgical Press,
Collegeville, Minnesota.

Printed in the United States of America.

ISBN 0-8146-6047-9

CONTENTS

INTRODUCTION

The Church year or, to use the term preferred in Latin documents, the liturgical year is the commemorative celebration, throughout a calendar year, of the saving deeds God accomplished in Jesus Christ. One Church document describes it this way: "The whole mystery of Christ, from his Incarnation to the day of Pentecost and the expectation of his coming again, is recalled by the Church during the course of the year" (GNLYC, no. 17; cf. CL, no. 102).

The term "Church year," which apparently occurs for the first time in German in a *Postille,* or sermon, of the Lutheran pastor Johannes Pomarius (Wittenberg, 1589), should not be interpreted as being a kind of ecclesiastical rival of the "civil year." After all, the "secular time" which the course of a year represents is itself a gift of the Creator, and Christians must accept it, live in it and shape it to their own purposes. Moreover, in this historical time God's saving will makes its presence felt in many forms. In Christ he has entered it in an especially clear and full way, so that all time has become God's time and a time of salvation, since his offer of salvation is directed to all periods of history and all human beings; in other words, it is universal The Church's task is to make known and accessible to all human beings of all times and places the saving work whose foundations have been laid in Christ. She does this in the proclamation of God's word, in the celebration of the sacraments, and in her many pastoral services that are intended to clear the way for faith, hope and love and to promote growth in grace.

The Christian feast, which is the thankful commemoration of the saving acts of Jesus, must be celebrated over and over if it is to perform its function of proclaiming salvation and making it present in each here and now. Given this need, and in order to avoid arbitrariness, it was natural to take advantage of the year as a unit of time that has its basis in the cycles of the cosmos, to give each feast its fixed place in this unit of time, and thus to assure a cyclical repetition of it. The fixing of particular dates in the cycle is suggested to some extent by scripture; for the rest it depends on conventions established in the course of history. In either case, the dates are not so binding as necessarily to exclude corrections and reforms.

It will be clear from what I have said that the celebration of the liturgical year is not to be understood exclusively as a retrospective concentration on a salvation already accomplished. On the contrary, those who already believe and have been redeemed in baptism must focus their efforts on consolidating this salvation, since it is always endangered. At the same time, they must regard themselves as being, in and by means of the liturgical celebration, witnesses to the salvation that is meant for all and as having an obligation to pave the way for its universal acceptance because they have a sense of responsibility for their fellow human beings and of solidarity with them. From both of these points of view the liturgical celebrations of the Church year look not only to the past but to the future as well. They have an eschatological aspect inasmuch as they look forward to the Lord's return and the complete fulfillment he will bring, and they also prepare the way for this coming.

The Church year is thus to be understood as the sum of all the liturgical feasts that have found their set place in the annual cycle. Wherever the liturgy is celebrated, Jesus Christ, the high priest of the new convenant, unites himself with the celebrating community in a common action that is directed to the salvation of believers and the glorification of the heavenly Father (cf. CL, no. 7). Christian faith thus takes concrete and effective form in the liturgical year, and this year becomes the comprehensive self-expression of the Church, while at the same time contributing to the consolidation and building up of Christian life.

Familiarity with the meaning and implementation of the liturgical year seems thus to be an urgent duty, the importance of which can hardly be exaggerated in this age of rampant secularization and widespread ignorance of Christian faith and values. The aim of this book is to explain the present form as well as the theological and spiritual substance of the liturgical year against the background of its historical development and thereby to stimulate Christians to fruitful participation in it. Anyone who celebrates the liturgical year with an intelligent faith experiences, year after year, a synthesis of the Christian message of salvation and a constantly repeated encounter with the Lord who seeks and accomplishes our salvation. Preaching and catechesis (including religious instruction) must endeavor, more than they have in the past, to make Christians informed interpreters of the liturgical cycle. The faithful will thus be helped to feel at home and secure in the Church.

The time seems ripe for a book that synthesizes the old and the new and, notwithstanding its scientific underpinning, proves understandable and readable to people outside the scholarly world.

Lest the book become excessively long, conciseness was required in the historical section and in the description and interpretation of individual Mass Propers. The same is true of bibliographical listings for the work as a whole and for particular questions. A special chapter is devoted to the Church's Liturgy of the Hours, which forms an important part of the liturgy as a whole; the chapter discusses its history, significance and revised form. It was not possible, however, to give well-deserved attention to the individual texts used in the Office during the course of a year, as the planned size of the book would have been substantially increased.

I intend this book as an aid to students of theology but also as a stimulus to preachers, catechists and instructors in religion, as well as the many groups and committees working in Christian communities. My hope is that it will not only increase knowledge but be helpful in achieving a more profound and vital integration into the mystery of Christ.

Mainz   Adolf Adam
                                                      October 1, 1978

ABBREVIATIONS

AAS	*Acta Apostolicae Sedis.* Rome, 1909–
AC	*Antike und Christentum* 1–6 (F. J. Dölger). Münster, 1929–50.
AL	*Archiv für Liturgiewissenschaft.* Regensburg, 1950–
ASS	*Acta Sanctae Sedis.* Rome, 1865–1908.
CCL	*Corpus Christianorum, Series Latina.* Turnhout, 1954–
CL	*Constitution on the Liturgy* of Vatican II (December 4, 1963).
CommALI	*Commentarius in Annum Liturgicum Instauratum,* published by the Consilium for the Implementation of the Constitution on the Sacred Liturgy.
CommNC	*Commentarius in Novum Calendarium,* published by the Consilium.
CSCO	*Corpus Scriptorum Christianorum Orientalium.* Paris, 1903–
CSEL	*Corpus Scriptorum Ecclesiasticorum Latinorum.* Vienna, 1866–
DACL	*Dictionnaire d'Archéologie Chrétienne et de Liturgie.* Paris, 1924–
DS	H. Denzinger and A. Schönmetzer, *Enchiridion symbolorum.* 36th ed. Freiburg, 1976.
EL	*Ephemerides Liturgicae.* Rome, 1887–
GCS	*Die griechischen christlichen Schriftsteller der ersten drei Jahrhunderte.* Leipzig, 1897–
Gd	*Gottesdienst.* Information und Handreichung der Liturgischen Institute Deutschlands, Österreichs und der Schweiz, 1967–
GILH	*General Instruction of the Liturgy of the Hours* (February 2, 1971).
GIRM	*General Instruction of the Roman Missal* (April 6, 1969)
GNLYC	*General Norms for the Liturgical Year and the Calendar* (March 21, 1969)
HD	*Heiliger Dienst.* Published by the Liturgical Institute of the Archabbey of St. Peter, Salzburg. 1947–

HK	*Herder-Korrespondenz.* Freiburg, 1946–
JL	*Jahrbuch für Liturgiewissenschaft.* Münster, 1921–41.
JLH	*Jahrbuch für Liturgik und Hymnologie.* Kassel, 1955–
Lect: Introd	Introduction to the *Lectionary for Mass* (Collegeville, 1970).
LJ	*Liturgisches Jahrbuch.* Münster, 1951–
LQF	*Liturgiegschichtliche Quellen und Forschungen.* Münster, 1909–40, 1957–
LTK	*Lexikon für Theologie und Kirche.* 2nd ed. Freiburg, 1957–67.
MD	*La Maison-Dieu.* Paris, 1945–
OHS	*Ordo hebdomadae sanctae instauratus* (November 16, 1955).
PG	*Patrologia Graeca,* ed. by J.-P. Migne. Paris, 1857–66.
PL	*Patrologia Latina,* ed. by J.-P. Migne. Paris, 1878–90.
PO	*Patrologia Orientalis,* ed. by R. Graffin and F. Nau. Paris, 1903–
RAC	*Reallexikon für Antike und Christentum,* ed. by Th. Klauser. Stuttgart, 1941 (1950)–
RGG	*Die Religion in Geschichte und Gegenwart.* 3rd ed. Tübingen, 1956–
SC	*Sources chrétiennes.* Paris, 1941–
TG	*Theologie und Glaube.* Paderborn, 1909–
TPG	*Theologisch-Praktische Quartalschrift.* Linz a. d. Donau, 1848–
TTZ	*Trierer Theologische Zeitschrift* (until 1944: *Pastor Bonus*). Trier, 1888–
ZAM	*Zeitschrift für Ascese und Mystik* (since 1947: *Geist und Leben*). Würzburg, 1926–
ZKT	*Zeitschrift für Katholische Theologie.* (Innsbruck) Vienna, 1877–

SHORT TITLES OF FREQUENTLY CITED LITERATURE

Auf der Maur
H. J. Auf der Maur, *Die Osterhomilien des Asterios Sophistes als Quelle für die Geschichte der Osterfeier* (Trierer theologische Studien 19; Trier, 1967).

Bihlmeyer
K. Bihlmeyer. *Die Apostolischen Väter.* Neubearbeitung der Funkschen Ausgabe (Tübingen, 1924).

Casel
O. Casel, "Art und Sinn der ältesten christlichen Osterfeier," JL 14 (1938), 1–78. [There is a French translation by J. C. Didier: "La fête de Pâques dans l'Eglise des Pères." *Lex orandi* 37. Paris, 1963.]

Croce
W. Croce, "Die Adventsliturgie im Lichte der geschichtlichen Entwicklung," ZKT 70 (1954), 257–96, 440–72.

Dölger
F. J. Dölger, "Die Planetenwoche der griechisch-römischen Antike und der christliche Sonntag," AC 6 (1941), 202–38.

Egeria
Egeria: Diary of a Pilgrimage, tr. by G. C. Gingras (Ancient Christian Writers 38).

Eisenhofer
L. Eisenhofer, *Handbuch der katholischen Liturgik.* 2 vols. (Freiburg, 1932–33).

Eisenhofer-Lechner
L. Eisenhofer and J. Lechner, *The Liturgy of the Roman Rite,* tr. by A. J. and E. F. Peeler (New York, 1961).

Flannery
A. Flannery (ed.), *Vatican II: The Conciliar and Postconciliar Documents* (Collegeville, 1975).

Franz
A. Franz, *Die kirchlichen Benediktionen im Mitteralter.* 2 vols. Freiburg, 1909. Reprinted: Graz, 1960.

Funk
F. X. Funk, *Didascalia et Constitutiones Apostolorum*. 2 vols.
Paderborn, 1905.

Jungmann
J. A. Jungmann, *The Mass of the Roman Rite. Its Origins and
Development*, tr. by F. A. Brunner. 2 vols. (New York, 1951–55).

Jungmann, "Advent"
J. A. Jungmann, "Advent und Voradvent. Überreste des gal-
lischen Advents in der römischen Liturgie," in idem, *Liturgisches Erbe und pastorale Gegenwart. Studien und Vorträge*
(Innsbruck–Vienna–Munich, 1960), pp. 232–94. [This essay is
not included in the English translation of this book: *Pastoral
Liturgy* (New York, 1962).]

Jungmann, *Liturgie*
J. A. Jungmann, *Gewordene Liturgie. Studien und Durchblicke*
(Innsbruck–Leipzig, 1941).

Kellner
K. A. H. Kellner, *Heortologie oder die geschichtliche Entwicklung
des Kirchenjahres und der Heiligenfeste von den ältesten Zeiten bis
zur Gegenwart* (Freiburg, 1911³).

Kirch
C. Kirch and L. Ueding, *Enchiridion fontium historiae ecclesias-
ticae antiquae* (Barcelona, 1965⁹).

Lengeling
E. J. Lengeling, *Die neue Ordnung der Eucharistiefeier* (Münster,
1970).

Mansi
J. D. Mansi, *Sacrorum Conciliorum nova et amplissima collectio*,
reprinted and continued by L. Petit and J.-B. Martin (Paris,
1899–1927). Reprinted: Graz, 1960.

Martimort
A.-M. Martimort (ed.), *La Prière de l'Eglise. Introduction à la
liturgie* (Paris, 1961).

Paschatis Sollemnia
B. Fischer and J. Wagner (eds.), *Paschatis Sollemnia. Studien zur
Osterfeier und Osterfrömmigkeit* (Basel–Freiburg–Vienna, 1959).

Radó
P. Radó. *Enchiridion liturgicum.* 2 vols. (Rome–Freiburg–
Barcelona, 1961).

Righetti
M. Righetti, *Manuale di storia liturgica* 2 (2nd ed.; Milan, 1955).

Rordorf
W. Rordorf, *Sunday: The History of the Day of Rest and Worship
in the Earliest Centuries of the Christian Church,* tr. by A. A. K.
Graham (Philadelphia, 1968).

Schmidt
H. A. P. Schmidt, *Hebdomada Sancta.* 2 vols. (Rome–Freiburg–
Barcelona, 1956–57).

Schmidt, *Introductio*
H. A. P. Schmidt, *Introductio in liturgiam occidentalem* (Rome–
Freiburg–Barcelona, 1960).

Schümmer
J. Schümmer, *Die altchristliche Fastenpraxis mit besonderer
Berücksichtigung Tertullians* (LQF 27; Münster, 1933).

Schuster
I. Schuster, *The Sacramentary (Liber Sacramentorum): Historical
and Liturgical Notes on the Roman Missal,* tr. by A. Levelis-
Marke. 5 vols. (New York, 1924–30).

Cosmic Time and Human Life

Our human life is closely bound up with its cosmic environ-
ment. Earth, the planet assigned us as our dwelling place, is like
a grain of dust in a lofty mountain range when measured
against the unimaginably vast dimensions of the universe. The
earth's course around the sun creates the measure of time we
call the year. The circuit which the moon makes around the
earth is translated into the month, a time unit of about 29½
days; this is why all months were originally either 29 or 30 days
long. The swift turning of the earth on its own axis we call a
day, which we subdivide into 24 hours. Thus the orderly reg-
ularities of astronomy yield objective divisions of time that
exercise a decisive influence on organic life by reason of the
alternation of light and darkness, heat and cold, that accom-
panies them.

We experience the period of the day with its bright and dark
hours; we experience the passage of the year with the climatic

variations proper to the four seasons, which are signaled by the two solstices at the beginning of summer and winter and the two equinoxes at the beginning of spring and autumn. The circuit of the moon around the earth gives the experience of a further division of time due to the phases of the moon: new moon, waxing half-moon, full moon, waning half-moon. In the industrial era we are perhaps hardly aware of these phases (except for sailors, herdsmen, hunters and astronomers), but they played an important role among the peoples of the Near Eastern and Mediterranean world. As we shall see later on, these "quarters of the moon" may have been the earliest basis for the elaboration of the seven-day week.

Just as the human race must get its bearings in and accommodate itself to the geographical space in which it finds itself so too it must accept its inescapable placement in these cosmically based divisions of time: the day, week, month and year. The regular recurrence of these provides us with units of time for measuring our life and experience and determines our behavior and activities. Deeply religious men and women among primitive peoples and in the civilized nations of antiquity regarded this temporal sequence as a gift or disposition of the cosmic heavenly powers. They considered certain times to be times of salvation, others to be times of danger or unlucky times. Thus created reality itself gave the impetus to a religious attitude that was variously shaped by the divisions of time, and to an annual religious calendar with its ritual sacrifices of thanksgiving, expiation and suppliant petition, with its prayers, rites and processions, and perhaps with its periods of abstention from work of any kind.

Given the purpose of this book, there would be no point in a detailed description of the annual religious calendars of the various primitive and civilized people. A great many distinctions would have to be made between the festivals and rites of, for example, nomads (herdsmen) and those of farming tribes or hunters and fishers; in addition, account would have to be taken of local variations and of changes occurring over the course of time. Common to all these peoples were the spring festivals that centered on the tilling of the fields and the departure of the flocks for their pastures, and the autumn festivals connected with the various harvests and the return of the flocks to the settlements.

Among all peoples "rites of passage" had a special role; that is, the festive rituals celebrated at key points in the life cycle. These were religious rites accompanying birth, weaning, puberty, marriage and death. Such events did not belong solely to the private sphere but were regarded as the concern of the entire tribe or community and were therefore celebrated in a public form.

In addition, many historical events—natural catastrophes, victories and defeats, settlement in a country, birthdays, coronations, and epiphanies (solemn visits) of famous rulers—leave a permanent impression on the consciousness of a people and lead to the establishment of institutionalized feasts and commemorations.

Primitive peoples and the peoples of antiquity saw in such events of private or public significance the action of celestial powers; consequently the festivals of those earlier times had a thoroughly religious character. Many festivals of the ancient civilizations, especially in the Mediterranean world, were "mystery festivals." That is, they reflected the fact that people thought of the fortunes of various deities as interwoven with processes of the natural world. By joining in the ritual celebration of these festivals they hoped to share in the life and fortunes of the particular deity.

The life of the Hebrew patriarchs must likewise have been marked by the religio-cultural ideas and attitudes of the countries of their birth. After Yahweh had intervened in a special act of providence to lead the descendants of Abraham and had made them his chosen people of the covenant, the Hebrews kept some of these traditions unchanged; many others they adapted to their new monotheistic faith or rejected and violently resisted because of their incompatibility with belief in a single God.

The Jewish Festal Calendar

Christians see God's covenant with the human race as having its roots and background in the Old Testament and as being the fulfillment and completion of the former covenant. Consequently, if we want a full and rounded understanding of the Christian liturgical year we must have some knowledge of the Jewish festal year. The latter underwent extensive historical development in which the old feasts were not only supplemented by new ones but to some extent changed their own meaning. I shall therefore limit my discussion for the most part to the festal calendar in the time of Jesus. According to the gospels and the Acts of the Apostles his passion and resurrection and the sending of the Spirit were closely linked with Jewish feasts and receive additional clarification and meaning from these.

Three preliminary observations are indispensable for an understanding of the Jewish festal calendar.

5

a) The calendar was a lunisolar one in which the solar year provided the overall temporal frame of reference but was divided according to the circuits of the moon around the earth ("months" in the original sense of synodic months). The new moon and full moon especially played an important role. Because the lunar month contains 29½ days (the Israelite months had alternately 29 and 30 days), a standard year with its twelve months had 354 days. This division of time evidently came from Babylonia, whence the Greeks likewise took it.

At an early date, however, it was recognized that such a year was not coextensive with the tropical solar year with its 365 days, 5 hours and approximately 49 minutes. The attempt was therefore made to bridge the gap with the help of intercalary months. In Israel this took the following form: after Adar, the month before the spring equinox, a second Adar was introduced every two or three years and given the name Veadar. This solution does not flow from an application of an astronomical rule, such as we find in the Athenian Meton of 432 BC which prescribed the introduction of seven intercalary months every nineteen years in order to maintain balance with the solar year. The Israelites went rather by appearances, especially observations of the sun's position, the ripeness of the grain, and other points of reference. A specially appointed court made the decision on intercalation.[1]

b) In Israel the *year* originally *began* in the autumn and specifically at the new moon after the autumn equinox. Babylonian influence caused the new year to be shifted to the day of the new moon after the spring equinox (Nippur calendar). This month, Nisan, headed the list of months.

In religious matters, however, the older new year continued to be observed. That is why down to our own time Jews celebrate the new year on the first day of the seventh month (Tishri).

c) All feast days *began on the evening* of the preceding day and lasted until the following evening.

1/ THE SABBATH

The sabbath plays a very important role in the festal year. It is the end and crown of the seven-day week and may be called the primordial feast day of the Jewish people: a day of rest but also of openness to Yahweh and his word. Its establishment as binding upon Israel must be traced back at least to the time of the exile; there is disagreement today about whether its roots are to be sought in a still earlier period. In all likelihood the forerunner of our seven-day week and of the sabbath is to be seen in the series of "unlucky" days that were observed in the pagan religions of the ancient East.

> This group of days contained multiples of seven: the seventh, fourteenth, twenty-first, twenty-eighth, and nineteenth days. On these days almost everyone was obliged "to do nothing" (*sabbatu*, in Accadian). . . . At first, the set of seven unlucky days had no significance as a measure of time. The month and not the week was the time unit. But it cannot be denied that we are at the beginning of a series of purifications that lead to the Jewish Sabbath. These will be noted later. The act of purification, in fact, was begun in the pagan world, if we can judge by the prescriptions of Lagos in 2500 B.C. Despite the text cited above, these days were sanctified by the offering of sacrifice.[2]

The origin of this series of unlucky days may very well have been the various phases of the lunar cycle as directly observable on earth: new moon, waxing half-moon, full moon, waning half-moon. (The number 19 in the series is explained as derived from the sum of seven times seven when a full month of 30 days is subtracted from it.) These are good reasons for thinking that the Israelites knew of the observance of unlucky days from the countries of their origin and that they purified it to fit in with their monotheistic religion.

The first redaction of the Decalogue stresses rest from work on the sabbath (the word "sabbath" is probably from the Hebrew *shabbat*, "to leave off, to rest"). It connects the sabbath closely with God's resting after the six days of his work of creation: "Remember the sabbath day, to keep it holy. Six days you shall labor, and do all your work; but the seventh day is a sabbath to the Lord your God; . . . for in six days the Lord made heaven and earth, the sea, and all that is in them; therefore the Lord blessed the sabbath day and hallowed it" (Ex 20.8-11).

Other passages of the Old Testament emphasize the social and economic function of the sabbath: "that your manservant and your maidservant may rest as well as you" (Deut 5.14); "Six days you shall do your work, but on the seventh you shall rest; that your ox and your ass may have rest, and the son of your bondmaid, and the alien, may be refreshed" (Ex 23.12). The sabbath is also to be regarded as a commemoration of the liberation from slavery in Egypt and as an obligatory sign of the covenant: "You shall remember that you were a servant in the land of Egypt, and the Lord your God brought you out thence with a mighty hand and an outstretched arm; therefore the Lord your God commanded you to keep the sabbath day" (Deut 5.15). The people of Israel are to keep the sabbath, observing it "throughout their generations, as a perpetual covenant. It is a sign for ever between me and the people of Israel" (Ex 31.16-17).

In view of this wide-ranging interpretation and insistent exhortation we can understand the failure to observe the sabbath being subject to very severe sanctions: "Every one who profanes it shall be put to death . . . Whoever does any work on the sabbath day shall be put to death" (Ex 31.14-15). In the postexilic period the prohibitions against work became increasingly comprehensive so that at times even self-defense on the sabbath was forbidden (cf. 1 Mac 2.34-38). The New Testament is still able to report numerous rigoristic prescriptions in contemporary Judaism; these compel Jesus to assert that "the sabbath was made for man, not man for the sabbath" (Mk 2.27).

The Jewish sabbath was not only a day of rest from work, on which the people sought to imitate "the repose of God" after his work of six days and to approach the Lord. It was also a day for "a holy convocation" and an "appointed feast of the Lord" (Lev 23.3 and 2). In the temple at Jerusalem special sabbath sacrifices were offered. (cf. Num 28.9-10). During the exile, when there was no temple, and later in places outside Jerusalem the Jewish communities met for a liturgy consisting of prayers and readings. The place of assembly was the synagogue which, in the opinion of many scholars, came into existence soon after the exile wherever a reasonably large number of Jews had settled. At these assemblies there were, among other things, readings from the Law and the prophets, as well as explanations of them.

The domestic life of devout families was and still is shaped by the sabbath. In addition to participation in the synagogal liturgy there was and is a richly detailed liturgy in the home that both expresses and nourishes deep faith and genuine piety.[3] "Without this constantly repeated rhythm of life from sabbath to sabbath the Jewish community of believers would be incapable of enduring through the ages and through all the trials that time brings with it and forces upon the community."[4]

2 / THE GREAT PILGRIMAGE FEASTS

Among the Jewish feasts celebrated in the time of Jesus there is a group known as pilgrimage feasts because every male Jew of twelve years and older was obliged each year to make the pilgrimage to Jerusalem for at least one of these feasts. The feasts in question were originally connected with the flocks and the soil, with the springtime and the harvest. Later on, they became connected with the commemoration of specific events in the Israelite history of salvation and were thus enriched with a new theological meaning.[5]

a / Passover (Pesach) and the Feast of Unleavened Bread (Matzot)

The two feasts had different origins but were later fused into a single feast. The change was all the easier since both were celebrated at the time of the first full moon of the spring. Passover originates in the nomadic custom of sacrificing a young male of the flock in the springtime, smearing its blood on the tent poles as protection against the action of evil spirits, and eating its flesh that has been roasted over an open fire. Behind the feast of Matzot is the rural practice of dedicating the first sheaf of barley to the divinity and then eating only unleavened bread for seven days, until "new leaven" has been gotten from the flour from the new harvest. In the account of Israel's exodus from Egypt the rituals for these two feasts have been conflated into a single cultic action and are interpreted as a visible sign of liberation from Egyptian servitude (Ex 12.1-28). The two feasts thus became a single commemorative feast that was to be celebrated annually: "You shall tell your son on that day, 'It is because of what the Lord did for me when I came out of Egypt.' And it shall be to you as a sign on your hand and as a memorial between your eyes, that the law of the Lord may be in your mouth; for with a strong hand the Lord brought you out of Egypt. You shall therefore keep this ordinance at its appointed time from year to year" (Ex 13.8-10).

After the exile the Passover meal acquired a more fully determined ritual form with a structure based on the order *(seder)* of the four cups. According to the treatise Pesahim of the Mishnah (a collection of oral traditions, put in writing in the second century AD) the meal proceeded as follows:

> At the beginning of the meal the first cup was filled with wine and water, and the most prominent of the diners spoke two formulas of blessing over it. . . . Then the first cup was drunk. Next, unleavened bread and green herbs were placed on the table; after washing his hands, the most prominent diner spoke a prayer of thanksgiving, tasted the food, and distributed it. At this point, the roasted Passover lamb was placed on the table. A second cup was mixed, and the meaning of the meal and the symbolism of the rites were explained by reference to the exodus from Egypt; the first part (Psalms 113 and 114.1-8) of the Hallel was sung. Then the second cup was drunk. After another washing of hands and a prayer of praise, the diners ate the Passover lamb and with it bitter herbs and unleavened bread which was dipped into the *haroseth* (a compote of various fruits). . . . The third cup followed; this was called the "cup of blessing" (1 Cor 10.6) because in connection with it a prayer of thanksgiving for the meal was recited. The fourth cup was accompanied by the second part (Psalms 115–118) of the Hallel, in which hope of the messianic restoration was expressed.[6]

Jews saw in this celebration of the Passover feast, especially as reformed after the exile, more than a historical commemoraton of a long past act of salvation. Rather they felt that they themselves shared in God's redemptive action and were therefore obliged to the same religious response as had been given by their forefathers when they left Egypt. To this very day Jews still adopt the same attitude, as can be seen from the contemporary ritual for the Passover feast. There we read: "In every generation let each man look on himself as if he came forth from Egypt. . . . It was not only our fathers that the Holy One, blessed be he, redeemed, but us as well did he redeem along with them."[7]

b/ The Feast of Weeks (Shavuot, Pentecost)

Seven weeks after the feast of unleavened bread (beginning of the barley harvest) the feast of (seven) weeks was celebrated in thanksgiving for the wheat harvest. Because the feast was celebrated on the fiftieth day (in antiquity the day after which a new stretch of time began counted as the first day of that new period) the feast was later given the name "Pentecost" ("the fiftieth [day]") (cf. Tob 2.1). Being a feast of thanksgiving after the heavy labor of the harvest, the feast of weeks was a joyous one and was celebrated with various sacrifices in the temple (Lev 23.15-21). Later on it was associated with the recall of the covenant at Sinai and giving of the ten commandments; it thus became one of the feasts commemorating the history of Israel's salvation.

c/ The Feast of Huts (Succoth) and the Feast of Joy in the Torah (Simchat Torah)

Like the first two, this third of the pilgrimage feasts was originally an agrarian feast, the feast of the grape harvest. It began with the full moon of the seventh month (Tishri) and lasted seven days (cf. Lev 23.33-36). It was a joyous festival, in keeping with its function of thanksgiving for the harvest.

> You shall keep the feast of booths seven days, when you make your ingathering from your threshing floor and your wine press; you shall rejoice in your feast, you and your son and your daughter, your manservant and your maidser-

vant, the Levite, the sojourner, the fatherless, and the widow who are within your towns. For seven days you shall keep the feast to the Lord your God at the place which the Lord will choose; because the Lord your God will bless you in all your produce and in all the work of your hands, so that you will be altogether joyful (Deut 16.13-15).

During this week-long festival the Israelites were to live in easily built huts or booths of green branches. In explanation of this custom the priestly tradition sought to link this agrarian feast, like the others, with the history of Israel's salvation: "All that are native in Israel shall dwell in booths, that your generations may know that I made the people of Israel dwell in booths when I brought them out of the land of Egypt" (Lev 23.42-43). Only after the beginning of the Christian period is there evidence of another custom connected with this feast: during processions the participants carried a piece of citrus fruit in their left hand and in their right a festive bouquet made of branches from various kinds of trees; this they waved in a solemn manner. However, the references in Leviticus 23.40 and 2 Maccabees 10.6-7 suggest that this custom had already been adopted in the prechristian period.

In the seventh/eighth century the joy characteristic of this week-long festival found a new climactic expression on the octave day in the closing feast or feast of joy in the Torah (Simchat Torah). On this day the annual reading of the Torah came to an end and a new beginning was made with the first verses of the Book of Genesis. The reader of the final verses of the Torah was regarded as "bridegroom of the Torah" and feted like a king.

3 / THE NEW YEAR FEAST (*ROSH HASHANAH*)

Following its older annual calendar[8] Israel celebrated the first day of Tishri (the day of the new moon in the first month of autumn) as New Year's Day. The prescriptions on this point are given in Leviticus 23.23-25 and Numbers 29.1-6, that is, in documents whose redaction is relatively late. The first of the two passages reads: "In the seventh month, on the first day of the month, you shall observe a day of solemn rest, a memorial

12

proclaimed with blast of trumpets, a holy convocation. You shall do no laborious work; and you shall present an offering by fire to the Lord" (Lev 23.24-25). The second passage adds further details.

It is to be noted that in neither passage does the name of the feast occur, while nothing at all is said of the occasion in earlier Old Testament writings. Consequently the question of the origin of the feast has raised many problems for scholars and given rise to numerous hypotheses we cannot discuss in this short account. A modern Jew offers the following interpretation:

> . . . a day of trumpet blasts: in this connection we should think not of a metal trumpet but of the shofar, or ram's horn, that still plays a central role in the synagogal liturgy of this day. The blowing of this horn is associated with the aborted sacrifice of Isaac. In place of the son a ram was offered, and its horn is now intended to remind God of the vicarious expiation for Isaac. . . . In Babylon the exiles came in contact with the feast of Marduk's enthronement, which was also a New Year's feast. They adapted this feast to their own worship of Yahweh. The day of horn-blowing became New Year's Day, and the liturgy is dominated by the thought of the enthronement of God the Judge, before whom, on this day of judgment, the book of merits and sins is laid open.[9]

4 / THE FEAST OF ATONEMENT (YOM KIPPUR)

This feast was celebrated on the tenth day of Tishri, that is, during the first moon of autumn. Although it was one of the more recently established feast days of prechristian Judaism, it became increasingly important. It was a day of strict rest from work, penitential "abstinence" and assembly for worship. Leviticus 16 gives a detailed description of the sacrificial ritual. On this day, and only on this day, the high priest was allowed to enter the Holy of Holies behind the curtain. First, he offered a bull in sacrifice for his own sins and those of the priests and then smeared its blood on the cover of the ark of the covenant. Next, he offered incense in the Holy of Holies. After this, one of two goats upon which lots had been cast was offered as a "sin offering . . . for the people," and its blood was poured out behind the curtain and in front of it. Finally, he used the blood of the bull and the goat in "atoning for the holy place and the tent of meeting and the altar" (16.20).

The high priest then laid hands on the second goat, the "goat for Azazel" (a demon? the devil?) or "scapegoat" as it was called later on, and made it the symbolic bearer of the people's sins. Then someone drove it out into the wilderness: "The goat shall bear all their iniquities upon him to a solitary land" (16.22).

Even after the destruction of the temple in 70 AD had put an end to ritual sacrifices, Yom Kippur continued to be a very important day in the Jewish calendar. The days between the first and the tenth of Tishri were days of penance. The day of atonement itself was marked by a strict fast, lengthy prayers and readings, and the repeated confession of the people's sins.

5 / THE FEAST OF THE DEDICATION OF THE TEMPLE (HANUKKAH)

The First Book of Maccabees tells how, after defeating their enemies, Judas and his brothers, along with the entire army, went up to Jerusalem in order to purify and rededicate the devastated and desecrated temple. They set up a new altar of burnt offering in place of the one that had been profaned. "They also rebuilt the sanctuary and the interior of the temple, and consecrated the courts. They made new holy vessels, and brought the lampstand, the altar of incense, and the table into the temple. Then they burned incense on the altar and lighted the lamps on the lampstand, and these gave light in the temple. They placed the bread on the table and hung up the curtains. Thus they finished all the work they had undertaken" (1 Mac 4.48-51). After this, on the twenty-fifth of Chislev (the ninth month) in the year 164 BC, or exactly three years after the desecration of the temple, the restored temple was dedicated anew and the first sacrifices were offered on the new altar of burnt offering. "They celebrated the dedication of the altar for eight days, and offered burnt offerings with gladness; they offered a sacrifice of deliverance and praise" (4.56).

14

"Then Judas and his brothers and all the assembly of Israel determined that every year at that season the days of the dedication of the altar should be observed with gladness and joy for eight days, beginning with the twenty-fifth day of the month of Chislev" (4.59).

Ever since then the Jews have celebrated this feast with great joy. Among the more prominent rituals were the carrying of decorated rods and green branches, to the accompaniment of songs of praise and thanksgiving, and the lighting of lights in every house. Each day of the week-long feast a new light was added to the number. For this purpose an eight-branched candelabrum, the Hanukkah candelabrum, was used. There is a basis for this ritual of lights in 1 Mac 4.50, but Jewish tradition also traces it back to a miracle connected with the purification of the temple by Judas Maccabaeus: "Only a single small jug of oil bearing the high priest's seal was found in the desecrated temple in Jerusalem. Such a supply of oil would keep the Menorah, or seven-branched candelabrum, burning only for a day, yet by a miracle the oil lasted for eight days, thus giving time for obtaining a supply of new and pure oil."[10] Hanukkah on the twenty-fifth of Chislev always occurs during Advent and, being the "feast of lights," is celebrated with special joy; for these reasons it is sometimes called the "Jewish Christmas."

6 / THE FEAST OF PURIM

This feast must have originated in some extraordinary deliverance of Jews in the Persian diaspora. The Book of Esther tells the story in great detail. When Haman, a great enemy of the Jews, planned their extermination, he decided on the day for this by casting lots (purim), thus giving the feast its name. After the deliverance of the people, Mordecai, an influential Jew at the royal court, ordered all Jews in the Persian empire henceforth to celebrate the 14th and 15th of Adar (last month of the year) as days of rejoicing, preceded by a day of fasting on the 13th. The Book of Esther itself suggests that the feast was one of joyous exuberance (cf. 9.19; 10.13). "It gradually turned into a carnival."[11]

Everyone went to the synagogue again [on the 14th and 15th of Adar], to listen to the reading of the book of Esther; while the story was being read the congregation would interrupt with curses against Aman and the wicked in general. . . . Apart from this reading, the feast was an occasion for the distribution of presents and of alms, and pious persons made these gifts with a religious intention; but otherwise, it was an utterly profane feast, taken up with banquets and amusements, and considerable liberty was allowed. The Rabbis allowed that anyone could go drinking until he could no longer tell the difference between "Cursed be Aman!" and "Blessed be Mardochai!" Later, the custom of putting on disguises was introduced, and the feast of Purim became the Jewish carnival. [12]

7 / THE DAY OF NATIONAL MOURNING (*TESHA-BEAB*)

On the ninth of Ab (a month that falls in our July–August period) Jews remember with sorrow four great national catastrophes, all of which occurred on the same day of the month: (a) destruction of the first temple in 586 BC; (b) destruction of the second temple in 70 AD; (c) crushing of the Jewish rebellion against Rome in 135 AD; and (d) expulsion of the Jews from Spain in 1492. The commemoration extends also to all the other catastrophes the Jewish people have suffered in the course of their sorrow-filled history, including those of the recent past. It is a day of strict fast. The mourning that marks the day finds liturgical expression in, among other things, the fact that the Lamentations of Jeremiah are read in the synagogue.

8 / ISRAEL'S NATIONAL INDEPENDENCE DAY

The most recently established Jewish feast commemorates the solemn proclamation, by the provisional government, of the founding of the state of Israel on May 14, 1948. It is celebrated in Israel as a national holiday with a special service in the synagogue.

Notes

1. Cf., among others, H. Daniel-Rops, *Daily Life in the Time of Jesus*, tr. by P. O'Brian (New York, 1962), p. 208.

2. Th. Maertens, O.S.B., *A Feast in Honor of Yahweh*, tr. by K. Sullivan (Notre Dame, Ind., 1965), pp. 31-32. [I have modified the translation at one point, since it mistakenly has "eighteenth" for "twenty-eighth."—*Tr.*]

3. Vivid descriptions and texts in R. R. Geis, *Vom unbekannten Judentum* (2nd ed.; Freiburg, 1977); F. Thieberger (ed.), *Jüdisches Fest. Jüdischer Brauch. Ein Sammelwerk* (2nd ed.; Berlin, 1967; reprinted, 1976).

4. Geis, op. cit., p. 62.

5. Details in R. de Vaux, *Ancient Israel: Its Life and Institutions*, tr. by J. McHugh (New York, 1961), pp. 484-508; Maertens, op. cit., pp. 62-151.

6. Summary from H. Haag (ed.), *Bibel-Lexikon* (Einsiedeln–Zurich–Cologne), art. "Paschamahl," col. 1269-70.

7. N. H. Glatzer (ed.), *The Passover Haggadah* (2nd ed.; New York, 1969), p. 49.

8. See above, p. 12.

9. Scholem Ben-Chorin, "Die Feste des jüdischen Jahres," TPQ 125 (1977), 160-61.

10. Ibid., p. 162.

11. Ibid., p. 161.

12. De Vaux, op. cit., pp. 514-15.

The Paschal Mystery of Christ as Heart of the Liturgical Year

1 / THE MEANING OF PASCHAL MYSTERY

The image of the heart signifies the innermost core or center of an organism, the starting point and terminus of the circulating blood. The heart is the vitalizing center without which life is impossible. As principal organ it supplies all areas of the body, even in their most minute parts, with the blood that is indispensable for life. In the context of our present subject the image of the heart tells us that the liturgical year did not come into existence on a draughtsman's table nor does it owe its existence to shrewd thinking and careful planning, but rather that it emanates, and derives its growth, from a heart, a center. This heart of the liturgical year is the passion and resurrection of Christ.

The passion–resurrection is the central wellspring of salvation for all human beings of every time. God accepted the self-emptying of Jesus and his obedience unto death as a sacrifice of expiation and reconciliation; he accepted it when he raised Jesus from the dead and glorified him (cf. Phil 2.6-9). The Second Vatican Council frequently speaks of this salvific activity of Jesus as the "paschal mystery," by reference to the Jewish feast of Passover on which Jesus was crucified.[1]

In this context *Pasch* (from the Hebrew *pesach*) means a "passing by" and a "passing through." As the Israelites were rescued from Egyptian slavery when the avenging angel passed by their homes and when they passed through the Red Sea and were subsequently led into the promised land, so Jesus by his passage through the sea of suffering and death led the new people of God to a communion of grace with the Father. The word mystery in this context does not mean something hidden (a secret) but the unfathomable saving action which God accomplished in Jesus. The paschal mystery gives believers a new access to the Father, a new kind of life as children of God within the communion of the body of Christ, and thus the promise of an eternal communion with the triune God.

If we were to translate the exotic phrase "paschal mystery" into plainer English, the best version might be "Easter act of salvation." But here we must not think solely of Jesus' resurrection on Easter morning; we must include the suffering and death of Jesus. In other words, "Easter act of salvation" embraces the entire "sacred three days of the crucified, buried and risen Lord"[2] from Holy Thursday evening to Easter Sunday inclusive.

The other stages of the theandric life of Jesus, prior to this central salvific action, also have a meaning for salvation. This is true of every stage or action from his incarnation to his ascension and his sending of the Spirit. The words of the Creed: "for us men and for our salvation" apply to all these events and actions of Jesus' life.

2 / THE PRESENCE OF THE PASCHAL MYSTERY IN THE LITURGY

The paschal mystery of Christ was a nonrecurring historical event and as such belongs to the past. Now, many historical events have a lasting effect, but they themselves cannot be brought into the present. Not so with the paschal mystery. For the innermost core of this mystery, namely, the self-giving of Jesus and his obedience unto death, is a present, active reality in the glorified God-man. Because his will to save extends to the entire human race, he wants all the human beings of every age and people to share in the fruits of his saving action:

> To accomplish so great a work Christ is always present in his Church, especially in her liturgical celebrations. He is present in the Sacrifice of the Mass not only in the person of his minister . . . but especially in the eucharistic species. By his power he is present in the sacraments so that when anybody baptizes it is really Christ himself who baptizes. He is present in his word since it is he himself who speaks when the holy scriptures are read in the Church. Lastly, he is present when the Church prays and sings, for he has promised "where two or three are gathered together in my name there am I in the midst of them" (Mt. 18:20) (CL, no. 7; Flannery, pp. 4-5).

This presence of Christ is not simply subjective and psychological but objective as well; it is not static but dynamic. In the words of Pius XII it is not a "cold and lifeless representation of the events of the past, or a simple and bare record of a former age. It is rather Christ Himself Who is ever living in His Church. Here He continues that journey of immense mercy which He lovingly began in His mortal life . . . with the design of bringing men to know His mysteries and in a way live by them. There mysteries are ever present and active."[3]

Due to the "mystery theology" of Odo Casel, a Benedictine monk of Maria Laach, the precise nature of this presence and efficacy became an object of extensive study and discussion in the present century. Casel's publications met with both approval and opposition, but on the whole they led to a deeper understanding of what happens in the liturgy.[4]

In order to underscore the presence of Christ's saving work in the liturgy, the Second Vatican Council quotes a sentence from the prayer over the gifts for the Second Sunday of Ordinary Time: "It is the liturgy through which, especially in the divine sacrifice of the Eucharist, 'the work of our redemption is accomplished'" (CL, no. 2; Flannery, p. 1). In the eucharistic celebration Christ is present with his sacrifice as the high priest of the new covenant in order to unite the participants with his own self-giving and bring them into communion with the Father.

The high-priestly action of Christ is also found in the celebration of the other sacraments. These too are a derivation and fruit of the paschal mystery and a saving encounter with Christ.[5] The same must be said of the liturgies of the word and prayer, including the "sacramentals" (consecrations and blessings), which the Christian community celebrates. For in the words of sacred scripture Christ himself speaks to us, and when we pray he leads us in prayer and prays with us, thus giving a greater value and efficacy to the actions of the Church.

It may help some of my readers if I clarify this truth of faith by a comparison. The sun above us ceaselessly emits its wealth of light and heat throughout the centuries and on every continent, city and village. It has done this for millions of years without ever exhausting its energy or diminishing its brilliance. In similar fashion Christ and his redemptive action have become a new sun of salvation; he emits his rays wherever a community gathers for its liturgical celebration and opens itself to him in faith and love. Thus he fulfills his promise: "Where two or three are gathered in my name, there am I in the midst of them" (Mt 18.20).

The early Christians had the same basic idea in mind when in their catacomb paintings they depicted a man striking a wall of rock with his staff, whereupon a powerful stream of water gushes forth. The primary referent was Moses who by the power of God worked such a miracle during the sojourn in the wilderness. But Moses was only a type and image of Christ, the leader of God's people under the new covenant. Christ caused the spring of redemption to send forth its water from the rock of Golgotha, and he continues to let it stream out wherever his community gathers for the celebration of the paschal mystery.

The paschal mystery, then, is the heart and center of the entire liturgy and thus of the Church year, which is shaped by the celebration of the mysteries of redemption. The paschal mystery is the wellspring whose waters flow through the liturgical year; it is the point on which the entire year turns. In the final analysis even the feasts and memorials of the saints are a great song of praise to the Pasch or Passover of the Lord.

The active influence of the paschal mystery on the liturgy is not, of course, to be interpreted as an automatic bestowal of grace; it takes the form rather of God's offer of grace to free, intelligent human beings. Because God takes seriously the freedom of the human person, he refuses to press, much less force, his offer of salvation in Christ on anyone. He does approach human beings and he desires to lead them to salvation. But he wants a meeting of partners with the human person who is in need of salvation. The "part" which the latter must contribute is faith in Jesus as the glorified Lord and in the Father who sent him.

"Faith," in this context, is to be understood as having its full New Testament meaning: faith as acknowledgment and confession and as trust and unlimited readiness for self-surrender to the Father. It is a faith that is characterized by love and that acts in love (cf. Gal 5.6) and is fulfilled by love; a faith that excludes every kind of self-sufficiency, arrogance, haughtiness, inordinate ambition and coldness. Whenever men and women open themselves in this manner to God's offer of salvation in Christ, the paschal mystery is operative and fruitful.

3 / SIGNIFICANCE AND CLASSIFICATION OF CHRISTIAN FEASTS

Feasts or festivals are as old as mankind. In his philosophical study of the concept of festivity Josef Pieper offers this solidly grounded definition: "To celebrate a festival means: to live out, for some special occasion and in an uncommon manner, the universal assent to the world as a whole.'"[6] However diversified feasts may be in their occasion and form, they are always celebrations of events that call for remembrance and gratitude. As we saw in Chapter I, this statement is true of periodically recurring festivals based on the annual cycle of nature, as well as of significant events in the life of individuals and families (rites of passage), local communities and more comprehensive groups. The basic "assent to the world" that is the presupposition and basis of every festive celebration includes, for the religious person, thankful praise of the creator, to whom the concrete occasion for the feast is referred. For this reason, all prechristian and nonchristian feasts are at bottom cultic feasts.[7]

The chapter on the Jewish festal calendar showed that feasts which originally celebrated the cycle of nature became increasingly secondary, to the point of almost complete absorption, to the commemoration of events in Israel's history of salvation, that is, to Israel's experiences of and salvific encounters with Yahweh, the God of the covenant. Because of their background and connection with the Jewish people and religion the first Christians had a detailed knowledge of these feasts which commemorated the saving acts of God. What could be more natural, then, than that after the experience of the Christ-event the redemptive act of Christ's Pasch should shed a new light on all the feasts of the Jewish faith and should even become the central feast for Christians and the main object of celebration? All the more since Christ himself imposed the permanent obligation of commemorating in the eucharist his redemptive obedience unto death and his self-giving for mankind: "Do this in remembrance of me" (1 Cor 11.24).

Later on, I shall be showing in detail how the paschal mystery of Christ was initially celebrated on Sunday as a weekly Pasch, until the feast of Easter was established as a yearly Pasch; Easter was introduced at the latest around the end of the first and the beginning of the second century. Historical development brought a further expansion of the basic theme of redemption as the entire Christ-event from the incarnation to the glorification and return of the Lord was made an object of festal commemoration. The Christian festal calendar also came to include the stages in the life of Christ's mother and the memorials of the martyrs and saints, in whose life and death the following of the Lord had become strikingly visible and the power of his Pasch had been operative.

We find a special group of feasts being celebrated since the Middle Ages: the "feasts of ideas." These do not focus on particular events of salvation but have as their object truths of faith, special aspects of Christian teaching and piety, or various titles of the Lord, his mother or a saint. Idea-feasts are also called "devotion feasts" or dogmatic, thematic and static feasts (in contrast to the "dynamic" feasts which have the redemptive actions of Christ for their object). Among the idea-feasts are, e.g., the feasts of the Trinity, Corpus Christi, the Sacred Heart of Jesus, Christ the King, the Precious Blood, the Holy Name, the Holy Family, and many feasts of Mary. This kind of feast can easily multiply out of control; in modern times efforts have been made to introduce feasts of "Christ the Worker," "Christ the High Priest," and "Christ the divine Teacher." There was even an attempt to introduce a feast of God the Father. Many of these feasts are also unnecessary duplications.

The supreme authority in the Church has successfully resisted many of these efforts. The Roman Commentary on the *General Norms for the Liturgical Year and the Calendar* shows great reserve toward these idea-feasts or devotion feasts and points out that they had their origin in private devotions and only gradually acquired a place in the universal festal calendar:

> As soon as legitimate authority acknowledged that the object of some private devotion was praiseworthy, the region or religious family in which the devotion had originated immediately asked that the diocese or order be allowed to celebrate it with a liturgical feast. Then the Supreme Pontiff, influenced by the large number of requests, extended the feast to the universal Church.[8]

It was in this manner that sixteen new idea-feasts—ten Marian feasts among them—entered the universal calendar since the end of the seventeenth century. The Commentary makes it clear that one goal of the reform is to reduce the number of such feasts or at least to limit them to the particular calendar of a local church or religious community.[9]

Even greater reserve is called for when the object of celebration is some event in Church history, the importance of which is to be underscored by means of a liturgical feast. Thus, the feast of the Transfiguration of Christ and the memorials of the Name of Mary and Our Lady of the Rosary—to name but three—were originally commemorations of victories over the Turks. The reform of the liturgical year has already eliminated some feasts of this group; for example, the feast of the Precious Blood (July 1) and the feast of the Motherhood of Mary (October 11), which Pius XI introduced in 1931 on occasion of the fifteen-hundredth anniversay of the Council of Ephesus, have been removed from the festal calendar.

Since a Christian feast is accompanied by the celebration of the liturgy, and especially of the eucharist, and reaches its climax in this celebration, it is not a mere festive remembrance but, as we saw above, brings the presence and application of the saving actions of Christ. Particular aspects of these actions may be singled out in prayers, songs, readings and special signs, but we should not forget that behind the rich multiplicity lies the unity of the paschal mystery, the coming of the Lord to his community, and the encounter with and participation in his redemptive grace. The individual and the entire community enter into a fuller communion with Christ, not least in the sense that their lives are increasingly conformed to that of Christ. In this way the annual cycle of Christian feasts serves the noble purpose of which St. Paul speaks in such exultant tones: "Those whom he foreknew he also predestined to be conformed to the image of his Son, in order that he might be the first-born among many brethren" (Rom 8.29).

The liturgical year evidently has an immanent dynamism of its own. It is not appropriate, therefore, to compare this year with a circuit in which we always return to our starting point and then set out again. A more apt comparison would be with a screw's thread, which leads ever forward, or with a spiral, in which each turn carries us a bit further from the starting point and "toward Christ." F. Peus' chart of the liturgical year provides a graphic illustration of this.[10] "First, no liturgical year is exactly like any other; and second, each cycle moves closer to the parousia, the last day, and the life of the world to come."[11] G. Künze, an Evangelical writer, expresses the same thought quite vividly:

> If you look back on a decade or more of life lived con-
> sciously in the Church, you may feel like a man who has
> climbed a conical peak that is much too precipitous to be
> tackled in a straight upward line. Mountain climbing of that
> sort is a sport for vacation time; the honest path of daily and
> yearly toil climbs slowly. We journey in a spiral up the
> peak, and the way leads gradually to the height.[12]

As liturgical feasts became more numerous and diversified in the course of the Church's history, there was a growing danger that the basic structure of the liturgical year might be obscured and that essentials might be lost from sight beneath peripheral special devotions. In many prescriptions of liturgical law the effort was made to counteract this tendency. In recent centuries, however, this very effort led to a complicated classification of feasts in which there were no less than six different ranks, with further subdivisions.

From the time of Pius V, who, as instructed by the Council of Trent, published a new Breviary (1558) and a new Missal (1570) there were the ranks of double of the first class, double of the second class, major double, double, semi-double, and simple.[13] Many doubles had an octave (a week-long feast); depending on the rank of the feast the octave could be privileged, ordinary, or simple. Privileged octaves, moreover, were divided into octaves of the first, second or third class. For example, Easter, as the supreme feast, was a double of the first class with a privileged octave of the first class, while Christmas had only a privileged octave of the third class.

Attempts to simplify matters had often been made since the time of Benedict XIV; they were repeated in 1955 and 1960 (Code of Rubrics of July 25, 1960). Only in 1969, however, did the revision commissioned by Vatican II (CL, no. 107) lead to a radical simplification which is set forth in the *General Norms for the Liturgical Year and the Calendar*. Here feasts are classified, according to their importance, as solemnities, feasts and memorials, the last-named being either obligatory or optional. Only the two solemnities of Easter and Christmas have an octave.

4 / THE STRUCTURE OF THE LITURGICAL YEAR

Without anticipating too much of what will be said later about the meaning and form of the individual feasts and seasons, I would like at this point to outline briefly the structure of the liturgical year; the outline will help the reader to keep the whole in mind as he deals with the parts.

Nowadays we consider the first Sunday of Advent to be the *beginning of the liturgical year;* this was not always the case. In fact, the Christian countries of the Middle Ages did not even agree on the beginning of the civil year. The Julian calendar of Gaius Julius Caesar (introduced in 45 BC) shifted the beginning of the Roman year from March 1, its ancient date, to January 1. Although the Julian calendar prevailed throughout the West, divergent starting points for the year were retained for a time: March 1, in the Frankish empire into the eighth century and in Venice as late as 1797; Easter, especially in France into the fifteenth century; Christmas, especially in Scandinavia and Germany into the sixteenth century; March 25 (feast of the Annunciation of the Lord, which was regarded as the actual date of the incarnation of Christ), especially in Italy but also in the ecclesiastical province of Trier; September 1, from the seventh century on in the Byzantine empire and regions under its influence.[14]

In the beginning there was no concept of a liturgical year or Church year that would accompany the civil year (this last beginning on various dates, as noted). From the tenth/eleventh century on, however, the practice gradually spread of placing the texts for the first Sunday of Advent at the beginning of sacramentaries; this permitted the development of the idea that the first Sunday of Advent begins the annual cycle of feasts.

From time to time regret is expressed that the date chosen as the first in the sacramentaries fostered the idea that the annual cycle of feasts is intended to set before the faithful the entire life of Jesus from his birth to his second coming.

> There is a widespread tendency, when instructing the people, to understand the liturgical year as a representation of the life of Jesus: from the expectation of his birth, through his incarnation, public ministry, suffering and resurrection, to his sending of the Spirit and second coming. Anyone can immediately see that this approach does not account for details of the liturgical year. But it is not even verifiable if we look only at the broad lines of this year[15]

"It [the liturgical year] is not a mystery play based on the life of Jesus and inserted, not too skillfully, into the framework of an annual cycle for our spiritual enjoyment."[16]

It is true enough that the Church's cycle of feasts was not thus conceived during the period of its historical development. The cycle grew out of the seed which is the paschal mystery, and became a great tree with many boughs, branches and leaves. At times it suffered from excessive and even uncontrolled growth because the gardener did not intervene to prune it. And yet in the last analysis every feast is an encounter with the exalted Lord in which we look back with grateful recollection at the historical accomplishment of salvation, while also looking to the future with hope and commitment and in solidarity with our fellow men who are being saved.

Our limited human capacity can be strained by an excessive number of feast days. This fact has been lost from sight at times, although the Roman authorities have not infrequently applied the brakes and resisted the pressure for new feasts from the various regional churches and religious communities. On the other hand, a multiplicity of feasts and memorials makes it easier to show forth special aspects and varied facets of the one mystery of Christ and thus permits the faithful to encounter the "many-sided figure of Christ" (A. Häussling) and the full extent of salvation. Care must be taken, of course, lest people be "unable to see the forest for the trees," that is, lest they lose sight of the whole because of a preoccupation with the parts.

Despite the uneasiness referred to above, we can still say of the reformed liturgical year what Pius XII said in his Encyclical *Mediator Dei* of 1947:

> In the sacred Liturgy, the whole Christ is proposed to us in all the circumstances of His life, as the Word of the Eternal Father, as born of the Virgin Mother of God, as He Who teaches us truth, heals the sick, consoles the afflicted, Who endures suffering and Who dies; finally, as He Who rose triumphantly from the dead and Who, reigning in the glory of heaven sends us the Holy Paraclete and Who abides in His Church forever: "Jesus Christ, yesterday and today; and the same forever."[17]

We realize, of course, that it is always the risen and exalted Lord whom we meet in the liturgy. It is also true, however, that in his transfigured theandric existence Christ retains the humility and spirit of sacrifice that marked his self-emptying as he entered our world (cf. Phil 2.6-8; Heb 10.5-9); he retains his spirit of surrender for the salvation of the world, his love of the poor and the weak and his efficacious word, "since it is he himself who speaks when the holy scriptures are read in the Church" (CL, no. 7).

I have already remarked several times that the paschal mystery is the source and center of the liturgical year. As a weekly pasch that is celebrated every Sunday, the paschal mystery pervaded the annual cycle even in apostolic times. It soon took form as well in the annual Pasch which gradually developed into the Easter cycle with its period of preparation and its festal ending. According to the *General Norms*, the Easter cycle begins on Ash Wednesday and ends, thirteen and a half weeks later, on Pentecost. The annual commemoration of Christ's birth likewise developed into a cycle of feasts with a time of preparation and a festal ending (first Sunday of Advent to the Sunday after Epiphany, which is the feast of Christ's baptism). These two cycles of feasts are the supporting pillars of the liturgical year. The thirty-three or thirty-four weeks between them, during which "the mystery of Christ in all its fullness is celebrated," are called "ordinary time" (GNLYC, no. 43). This period begins on the Monday after the feast of the baptism of Jesus and ends on the Saturday before the first Sunday of Advent.

The two cycles of feasts, ordinary time and the other solemnities and feasts celebrating the mystery of redemption, are also known as the "temporal cycle" *(Temporale)* or "Proper of the time" *(Proprium de tempore)* (GNLYC, no. 50). This cycle is to be preserved intact and to "maintain proper preeminence over particular celebrations" (ibid.).

The calendar of saints' feasts is called the "sanctoral" (Latin *sanctus*, "saint"). In regard to the sanctoral a distinction is to be made between the general calendar of the Roman rite and "particular calendars" that must be approved by Rome, i.e., the regional calendars of areas possessing a common language, diocesan calendars, and the calendars of religious orders.

In view of the relations between its essential parts the liturgical year has been compared to the structure of a *cathedral*: the Easter cycle forms the central nave, the Christmas cycle is the atrium, and sanctoral cycle functions as a "circlet of chapels."[18] In using this comparison we should not, however, forget that in the last analysis the paschal mystery is celebrated in every liturgical feast and that in every feast the Lord who emptied himself, sacrificed himself in an obedience unto death, and is now glorified, is present to his community and acts efficaciously in it.

Notes

1. The CL alone uses the phrase seven times (articles 5, 6, 61, 104, 106, 107, 109); it occurs also in the *Pastoral Constitution on the Church in the Modern World* (articles 22, 38), the *Decree on the Training of Priests* (article 8), and the *Decree on the Church's Missionary Activity* (article 14).

2. Augustine, *Epist.* 55, 24 (CSEL 34/2:195).

3. Pope Pius XII, Encyclical Letter *Mediator Dei* on the Sacred Liturgy (November 20, 1947), no. 163, in the Vatican Press translation (Washington, D.C., 1947), p. 56.

4. Cf., e.g., his books *Liturgie als Mysterienfeier* (Freiburg, 1921, with later editions); *The Mystery of Christian Worship* (Westminster, Md.,

1962; 1st German ed., Regensburg, 1932); and his essays "Das Mys-
teriengedächtnis der Messliturgie im Lichte der Tradition," JL 6 (1926),
113-20; and "Mysteriengegenwart," JL 8 (1928-29), 145-224. [There is a
French translation, by J. Didier, of the first of these two essays: *Faites
ceci en mémoire de moi* (Lex orandi 34; Paris, 1962).]

5. Detailed discussion in A. Adam, *Sinn und Gestalt der Sakramente*
(Würzburg, 1975).

6. J. Pieper, *In Tune with the World: A Theory of Festivity*, tr. by R. and
C. Winston (New York, 1965; Chicago, 1973), p. 23.

7. We cannot go more deeply here into the theory of festivity and
feasts, but there is an extensive literature on the subject. In addition
to Pieper's book (n. 6), cf. C. M. Edsman, "Feste und Feiern, I. Re-
ligionsgeschichtlich," RGG 2 (3rd ed.; Tübingen, 1958), 906-10; J. A.
Jungmann, "A 'Feast of the Church,'" in his *Pastoral Liturgy* (New
York, 1962), pp. 387-407; H. Fortman, *Vom bleibenden Sinn christlicher
Feste* (Vienna, 1969); Th. Klauser, "Fest," RAC 7 (1969), 747-66;
H. Cox, *The Feast of Fools: A Theological Essay on Festivity and Fantasy*
(Cambridge, Mass., 1969); G. M. Martin, *Fest und Alltag, Bausteine
zu einer Theorie: des Festes* (Stuttgart, 1973); A. Häussling, "Das ter-
mingebundene Fest. Überlegungen anlässlich einer bedeutenden
Heortologie," LJ 24 (1974), 209-19; W. Dürig, *Das christliche Fest und
seine Feier* (2nd ed.; St. Ottilien, 1978).

8. Cap. II, sect. I. 1, in *Calendarium Romanum* (Vatican City, 1969),
p. 66.

9. Ibid., p. 67.

10. The chart is a frontispiece in T. Kampmann, *The Year of the Church:
Mystery, Form, Catechesis*, translated from the German by Sr. M. C.
Hemesath, O.S.F. (Westminster, Md., 1966).

11. [I have translated this sentence of Kampmann from the German
original as given by Adam. The English translation referred to in n. 10
reads somewhat differently; cf. p. 52—Tr.]

12. "Die gottesdienstliche Zeit," in K. F. Müller and W. Blankenburg
(eds.), *Leitourgia. Handbuch des evangelischen Gottesdienstes* 1 (Kassel,
1954), 532. Cf. also A. Adam, *Erneute Liturgie* (3rd ed.; Freiburg, 1976),
pp. 56-57.

13. The term "double" *(duplex)* referred originally to the double Office
that had to be read when an important feast fell on a weekday *(feria)*;
on these days both the ferial and the festal Offices had to be read.

14. Cf. E. Meyer, "Christliche Zeitrechnung," RGG 1 (1957), 1815-16.

15. R. Berger, "Jahr der Kirche–Jahr des Herren. Stationen auf dem
Weg der Gemeinde durch die Zeit," Gd 10 (1976), 165.

16. A. Häussling, "Solange Gott Heil anbietet, gibt es seine Feste. Vom Sinn des Kirchenjahres," *Lebendige Seelsorge* 20 (1969), 206.

17. No. 163, in op. cit., p. 56.

18. B. Fischer (following B. Botte), "Kirchenjahr, I. Liturgisch," LTK 6 (1961), 225-26.

Sunday as the Original Celebration of the Paschal Mystery

The New Testament has a good deal to say about the paschal mystery as the central act of salvation and about the resultant incorporation of baptized believers into the new people of God and the body of Christ. It tells of liturgical gatherings of Christians which have as their focal point the celebration of the Lord's Supper (1 Cor 11.20 ff.); in this, "the cup of blessing" and "the bread which we break" become a participation in the body and blood of Christ (1 Cor 10.16). The New Testament says nothing, however, about the celebration of Christian feasts and does not even make it clear whether the apostolic communities were already celebrating the Jewish feasts of Passover and Pentecost as Christian feast days because of the saving events that had occurred on these occasions.[1]

1 / ORIGIN AND INTERPRETATION OF SUNDAY

The New Testament does, however, present us with the first component of a liturgical year that will develop only very gradually. This component is the celebration of Sunday, the first day of the Jewish week. This was the day of the Lord's resurrection, as all the evangelists agree (Mt 28.1 ff.; Mk 16.1 ff.; Lk 24.1 ff.; Jn 20.1 ff.). It was also the preferred day for his appearances to his disciples (Mt 28.9; Lk 24.13 ff., 36; Jn 20.19 ff.), the day on which he bestowed on them the promised gift of the Holy Spirit (Acts 2.1 ff.; Jn 20.22), and the day on which he sent them forth, in the power of the Spirit, as the messengers and ministers of salvation (Jn 20.21-23; Acts 1.8 with 2.4). The first day of the week was thus singled out by Christ himself and set apart as the day of the resurrection and the sending of the Spirit. It stood out in the minds of the early Christians as "the day which the Lord has made" (Ps 118.24). On this day, the Christian community regularly gathered in the evening (the hour of the principal meal) "to break bread" (Acts 20.7). It was also the day on which, at Paul's bidding, each member of the communities at Corinth and in Galatia was to contribute something to a relief fund for the impoverished community of Jerusalem (1 Cor 16.1-2).

The Sunday assembly of the community certainly did not follow any uniform ritual in apostolic times:

> A reflection of the variety of forms taken by the early Christian liturgy can be seen in 1 Corinthians 14 (see 14.6 which mentions revelation, knowledge, prophecy and teaching, and 14.26 which speaks of hymns, revelations, tongues and their interpretation, as well as thanksgiving and praise). The fact, moreover, that the richly differentiated spiritual gifts listed in 1 Corinthians 12 evidently played a role in community gatherings allows us to conclude to the variety and flexibility of these "specifically Christian" assemblies—a conclusion justified by the very fact that in 1 Corinthians 14 Paul is forced to warn against disorder in the exercise of this multplicity.[2]

And yet it is impressive to see how the same Paul in 1 Corinthians 11.17-34 makes the Lord's Supper the central act of the community's assemblies. The Supper is connected with an ordinary meal, yet it is not the latter but the "celebration of the Lord's Supper" that is the real focus of the gathering ("if any one is hungry, let him eat at home," v. 34). We must think of this celebration, like the last supper of Jesus on the eve of his passion, as being accompanied not only by a regular meal but also by a variable garland of elements which we now see as part of the liturgy, elements that include reading, discourse, dialogue, and so on (cf. above on 1 Cor 14).

The oldest extrabiblical witnesses confirm the central place assigned to the eucharistic celebration in the Sunday assemblies of the early Christians. Here are some examples.

A letter of Pliny, governor of Bithynia, to Emperor Trajan, tells us that the Christian communities of Bithynia assembled twice on Sunday: in the early morning for a kind of liturgy of the word, at which baptism may also have been administered[3] and in the evening for a meal.[4] Under the pressure, evidently of imperial decrees forbidding suspicious gatherings in the evening,[5] the communities transferred their evening liturgy to the early morning. This meant that the external framework of a regular meal was discarded and that the kind of Sunday liturgy developed which Justin Martyr describes around the middle of the second century[6] and which became the prototype of the Sunday liturgy of later times: a liturgy of the word in which there were scripture readings, a sermon and prayers, and a eucharistic celebration in the strict sense of the term.

The first Christians took participation in these liturgies for granted. The services expressed their membership in Christ's body; they were a time for sharing in his body and blood (cf. 1 Cor 10.16-17); they were an occasion for voicing joyous anticipation of his return (this anticipation finds expression in the early Christian prayer "Marana tha—Our Lord, come!"[7] It was here that Christians experienced the fraternal communion of the redeemed, nurtured their faith with the witness given by their brothers and sisters, and strengthened one another in hope and fidelity.

There was no need of a "positive commandment of the Church" declaring attendance to be a strict duty. The obligatory nature of attendance had deeper foundations than that. Only when the image of Christ grew dim in hearts and the hope of his return weakened and the way was thus prepared for apostasy did Church authorities intervene with warnings and exhortations, as in the Letter to the Hebrews: "Let us hold fast to the confession of our hope . . . not neglecting to meet together, as is the habit of some, but encouraging one another, and all the more as you see the Day drawing near" (10.23, 25). The *Didache* (Teaching of the Twelve Apostles), a postbiblical but very ancient Christian document which "provides important information about life in the period ca. 80–130,"[8] makes it clear that attendance at the Sunday eucharist was regarded as a duty; the text says: "Assemble on the Lord's Day, break bread and give thanks, after you have first confessed your sins so that your sacrifice may be pure."[9]

Ignatius of Antioch makes the celebration of Sunday a badge of identification for Christians and a sign distinguishing them from those who follow the old order and still celebrate the sabbath. Christians have been reborn to a new hope and "they live in observance of the Lord's Day on which our life dawned through him and his death"; they have no life apart from him.[10] Here, at the beginning of the second century, we already find expressed what the martyrs of the North African town of Abitina will confess, despite torture and threats of death, at the beginning of the fourth century: "We cannot live without the *dominicum* [Sunday Lord's Supper]."[11]

The exhortation in the Syrian *Didascalia of the Apostles* (middle of the third century) shows the extent to which the celebration of Sunday had become essential to Christian existence in the consciousness of the age of the martyrs:

> Since therefore you are the members of Christ, do not scatter yourselves from the Church by not assembling. Seeing that you have Christ for your head, who as He promised is present and in communion with you, be not then neglectful of yourselves, and deprive not our Savior of His members, and do not rend and scatter His body. And make not your

worldly affairs of more account than the word of God; but on the Lord's day leave every thing and run eagerly to your Church; for she is your glory. Otherwise, what excuse have they before God who do not assemble on the Lord's day to hear the word of life and be nourished by the divine food which abides for ever?[12]

But even though this conviction was prevalent in the early Church, it appears that in many communities there were even then individuals of weak and inconsistent faith and that an effort was made to counter these defects by disciplinary measures. Thus the Council of Elvira (Spain) in about the year 300 addressed itself to the problem of members of the community "who are negligent in attendance at church" and decreed: "If anyone living in the city fails to attend church on three Sundays, he is to be excommunicated for a short time, so that it will be clear he has been taken to task."[13]

It is worth bearing in mind that in the first three centuries of Christianity there is never any mention of abstention from work on Sunday. In the world of that time Sunday was a day of work like any other. The Jews, however, kept Saturday as a day of rest, and the custom was spreading among pagans of not working on Saturn's day (Saturday), perhaps under the influence of the Jewish sabbath observance.[14]

Christians were thus forced to hold their Sunday liturgy in the late evening or, after the prohibition by Emperor Trajan, in the early morning. There is probably a reference to the limitations of time in Justin's remark that in the liturgy the sacred scriptures are to be read "as long as time allows." [5] Because the liturgical assembly had to end by daybreak attendance at it meant a good deal of inconvenience and self-discipline. It is not surprising, therefore, that despite the enthusiastic faith of the early Christians an occasional admonition about attendance at worship should seem necessary.

2 / EARLY CHRISTIAN NAMES FOR SUNDAY

The significance which the early Christians attached to Sunday may be judged by their names for it. I have already noted that the earliest Christian writings speak of it simply as the *first* day of the week; in this they are following Jewish custom. This manner of listing the days of the week is already to be found in the first scriptural account of creation in which the creation of light and its separation from the darkness are assigned to the first day of creation. It was natural, therefore, to connect this "day of light" with the "new creation" of which Paul writes in 2 Corinthians 5.17: "Therefore, if any one is in Christ, he is a new creation; the old has passed away, behold, the new has come." Due to the resurrection of Jesus on this day the new light has shone "that enlightens every man" (Jn 1.9).

We find a specifically Christian name used in Revelation 1.10 and very frequently from then on: "Lord's day" *(kyriakē hēmera)*; in other words, the day that is especially associated with Christ the Lord *(Kyrios)*. The name immediately suggests a reference to the resurrection of Jesus which gave this first day of the week a peculiar significance. But there are good reasons for thinking that the name was in fact inspired by the older term "Lord's Supper" *(kyriakon deipnon)*, i.e., the eucharist that was celebrated as the central action of the Christian assembly. It is noteworthy that, apart from Revelation 1.10, the Greek word *kyriakos* ("of or with reference to the *Kyrios*") occurs with reference to Christ only in 1 Corinthians 11.20 where it describes the eucharistic meal. Both references—to the resurrection of Christ and to the Lord's Supper—are essential to Sunday as the day commemorating the paschal mystery, "the day on which our life dawned through him and his death."[16] The name "Lord's day," with its rich freight of meaning, became widely used and, via its Latin form *dies dominica* (or simply *dominicum*) has remained until the present day in the Romance languages: *domenica* (Italian), *domingo* (Spanish and Portuguese), *dimanche* (French).

An early Christian name little used today is "the eighth day." After the six days of creation and the sabbath on which God "rested from all his work which he had done" (Gen 2.3), the day of resurrection following the sabbath was regarded by Christians as an eighth day. This day is the first of a new and greater creation that will lead to an eternal sabbath rest of fulfillment. This richly symbolic name may perhaps have a further reference: it is possible, on the one hand, that baptism was administered on Sunday mornings even in the very first days of Christianity, [17] while, on the other, the symbolic number eight was also linked to baptism at an early date (typology of circumcision on the eighth day; typology of the story of the flood with its eight survivors). Still another influence may have been the chiliastic conception (widespread in the early centuries) of the present world as destined to last for seven times a thousand years and to be followed by the eighth day of an everlasting new creation. [18]

The oldest witness to this designation is the *Letter of Barnabas:* "Therefore with joy we celebrate the eighth day on which Christ arose and entered heaven." [19] Justin Martyr sees in the commandment of circumcision on the eighth day a reference "to the true circumcision in which Jesus Christ our Lord, who arose from the dead on Sunday, circumcised us from error and sin." He adds this explanation: "Sunday is the first day of the week, but it is also numbered as the eighth day when it returns at the end of the weekly cycle; yet it does not cease to be the first." [20]

This designation, "eighth day," should not lead us to the false conclusion that Sunday was really the last day of the Christian week since it was regarded as an eighth day at the end of the Jewish week. This was J. A. Jungmann's view in an early essay:

> There could be no clearer expression of the idea that the Christian week ends rather than begins on Sunday. . . . The persistent zeal which sought and found ever new biblical images and references to the mystery of Sunday as "the eighth day," shows how people at that time saw Sunday not as the beginning but as the conclusion of the Christian week. Sunday brings the joy of resurrection and is a fulfillment, and because it is a fulfillment it is primarily related not to the following weekdays . . . but to the preceding days of earthly journey and penance. [21]

But the meaning of this name for Sunday is evidently that "the eighth day" leaves behind the old week proper to the first creation and marks the beginning of a new creation. The decisive thing is not the retrospective consideration of the past, no matter how much this past may have represented a preparation, but the prospect of a new reality which is now beginning and of which Paul says: "Therefore, if any one is in Christ, he is a new creation" (2 Cor 5.17). This interpretation is confirmed by, among other things, the way in which the Roman liturgy has always regarded Monday as the second day of the week. As compared with this long practice, the fact that during the Middle Ages the Slavs, Balts and Hungarians adopted names for the weekdays which made Monday the first day of the week is of little significance.[22]

Inasmuch as the name "the eighth day" did not survive into later centuries, it is all the more noteworthy that the Second Vatican Council revived it. In its *Constitution on the Sacred Liturgy* the Council says: "By a tradition handed down from the apostles, which took its origin from the very day of Christ's resurrection, the Church celebrates the paschal mystery every eighth day, which day is appropriately called the Lord's Day or Sunday" (CL, no. 106).[23]

Another name, first used by Tertullian at the beginning of the third century, is "day of the Lord's resurrection."[24] This name is later used by many Greek writers in the form "resurrection day" *(anastasimos hēmera)* and makes it clear that Sunday is a weekly celebration of the Pasch.[25] This name for Sunday is used today in many Slavic languages, e.g., the Russian *woskresenie*.

The name "Sunday," used in Germanic languages for the first day of the Jewish week, originates in the Greco-Roman week in which the days were named after the planets, a practice which gradually arose in the first century AD and by about the beginning of the third century had become universal in the Mediterranean world. Behind it is the ancient idea that there were seven planets (the sun being one of them) and that they all revolved around the stationary earth. Divine powers were attributed to them and they were even honored as deities. The days of the week were listed in the following order (Greek names in parentheses): Saturn (Kronos), Sun (Helios), Moon (Silene), Mars (Ares), Mercury (Hermes), Jupiter (Zeus) and Venus (Aphrodite).[26]

Even before becoming acquainted with this planetary week Christians already thought of Christ as "sun of righteousness" (Mal 3.20 [4.2]), "light of the world" (Jn 8.12; 9.5; 12.46), "light for revelation to the Gentiles" (Lk 2.32), and as the "light of men" (Jn 1.4), who, as "true light," "enlightens every man" (Jn 1.9). But this application of light and sun symbolism was reinforced as the planetary week—and with it the name "Sunday" (*dies solis*)—became part of daily life. At the same time, Christians saw in this symbolic name for Christ a way of countering the increasingly popular religion of Mithras with its cult of the sun, as well as the veneration of the "unconquered sun" (*sol invictus*) which had its center at Emesa; in 274 the Emperor Aurelian made the birthday of the unconquered sun (i.e., the day of the winter solstice) a holiday throughout the empire. This holiday would later play an important role in the establishment of the feast of Christmas.

A further point is the fact to which I alluded earlier: that the application of the sun symbolism to Christ was facilitated by the Christian interpretation of the creation story which has the light coming into existence on the first of the seven days of creation.

As the name "Sunday" became accepted throughout the Greco-Roman world, it also began to appear in Christian writings, although hesitantly at first. Justin Martyr is the first to use it, but in the form of "the day named after the sun" (or "the so-called day of the sun").[27] About fifty years later Tertullian uses the name without any such qualification and thus shows that it is now in general use.[28] St. Jerome, toward the end of the fourth century, provides the classic Christian interpretation of it: "The Lord's day, the day of the resurrection, the day of Christians: that is our day. It is called the Lord's day because on it the Lord ascended victoriously to the Father. When pagans speak of it as the day of the sun, we gladly agree, for on this day the light of the world, the sun of justice, arose and salvation is hidden in the shelter of his wings."[29] Right down to the present, however, the Church in its official language has preferred the name "Lord's day."

3 / POSTCONSTANTINIAN DEVELOPMENTS

The law which Emperor Constantine promulgated on March 3, 321 marks an important turning point in the history of the Christian celebration of Sunday. It decrees that "the venerable day of the sun" is to be a day of rest for all judges, for city folk and for business people. The rural populace, however, may go about their work, lest they fail to take advantage of the hours of good weather.[30] A few weeks later, on July 3, 321, the emperor added a further law which exempted the manumission of slaves (an action regarded as desirable) from the law of Sunday rest.[31]

The edicts, which represented an important step in the development of an Imperial Church, greatly facilitated the celebration of the Sunday liturgy and, at the same time, provided an opportunity for welfare work and for the refreshment of body and spirit. On the other hand, the danger of idleness and misuse of Sunday soon became evident. Thus Ephraem the Syrian writes in a sermon for the Easter vigil: "we sin on the day of rest more than on other days. While we abstain from work on the land, we run grave danger of being condemned, since we go into trading establishments."[32]

Constantine's law had the further consequence that rest from work became increasingly the focal point in the sanctification of Sunday and even the essential criterion of it. "Servile work" (*opera servilia*) on Sunday was considered a serious violation of both civil and Church law and was visited with ever harsher punishments. In this context appeals were occasionally made to the Old Testament sabbath laws, although many Christian writers had earlier made it clear that the sabbath laws were part of Jewish ceremonial law and did not bind Christians. A Coptic fragment from the sixth century, erroneously ascribed to Peter of Alexandria, reads as follows: "Cursed is he who on the holy day of the Lord performs any business, except that which is beneficial to the soul, and also the care of cattle."[33]

The Council of Orleans (538) dissociates itself from the Jewish sabbath ordinances but under threat of punishment forbids any work in the fields, "in order that people may more easily be able to attend church and devote themselves to the grace of prayer."[34] A few years later the Council of Narbonne (589) prescribes severe punishments for those who do any work on the Lord's day: "If anyone dares to do this, he shall, if he is a freeman, pay the city judge six pieces of gold; if he is a serf, he shall receive a hundred lashes."[35] Thus the impression was increasingly given that Sunday was a continuation of the Jewish sabbath, even though the early Church had protested so vehemently against such a view.

The scholastics of the High Middle Ages again clearly distinguished Sunday from the Jewish sabbath and based the prohibition of servile work on the fact that it facilitated attendance at Sunday worship.[36] Yet it cannot be denied that in subsequent centuries much too much attention was given to the prohibition of work on Sundays, especially by the casuists in moral theology, and that this helped obscure the christological meaning of Sunday.

In the Late Middle Ages (late scholasticism) and in modern times a stronger emphasis was placed on the Sunday Mass obligation, and the violation of it was declared to be a serious sin.[37] The Code of Canon Law of 1917–18 enjoined this duty in Canon 1248 with this lapidary sentence: "Mass is to be heard on all holy days of obligation [according to Canon 1247 §1 Sunday is such a day]."

4 / SUNDAY TODAY

Not the least merit of Vatican II and of the theological and practical study that preceded it was that they restored the original meaning of the Christian Sunday. They did so at a time when the people of "postindustrial society" are besieged as it were by the leisure time available to them; when, for example, the roads are choked with endless processions of cars taking people on their quest of recreation and diversion; when Sunday morning television programs vie in soliciting their attention and supplying families with amusement, information, and participation in all sorts of world events, science, art, sports, and so on; when the so-called "second Enlightenment" is undermining the faith of many baptized persons and greatly weakening their consciousness of the Christian character of Sunday and the sanctification of it that their faith calls for. In the midst of this situation Vatican II reminds us that in keeping with an apostolic tradition which originates on the day of Christ's resurrection, the paschal mystery is celebrated on Sunday. On this day "Christ's faithful are bound to come together into one place. They should listen to the word of God and take part in the Eucharist, thus calling to mind the passion, resurrection, and glory of the Lord Jesus, and giving thanks to God. . . . The Lord's Day is the original feast day, and it should be proposed to the faithful and taught to them so that it may become in fact a day of joy and of freedom from work. . . . Sunday . . . is the foundation and kernel of the whole liturgical year" (CL, no. 106; Flannery, pp. 29-30).

The Joint Synod of the Dioceses of the Federal Republic of Germany has taken up the ideas of Vatican II, explored them further and given them concrete application. In its resolution on the liturgy (November 21, 1975)[38] the Synod observes: "The weekly Christian celebration is essentially a 'sign' of the salvific reality of the 'new' creation that began with the resurrection of Christ." "As a feast of the Christian community, a day of eucharistic celebration, and a day of Christian anticipation of what is to come" Sunday is "indispensable, and no other day of the week can be substituted for it" (2.1). The Synod lists the following as important functions of Sunday for the people of our day: strengthening their faith, fitting them for worship and for service in this world, liberating them from the manifold pressures of a manner of life that is determined by industrial mass-society, and preventing their enslavement and isolation by the world of work. "Therefore Christians defend Sunday as a day of festivity and repose; Sunday is important not only for the community but for the whole of society" (2.2). The Synod believes it possible to make Sunday once again a "real festive day" if "our actions bring relaxation and joy but at the same time serve to foster leisure and meditation." "Exchange of ideas, dialogue and play, shared undertakings: all these can break through the isolation from which so many people suffer today. Sunday celebrated together can thus help many to rediscover the value of community" (ibid.).

46

The Synod regards the Sunday eucharist as a fundamental duty of the community as well as an obligation which faith imposes on the individual conscience. "For this reason all of the faithful have the duty of regularly taking part in the Sunday liturgy as an expression of gratitude and love for God and of responsibility to themselves and the community, and also in order to represent and make up for those who absent themselves from the liturgy or do not know the Lord. Even though many object to speaking of this unique expression of faith as the 'Sunday obligation,' yet now as in the past Christians commit a serious offense against both God and the community when they neglect the Sunday eucharist without a serious reason" (2.3).

This clear and unequivocal declaration of the Synod is especially important in view of contemporary efforts to come up with alternatives for Sunday Mass: liturgies of the word, works of charity to the neighbor, or various gatherings (including a communal meal) that would promote community. Those who seek to downgrade the importance of Sunday Mass in favor of the supposed priority of service to the world should reflect on the fact that service and commitment in and for the world soon dissipate and dry up unless they are continually fed by love of Christ. But the source of this love is made available to us above all in the celebration of the eucharist, in which we are united to Christ in his self-giving to the Father for the salvation of the human race. An important purpose of the "Sunday obligation" is to make it possible for the waters of this spring to flow into us anew every Lord's Day. The Sunday obligation is therefore not to be regarded as just one of many "positive laws of the Church" but rather an inherent and necessary consequence of Christ's redemptive self-sacrifice for us and the salvation of the human race.

The special emphasis placed on the Sunday eucharist is not at all meant to exclude or downgrade other forms of liturgical assembly, such as vespers, devotions, liturgies of the word or of preaching, and shared prayer. Without these the liturgical life of the communities would be impoverished. They are an expression of a common faith, hope and love and also foster the growth of these basic Christian attitudes. They attest, deepen and intensify *koinonia* (= communion; cf. 1 Cor 1.9; Acts 2.42) with Christ and with the brothers and sisters.

Similarly, all forms of socio-caritative service to our fellow human beings—for example, visiting the sick and the lonely—should not lose their traditional connection with Sunday. The Joint Synod makes reference to an important form of service to the neighbor on Sunday when it says: "Finally, we should not forget that for many people (working mothers, employees in service jobs, health-care personnel in homes and hospitals), Sunday is not a day of rest. The way in which such people are overworked challenge Christians to help carry their neighbors' burden and generously enable them to have a free Sunday or a few free hours (for example, by substituting for them on a Sunday, or taking care of their children)" (2.2).

In view of all this, it can rightly be regarded as a curtailment of the sanctification proper to Sunday when people are satisfied with attending Mass on Saturday evening and then habitually using Sunday exclusively for their private interests and without any effort to give the day a Christian character. Thus Hermann Cardinal Volk writes: "Part of Christian family life should be the sanctification of Sunday, and this does not consist simply in attendance at Mass. To attend Mass on Saturday evening so as to have no religious obligation to fulfill on Sunday is an abuse of the privilege of Mass on the preceding evening; for Sunday is meant to be sanctified even when this privilege is used" (Pastoral Letter for Lent 1978, no. 2).

It should be noted, however, that we live in an age when many members of the family, due to their work or to attendance at out-of-town schools, are often unable to meet during the week for a common meal and for other shared experiences. The cultivation of family life on Sunday through a shared meal or recreation or an outing is therefore an important Christian concern, and one whose value, even in terms of the sanctification of Sunday, should not be underestimated.

Another area in which emphasis has shifted in the present-day Church is the character of the liturgical celebration of Sunday. The veneration of the saints, which had undergone such a luxuriant development since the Middle Ages, and the addition of a good many "feasts of devotion" had led to the suppression of many Sunday Masses in favor of saints' feasts and other memorials. Vatican II responded to this situation by asserting the priority of the Sunday liturgy: "Other celebrations, unless they be truly of the greatest importance, shall not have precedence over Sunday, which is the foundation and kernel of the whole liturgical year" (CL, no. 106; Flannery, p. 30).

The *General Norms for the Liturgical Year*, which went into effect in 1969, give concrete form to this principle by stipulating that only a solemnity or a feast of the Lord can replace the liturgical celebration of Sunday. "The Sundays of Advent, Lent, and the Easter season, however, take precedence over all solemnities and feasts of the Lord. Solemnities that occur on these Sundays are observed on the preceding Saturday. By its nature, Sunday excludes the permanent assignment of another celebration" (nos. 5-6). Exceptions to this last rule are the feasts of the Holy Family and the Baptism of the Lord as well as the solemnities of the Blessed Trinity and Christ the King (no. 6). In addition, in places where the three solemnities of Epiphany, Ascension and Corpus Christi are not holy days of obligation, they are assigned to a Sunday: the Epiphany of the Lord to the Sunday between January 2 and January 8, and the other two to the Sundays following upon the date of the feast.

These new regulations in defense of the Sunday liturgy are in danger of being frustrated once again by well-intentioned initiatives that tend to give many Sundays a special theme and purpose which are foreign to Sunday itself. We may add the widespread practice of celebrating on Sundays "motif Masses" or theme Masses that are meant to "raise people's consciousness" with regard to ecclesial or social problems and prepare them for appropriate "actions." To this end special readings are chosen and special prayers written, which then replace those of the official Sunday liturgy.

It is quite true, of course, that the liturgical celebration should not be carried out in an isolated "ivory tower," far removed from everyday life. The message of Jesus and his self-giving for the salvation of the world, which we celebrate in the liturgy, oblige Christians of every generation to avoid all self-satisfaction and bovine contentment and to seek rather to build the world and solve its problems in a Christian manner. But these goals can certainly be achieved, and, on the whole, better achieved, if the prescribed Sunday liturgy is retained and topical problems of the day are brought into the introduction or the Kyrie acclamations or the homily or the general intercessions. In exceptional situations, the competent ecclesiastical authorities, and they alone, can allow or prescribe special Mass formularies for specific purposes on Sundays that do not already have a special character of their own.[39]

If a green light were given to this kind of alienation of the Sunday liturgy and this kind of more or less subjective assignment of theme to it, the Sunday liturgy and thus Sunday itself would be in danger of "losing its festive and liberating character, for this is always closely linked with the absence of utilitarianism and ulterior intentions. Sunday and its liturgy are already being undermined at the anthropological level. If there is anything of which the congregation must be made aware in the celebration of Mass, it is Jesus Christ whom the Church proclaims as Savior and Liberator. The encounter with him in word and sacrament begets a renewed faith and the kind of responsible faith-inspired activity that is likewise always a grace. Now that the liturgical celebration of Sunday has been rescued from superimposed memorials of the saints, it must not be allowed—in the celebration of the community Mass—to pass from that frying pan into the fire of utilization for the solution of concrete ecclesial or social problems and the provision of financial means to such ends. A good pastoral end does not justify bad liturgical means."[40]

The new Missal (Sacramentary) has especially enriched the Sunday liturgy by providing it with a number of prefaces. According to a 1759 decree of the Congregation of Rites under Pope Clement XIII the preface of the Blessed Trinity was to be used on all Sundays that did not have a special preface of their own.[41] This law applied not only to the Sundays of Ordinary Time but even to the Sundays of Advent. As a result the trinitarian aspect of Sunday was further emphasized while its original meaning as weekly celebration of the Christian Pasch was obscured. The eight new prefaces do greater justice to this proper meaning and substantially enrich the Sunday liturgy with their many themes. Here are the titles which the Missal gives to these prefaces: 1. The Paschal Mystery and the People of God; 2. The Mystery of Salvation; 3. The Salvation of Man by a Man; 4. The History of Salvation; 5. Creation; 6. The Pledge of an Eternal Easter; 7. Salvation through the Obedience of Christ; 8. The Church United in the Mystery of the Trinity.

A regrettable break with Christian tradition is to be seen in recommendation R 2015 of the International Organization for Standardization, an agency connected with the United Nations Organization. This document urges that beginning on January 1, 1976, Sunday be regarded as the last day of the week in the economic and technical sphere and thus in the whole public realm. The result was that beginning on January 1, 1976 calendars in some major areas in the world placed Sunday at the end of the week, as the "week-end" on which people rest in order then to begin a new week on Monday.

Thus the International Union of Liturgical Commissions in the German-speaking countries rightly regarded this change as a radical attack on "the interpretation and observance of Sunday as the day of 'Christ's resurrection on the first day of the week.' "[42] "As the 'Lord's Day,' the first day of the week should give a special cast to the entire week that begins with it and should set a stamp on daily Christian life. The incongruous effects the change would produce may be seen, for example, in the fact that the first Sunday of Advent would be separated from Advent and the new liturgical year, and Palm Sunday from Holy Week."[43]

Unfortunately, the new organization of the calendar means that in the consciousness of the general public Sunday will degenerate even more into a characterless "weekend," especially since the name "Sunday" conveys no hint of the religious and specifically Christian significance of the day.

5 / THE LITURGICAL CHARACTER OF THE WEEKDAYS

Unlike Sunday, it was only gradually and in a nonuniform manner that the weekdays acquired a liturgical character of their own. The emphasis on Sunday as resurrection day, on which the redemption was crowned and completed, left the other days of the week initially disregarded. An early exception to this general pattern was Wednesday and Friday. Thus the *Didache* or *Teaching of the Twelve Apostles* contains the instruction that Christians are to fast, not on Mondays and Saturdays like the "hypocrites" (cf. Mt 1.16) but on Wednesdays and Fridays.[44] A reason for this fast (a practice known to Tertullian[45]) is given in the Syriac *Didascalia,* which dates from the first half of the third century. Here the Wednesday fast is connected with the betrayal of Judas, and the Friday fast with the death of Jesus on the cross.[46] Similarly the Saturday fast that began to be observed in Rome at a very early date was connected with the mourning of the apostles over the death of Jesus.[47]

It is clear from all this that the events of holy week played an important role in developing the liturgical character of the weekdays. Finally, in the Middle Ages, Thursday too was given an unmistakable Christian accent as memorial of the institution of the eucharist at the Last Supper of Jesus and of the passion that began with the agony in the garden.[48] "Just as Sunday represented a weekly Easter, so the whole week appeared to be a faint copy of Holy Week. The great facts of the story of redemption were to be set before the eyes of the people, not only once a year, but in the course of the weekly cycle as well."[49]

This characterization of most weekdays by giving them a reference to the events of salvation history was obscured for a time in the Middle Ages, beginning with Alcuin († 804), by the introduction of a series of votive Masses that followed a different inspiration. Especially prominent were veneration of the Blessed Trinity and the saints and a concern for perfection and the salvation of the soul. The attempt to link the incarnation and earthly life of Jesus with the days of the week had no lasting success.[50] Finally, due to the posttridentine unification and codification of the liturgy, especially as this took shape in the 1570 Missal of Pius V, the following set of votive Masses was developed and, with a few later additions, remained in effect for exactly four hundred years, until the 1970 Missal of Paul VI:

MONDAY	Trinity
TUESDAY	Angels (including Guardian Angels)
WEDNESDAY	Apostles; from 1920 on, also St. Joseph and Saints Peter and Paul
THURSDAY	Holy Spirit; from 1604 on, also the eucharist; from 1935 on, also the high priesthood of Christ
FRIDAY	Cross; from 1604 on, also the passion of Christ
SATURDAY	Mary

The new Missal of 1970 has sixteen votive Masses,[51] among them all the ones just listed. The new Missal makes no effort, however, to associate them with particular days of the week. The individual pastor is left more or less free to decide whether or not he will continue to follow the essentially medieval practice of celebrating particular Masses on specified days of the week.[52]

Notes

1. Cf. F. Hahn, *Der urchristliche Gottesdienst* (Stuttgart, 1970), pp. 64-65.

2. W. Thüsing, "Eucharistiefeier und Sonntagspflicht im Neuen Testament," Gd 5 (1971), 11.

3. Cf. Rordorf, pp. 253-73.

4. The text of Pliny's letter and Trajan's response is available in, e.g., Kirch, pp. 22-24 (nos. 28-31).

5. The reference is to the prohibition against hetairies (from Greek *hetairos*, "companion"), i.e., groups of friends, but in the sense of secret societies.

6. *Apologia I* 67, 3-6, in E. J. Goodspeed (Göttingen, 1914), pp. 75-76.

7. 1 Cor 16.22; *Didache* 10, 6; cf. Rev 22.20.

8. Hahn, op. cit., p. 65.

9. 14, 1 (Bihlmeyer, p. 8).

10. *Ad Magnesios* 9, 1-2 (Bihlmeyer, p. 91).

11. *Passio SS. Dativi, Saturnini Presbyteri et aliorum*, in P. F. de Cavalieri, *Note agiografiche*, fasc. 8 (Rome, 1935), pp. 499 ff.

12. II, 59, 2 (Funk 1:170-72), tr. in R. H. Connolly, *The Syrian Didascalia* (Oxford, 1929), p. 124 [I have modified Connolly's translation to fit the Latin text, which Adam's version reflects.—*Tr.*].

13. Canon 21 (Kirch, p. 202).

14. Cf. Dölger, pp. 217-22.

15. *Apologia I* 67, 3 (Goodspeed, p. 138).

16. Ignatius of Antioch, *Ad Magnesios* 9, 1 (Bihlmeyer, p. 91).

17. Cf. above, p. 37.

18. Rordorf, pp. 275-85.

19. 15, 9 (Bihlmeyer, p. 29).

20. *Dialogus* 41, 4 (Goodspeed, p. 138).

21. "Beginnt die christliche Woche mit dem Sonntag?" ZKT 55 (1931), 605-21, cited here according to the later, expanded version in Jungmann, *Liturgie*, pp. 206-31 at pp. 217 and 219.

22. Particulars in Jungmann, ibid., pp. 220-221. Pascher, pp. 30-36, offers sound arguments against Jungmann's thesis. Recently A. Heinze, "Der Tag, der Herr gemacht hat. Gedanken zur Spiritualität des Sonntags," TG 68 (1978), 40-61, shows sympathy with Jungmann's thesis when he summarizes: "The secular view of Sunday as 'weekend' and the Christian view of Sunday are thus not as irreconcilable as they might seem to be at first glance" (p. 59).

23. [To fit the context here I have changed one word in the Flannery translation, which has "seventh day" for the Latin *octava die*.—*Tr.*]

24. *De oratione* 23 (CCL 1:271).

25. Particulars in, e.g., H. Dumaine, "Dimanche," DACL 4 (Paris, 1921), 884-86.

26. Cf. Dölger, pp. 202 ff.

27. *Apologia I* 67, 3.7 (Goodspeed, pp. 75-76).

28. E.g., *Ad nationes* I, 13, 1 (CCL 1:32).

29. *In die dominicae Paschae homilia*, in G. Morin (ed.), *Anecdota Maredsolana* III/2 (1897), 418.

30. *Codex Justinianus* III, 12, 2, cited in Dölger, p. 229.

31. *Codex Theodosianus* II, 8, 1, cited in Dölger, ibid.

32. *Sermo ad noctem dominicae resurrectionis* 4, in T. J. Lamy, *S. Ephraemi Syri hymni et sermones* I (1882); cited in Rordorf, p. 169.

33. Cited in Rordorf, pp. 171-72.

34. Kirch, p. 1038.

35. Canon 4 (Mansi 9:1015).

36. Details in H. Huber, *Geist und Buchstabe der Sonntagsruhe. Eine historisch-theologische Untersuchung über das Verbot der knechtlichen Arbeit von der Urkirche bis auf Thomas von Aquin* (Salzburg, 1957), pp. 194-222.

37. Extended discussion in G. Troxler, *Das Kirchengebot der Sonntagsmesspflicht als moraltheologisches Problem in Geschichte und Gegenwart* (Fribourg, 1971), pp. 159 ff.

38. Published in L. Bertsch *et al.* (eds.), *Gemeinsame Synode der Bistümer in der Bundesrepublik Deutschland. Beschlüsse der Vollversammlung. Offizielle Gesamtausgabe* (3rd ed.; Freiburg–Basel–Vienna, 1976), pp. 196-225.

39. Cf. GIRM, nos. 331-32. The new Missal specifies only one exception: the annual World Mission Sunday, in which according to the introductory rubric one of the two Masses for the Spread of the Gospel is to be used (no. 14 among the Masses and Prayers for Various Needs and Occasions), unless the day happens to be a Sunday of Advent, Lent or the Easter season, or a solemnity. The justification for this exception is rightly seen to be the fact that this Mass formulary emphasizes the resurrection of Christ, which must become the source of salvation for all peoples. Cf. Eissing, "Sonntag in Gefahr," Gd 10 (1976), 124.

40. Eissing, ibid., pp. 125 and 127. Cf. also Ph. Harnoncourt, "Motivmessen und Votivmessen," Gd 8 (1974), 121-23; A. A. Häussling, "Messhäufigkeit and Motivmessen," in Th. Maas-Ewerd and K. Richter (eds.), *Gemeinde im Herrenmahl* (Freiburg, 1976), pp. 143-49; K. Richter, "Die liturgische Feier des Sonntags im Kirchenjahr," TG 68 (1968), 23-39. In the last-named article references are given to further literature; most recently, H. B. Meyer, "Zuerst der Sonntag . . . ," Gd 12 (1978), 185-86, where reference is made to a "good and practical arrangement" followed in Switzerland.

41. January 3, 1759, in A. Gardellini (ed.), *Decreta authentica Congreg. S. Rit.* 5 (Rome, 1825), p. 23, no. 4126.

42. Cf. "Erster oder letzter Tag der Woche?" Gd 9 (1975), 90 ff. at p. 90. The information and citations in this and the next paragraph are from this article. Cf. also F. Schulz, "Gefährdeter Sonntag," JHL 20 (1976), 158-65.

43. Gd 9 (1975), 90.

44. 8, 1 (Bihlmeyer, p. 5).

45. *De ieiunio* 10 (CCL 2:1267-68).

46. V, 14, 4 ff. (Funk 1:276-78).

47. Innocent I, *Epist.* 25, 4 (PL 20:255).

48. Cf., e.g., Honorius of Autun († ca. 1150), *Gemma animae* II, 67-68 (PL 172:640 ff.).

49. J. A. Jungmann, "The Weekly Cycle in the Liturgy," in his *Pastoral Liturgy* (New York, 1962), p. 253.

50. Details on these various points in Jungmann, ibid., pp. 264 ff.

51. The Missal numbers only 15, but a Mass for Jesus Christ the High Priest is given as a second Mass of the Holy Eucharist.

52. G. Schreiber, *Die Wochentage im Erlebnis der Ostkirche und des christlichen Abendlandes* (Cologne–Opladen, 1959), provides a detailed study of the way in which popular devotion and folklore treated the various weekdays. In his *Sakramentalliturgie* 2:288-89, H. Reifenburg offers a novel suggestion regarding "motifs for weekdays."

Easter and the Easter Cycle of Feasts

Inasmuch as the Roman liturgy makes Advent the beginning of the liturgical year it might seem natural to begin our study of the feasts with the Christmas cycle. On the other hand, the paschal mystery is the absolutely fundamental fact of our faith and the center to which all liturgical feasts are related. Both theologically and historically the entire liturgical year springs from the paschal redemptive action of Christ and the celebration of this action. Thus there are substantial reasons for beginning not with the Christmas cycle but with the Easter season.

1 / ORIGIN, DATE, NAMES

In addition to Sunday as the regularly recurring memorial day of the death and resurrection of Christ, there seems also to have been at a very early period an annual commemoration of the Pasch. Although the New Testament writings make no clear reference to such a commemoration, at least Paul in 1 Corinthians 5.7-8 leaves no doubt that in the minds of believers at that time the Jewish Passover had taken on a new meaning for Christians: "For Christ, our paschal lamb, has been sacrificed." Those united to Christ are free of "the old leaven" and have become new "unleavened bread": "Let us, therefore, celebrate the festival, not with the old leaven, the leaven of malice and evil, but with the unleavened bread of sincerity and truth." This new meaning assigned to the Jewish feast suggests that during the days of the Jewish Passover the apostolic communities celebrated the memory of the Christian paschal mystery with heightened intensity. It is also probable, however, that Jewish-Christian communities only gradually broke away from the Jewish feast as a memorial of salvation history.

This suggestion is confirmed not only by a number of literary testimonies from the second century[1] but also by the "paschal controversy" of the second half of that century. This domestic ecclesiastical debate focused on the question of whether the annual commemoration of the paschal mystery should be celebrated on the fourteenth day of Nisan, i.e., the first day of the full moon in the first month of spring, no matter which day of the week this should turn out to be, or whether it should rather be celebrated on the first Sunday after the fourteenth of Nisan. The first alternative was defended chiefly by Christians of Asia Minor and Syria, who were called "Quartodecimans" because of their view. Rome and most other local Churches opted for the second alternative. Both groups, the former represented especially by two bishops of Asia Minor, Polycarp of Smyrna († between 155 and 168) and Polycrates of Ephesus († ca. 200), and the latter by Pope Anicetus († 166) and Victor I († ca. 200), appealed to apostolic tradition in defense of their Easter practice, although for each side different apostles were taken as embodying the tradition.

From this controversy we may conclude that while a Christian feast of Easter is expressly mentioned only in the second century it was already being celebrated in the first. As is clear from the *Ecclesiastical History* of Eusebius of Caesarea, who gives us details of the controversy based on the documents at his disposal,[2] both parties celebrated a liturgy, including a eucharistic meal, which marked the end of a preceding period of fasting. Despite the difference in date both feasts had the same object, namely, the paschal mystery in the comprehensive sense of this term. The Quartodecimans, however, laid greater emphasis on the redemptive death of Christ, while Rome and the other churches stressed more the resurrection and exaltation of Christ.

The first ecumenical council of Nicaea (325) put an end to the discussion of the date of Easter by prescribing that it should be celebrated on the first Sunday after the first full moon of spring.[3] This decree prevented the Christian feast of Easter from being celebrated at the same time as the Jewish Passover, since if the fourteenth of Nisan falls on a Sunday Easter is celebrated on the following Sunday. On the other hand, this arrangement, based on the phases of the moon and therefore out of step with the increasingly popular solar reckoning of time, meant that the date of Easter could vary over a five-week period (March 22–April 25). In consequence, a rather lengthy part of the liturgical cycle is dated differently each year, so that we speak of "movable" feasts and seasons.

In modern times there has been a growing desire for a fixed date of Easter. The wish is based, first of all, on the fact that the feast of the resurrection of Jesus celebrates a historical event and that, given our solar calendar, the feast would more appropriately be celebrated on the same date in the solar year. A further consideration is that because of the great variation in the date of Easter the dates of many other feasts vary widely, with some of them falling on a weekday (Easter Monday and Pentecost Monday, Ascension, Corpus Christi). This variation in dates also entails many disadvantages in the secular sphere. The growing assimilation of peoples and continents and their modern economies calls for a fixed and easily grasped chronological order with a uniform rhythm of workdays and holidays, times of work and times of leisure. For statistics on work, productivity schedules, and long-range planning the irregular occurrence of Christian holy days raises difficulties that merit serious consideration.

It is certainly not a good thing for Christians to belittle such considerations of the secular order, which are in fact considerations relating to the common good. For this reason Vatican II issued the following declaration in an Appendix to the Constitution on the Liturgy:

> The Sacred Second Vatican Ecumenical Council, recognizing the importance of the wishes expressed by many concerning the assignment of the feast of Easter to a fixed Sunday and concerning an unchanging calendar, having carefully considered the results that could follow from the introduction of a new calendar, declares as follows:
>
> 1. The sacred Council is not opposed to assigning the feast of Easter to a fixed Sunday in the Gregorian Calendar, provided those whom it may concern give their assent, especially the brethren who are not in communion with the Apostolic See.
>
> 2. The sacred Council likewise declares that it does not oppose efforts designed to introduce a perpetual calendar into civil society (Flannery, p. 37).

An important question that arises in connection with any effort to fix the date of Easter is whether the date of Christ's resurrection can be determined beyond dispute. Despite all the difficulties involved in the chronology of the life of Jesus many scholars attribute a high degree of probability to Friday, April 7, 30 AD, as the date of the crucifixion of Jesus.[4] This means that Sunday, April 9, 30 AD, would be the probable date of the resurrection. This date comes in almost the exact middle of the range of variation hitherto allowed, i.e., March 22 to April 25, and on this account would seem appropriate. In the two widespread plans for reform that have been drawn up for a new date of Easter, namely, the Sunday after the second Saturday in April (April 9 to 15)[5] or else the second Sunday in April (April 8 to 14),[6] account has been taken of April 9 as the probable historical date.[7]

As for the agreement of the separated brethren, which the Council calls for as a prerequisite, there should be no great difficulties in regard to the major Reformation Churches.

Luther had already shown his unhappiness with the great variation in the date of Easter. He calls movable feasts "wobbling feasts" and expresses his view thus:

> How much better it would have been if they had let Moses' law regarding Easter die altogether and had retained nothing of the old garment. . . . They should instead have reckoned and noted the days of the passion, the burial, and the resurrection by the course of the sun and set a fixed day for these, as they did with Christmas, New Year's, the day of the Magi, Candlemas, the Annunciation of Mary, the Feast of St. John, and other festivals, which they call fixed, not wobbling festivals.[8]

Zeller, who cites in part these words of Luther, sees a true understanding of "the freedom of a Christian" as implying a readiness to accept a fixed date for Easter, although he too rightly prefers that "any solution" be sought "within ecumenical unity."[9]

It may be more difficult to win the agreement of the Eastern Churches. The Panorthodox Congress of Istanbul in 1923 expressed a readiness in principle to accept a stricter determination of the date of Easter, provided the other Christian Churches are in agreement. But the reactions to the introduction of the Gregorian Calendar, which the Congress decreed, suggest that there are still major difficulties to be overcome.

Thus, because of the refusal of the Orthodox Churches, the World Council of Churches at its Fifth Assembly in Nairobi, November 23–December 10, 1975, was frustrated in its efforts to determine a universally acceptable date for Easter. In response to a questionnaire (1965 ff.) the vast majority of member Churches had already voted in favor of a fixed, common date for Easter.[10] But the Orthodox Churches declared that they felt bound by the traditional way of calculating the date of Easter until such time as all the Orthodox Churches expressly agreed on a change; this agreement has not yet been achieved. In view of this Orthodox position the World Council stated that at this stage of development a specific recommendation would not lead to a common date of Easter in all Churches.[11]

Vatican II, in its *Decree on the Eastern Catholic Churches (Orientalium Ecclesiarum)*, states that until the desired agreement is achieved "it is left to the patriarchs or to the supreme ecclesiastical authorities of the place to consult all parties involved and so come to an unanimous agreement to celebrate the feast of Easter on the same Sunday" (no. 20; Flannery, p. 448). As a result of this proposal the Greek Catholics and most of the Copts of the Latin and Eastern rites as well as the Ethiopians have decided to celebrate Easter for the time being according to the old, unreformed Julian Calendar.[12] Continued efforts should nonetheless be made to keep the discussion alive and to make people aware from time to time of the more cogent arguments.

Another and indeed the most important of these arguments is the fact that the ceremonial laws of the Old Testament were abrogated by the death of Christ. Among these laws is the regulation on the lunar determination of the Jewish Passover. In several passages of his letters Paul leaves no doubt that a Christian may not submit to the ceremonial laws of the Old Testament. "Therefore let no one pass judgment on you in questions of food and drink or with regard to a festival or a new moon or a sabbath. These are only a shadow of what is to come; but the substance belongs to Christ" (Col 2.16-17; cf. 2.20).

The question of a perpetual calendar, to which the Appendix of the *Constitution on the Liturgy* refers, will be taken up in the final chapter of this book.

As far as the names for the feast of Easter are concerned, Latin took over the Aramaic and Greek word *pascha,* which was derived from the Hebrew *pesach*. The meaning of this last was explained earlier (Chapter III, 1). The Latin name has been kept down to the present not only in the Romance languages but also in Low German, Dutch, Danish and Norwegian.

The origin of the English word *Easter* (German: *Ostern*) is disputed. The explanation given by Venerable Bede († 735), that the name is derived from an Anglo-Saxon spring goddess named Eostre,[13] is doubted by many scholars because it is highly unlikely that any such goddess was ever venerated.[14] Others derive the word from Middle High German *Urständ*, i.e., "Resurrection," or else they prefer a derivation from *East*.

A derivation from *East* is already to found in Honorius of Autun: "Just as the sun, after setting in the West, rises again in the East, so did Christ, the sun of justice, rise again in the East after his descent into death."[15]

According to modern scholarship, *Easter* is to be derived from the Christian phrase *hebdomada in albis* ("week in white vestments"). They claim that people misunderstood the *in albis* as a plural of *alba;* "dawn," and translated it (in Old High German) as *eostarun*.[16] In this explanation, too, the idea of Christ as the sun that rises in the East is in the background.

2 / THE PASCHAL OR EASTER TRIDUUM

Our discussion of the paschal controversy has brought out the fact that the early Church celebrated the Pasch in its total extent and meaning on a single day or in the course of a single Easter Vigil. In the following, almost lyrical passage the well-known liturgical scholar, Odo Casel, sums up what the Christians of the first three centuries thought about the content and high dignity of the Easter celebration:

> The feast of Easter is thus the cultic proclamation and representation of the redemptive action which Christ accomplished in his death and glorification, namely, the conquest of sin through the cross and thereby the reconciliation of the human race with God, but thereby too the establishment of the Church, which is redeemed by the blood of Christ and wedded to her Bridegroom by the Spirit of the Lord. Consequently, Easter is also the sacrament of passage from the world to the life of God, or of the entry of the redeemed human race into the kingdom of God and everlasting life with God. In short, Easter is the cultic mystery of the saving work which God accomplished in Christ on behalf of the Church. Easter is therefore rightly regarded as *"the* feast" at the center of the year, which symbolizes the world-year, the latter in its turn being a created image of God's eternity.[17]

From the fourth century on, as the result of a more historically oriented approach and a more representational type of presentation, the concentrated fullness of meaning proper to this feast of Easter was gradually broken down into its components and presented as a series of partial aspects. The Easter Vigil—"the mother of all holy vigils" (Augustine)—was originally marked, until midnight, by fasting and by mourning over the death of Christ. Only then was free rein given to joy at the Lord's resurrection and exaltation. The fourth century, however, saw the development of "the most holy triduum of the crucified, buried and risen Lord."[18] Since that time, the liturgical celebrations of these days have together made up the annual celebration of the paschal mystery. The new *General Norms for the Liturgical Year* confirms this interpretation when it says: "The Easter triduum of the passion and resurrection of Christ is thus the culmination of the entire liturgical year" (no. 18). This triduum "begins with the evening Mass of the Lord's Supper, reaches its high point in the Easter vigil, and closes with evening prayer on Easter Sunday" (no. 19).

During the 1600 years of its history the celebration of the triduum had come to be much in need of reform. We need only recall that the entire Easter Vigil celebration had been moved ahead to the early morning hours of Holy Saturday and had thus lost much of its natural symbolic power (for details, see below, section 2,c of this chapter). A decree of the Congregation of Rites, February 9, 1951, allowed it to be restored to the night before Easter "by way of experiment." Four years later, on November 16, 1955, the famous General Decree of the Congregation of Rites on the Restoration of Holy Week appeared; it was a substantial anticipation of the postconciliar liturgy that would be found in the new Roman Missal of 1970. The following presentation is based on the English translation of the Roman Missal comprising the Lectionary and Sacramentary, approved for use in the United States in 1970 and 1974, respectively.

a/ The Celebration on Holy Thursday Evening

The idea found in Judaism and antiquity that a day has already begun on the previous evening is still at work in the liturgy to the extent that the celebration of solemnities and Sundays begins with vespers on the preceding day. Consequently, it is not strange that Holy Thursday evening should be part of Good Friday or the first day of the Easter triduum. This collocation is justified and meaningful in terms of content, since at the Last Supper Jesus sacramentally anticipated the self-giving that would be embodied in his sacrificial death on the cross. The washing of the feet on Holy Thursday evening is another clear sign of his self-sacrificing love in the service of others. Furthermore, his agony in the Garden of Olives, his betrayal to his enemies, and his capture mark the real beginning of his passion.

The liturgy of Holy Thursday evening is above all a commemoration of the Last Supper of Jesus and the institution of the eucharist, as well as of the washing of the feet, which symbolizes the servant aspect of his love. The whole community should take part in this evening Mass. Normally, no other Masses, except for the bishop's Chrismal Mass in the Morning, are to be celebrated.

The entrance antiphon, taken from Galatians 6.14, gives the overall theme of the entire Easter triduum: "We should glory in the cross of our Lord Jesus Christ, for he is our salvation, our life and our resurrection; through him we are saved and made free." In these words, the full scope of the paschal mystery finds expression, as the joy and jubilation of the resurrection and redemption echo even in the suffering of the crucifixion.

"During the singing of the Gloria, the church bells are rung and then remain silent until the Easter Vigil, unless the conference of bishops or the Ordinary decrees otherwise" (rubric). This silence of the bells during the Easter triduum is a practice that goes back at least to the Carolingian period. Amalarius of Metz († ca. 850) sees in it a sign of humility that imitates the Lord in his humiliation; in his view, wooden noisemakers (clappers; Latin *crepitacula* and *tabulae*) are better suited than bells to express, during the final days of Holy Week, the humble self-emptying of the Lord. [19] According to other authors, "the silencing of the bells and the use of the wooden clapper in their place is a survival from those times when bells were as yet unknown in Church usage."[20]

During this same period, churches in many places abstain from the use not only of bells but also of the organ, which since the end of the Middle Ages has increasingly become *the* instrument for liturgical music. The motives for the abstention are probably the same in both cases. In regard to both of these instruments of festive sound people spoke of a "fast of the ears," just as they spoke of a "fast of the eyes" in connection with the veiling of crosses, statues and pictures during passiontide. However, neither the old nor the new Roman Missal makes any corresponding reference to the organ; mention was made of it only in a decree of the Congregation of Rites.[21]

The opening prayer focuses on the eucharist as sacrifice and as feast of love; it asks "that in this Eucharist we may find the fullness of love and life."

The Old Testament reading (Ex 12.1-8. 11-14) tells of the killing and eating of the Passover lamb, whose blood on the doorposts and lintels of their homes became a saving sign for Israel. This nocturnal meal taken by Israel in Egypt marked the beginning of the exodus from slavery and of the series of divine saving actions that reached its climax in the establishment of the covenant on Sinai.

The responsorial psalm (116) not only expresses gratitude for this past liberation of Israel, but in the response: "Our blessing-cup is a communion with the blood of Christ" (cf. 1 Cor 10.16) also gives thanks for the "cup of salvation," for the fulfillment of the Old Testament prefiguration in the paschal mystery of Christ, and for the Lamb who is slain and takes away the sins of the world (cf. Jn 1.29).

The second reading continues this idea, for it contains the account of the institution of the eucharist according to 1 Corinthians 11.23-26. The second intermediate song prepares the way for the gospel of the washing of feet by proclaiming the "new commandment": "Love one another as I have loved you" (Jn 13.24). The gospel pericope, John 13.1-15, tells us of the interior attitude of Jesus: his purpose is to serve, not to dominate. The washing of the disciples' feet, usually something done for guests by slaves, becomes a clear sign of the fact that Jesus loves the human race without limit, even to the point of sacrificing himself in death on the cross.

The Lord's admonition at the end of this passage cannot be missed: "If I then, your Lord and Teacher, have washed your feet, you also ought to wash one another's feet. For I have given you an example, that you also should do as I have done to you." This instruction of the Lord and the phrase "new commandment *(mandatum)*" led to speaking of the washing of the feet as the *Mandatum*. The important thing, of course, is the love that lies behind the symbolic washing of feet and the manifold expression of this love in manifold service to the brethren. But the Church has never lost sight of the concrete biblical sign the Lord had used in expressing his love.

As early as the fourth century we find a washing of feet as part of the baptismal rite in the West (except for Rome). This practice gradually disappeared due to the spread of the Roman liturgy, but the washing of feet came into use again in monasteries as a service to the poor and the brethren of the community. The seventeenth Council of Toledo (694) forthrightly requires that this solemn action be performed on Holy Thursday in all churches of Spain and Gaul. Every bishop and priest is to wash the feet of his subjects after the example of Christ.[22] This rite is attested for Rome since the twelfth century.[23] While the Missal of Pius V (1570) placed the washing of the feet at the end of Mass, the new 1955 Order for Holy Week places it after the gospel and homily. This practice is continued in the Missal of 1970. Before the reform of 1955 the rite was obligatory only in cathedrals and abbey churches, but the new Order intends it for all liturgical assemblies, "depending on pastoral circumstances."

The *rite* is a simple one: "The men who have been chosen are led by the ministers to chairs prepared in a suitable place. Then the priest (removing his chasuble if necessary) goes to each man. With the help of the ministers, he pours water over each one's feet and dries them"(rubric). The traditional number twelve, which the revised rite of 1955 had kept, has been dropped in the new Missal. During the washing of the feet, some of the antiphons provided in the Missal (six in all) or some other suitable songs are sung. Since there is no creed, the general intercessions follow immediately.

During the preparation of the gifts "there may be a procession of the faithful with gifts for the poor" (rubric). The hymn given in the Sacramentary, "The love of Christ has gathered us," as well as the antiphon, "Where charity and love are found, there is God," provide motivation for this practical love of neighbor, which is one of the concrete forms into which the symbolic gesture of washing the feet can be translated.

The preface extols the eucharistic celebration which Christ instituted on this evening. If the first eucharistic prayer is used (any eucharistic prayer may be chosen), there are special inserts for this evening, in which reference is made to the institution of the eucharist and the sacrifice of Christ. The introduction to the words of institution is expanded (in the Roman Missal) to read: "The day before he suffered for our salvation and the salvation of all, that is today . . ."

After the concluding prayer the presanctified gifts for the Good Friday liturgy are carried in solemn procession to the tabernacle of a side altar or to a side chapel. Then all ornaments are removed from the main altar (stripping of the altar). Adoration of the reserved sacrament is to be retained as far as is practicable, although without any solemnity once midnight is past.

This custom has a very long history going back to the second century. Irenaeus of Lyons († ca. 200) already says that many people fasted for the forty hours before Easter, that is, for a period equal (in round numbers) to the time of Christ's repose in the tomb; Augustine confirms the existence of this practice.[24] The purpose of this fast, which according to other witnesses was accompanied by liturgies, was to honor "the bridegroom who has been taken away" (cf. Lk 5.35). In the tenth century the custom arose, especially in England, of wrapping the crucifix or a corpus alone in a cloth and laying it in a symbolic tomb after the veneration of the cross on Good Friday. In many areas consecrated hosts were added to the crucifix. Later on, the event of the resurrection was acted out at this "holy sepulcher" in the form of the "Easter plays." Modern celebrations of the resurrection, often dramatic in character, probably had their origin here.

Once the Easter Vigil was pushed ahead to Holy Saturday morning (see blow, c), the forty hours of prayer were begun on Holy Thursday evening in order to get them in before the vigil service. Even the Congregation of Rites allowed the place where the presanctified gifts were reserved to be called "the holy sepulcher." We should also mention that a forty-hour prayer of adoration before the Blessed Sacrament also occurs outside the Easter triduum (it is first attested in 1527 at Milan).

The eminent liturgical scholar, J. A. Jungmann, observes: "Both forms [of forty hours devotion] would profit by bearing in mind the original idea that inspired the practice, namely, absorption in the mystery of redemption at the point where the freely accepted humiliation of the God-man is greatest."[25]

b/ The Good Friday Liturgy

Good Friday,[26] the day of Christ's death (the 14th of Nisan, which fell on a Friday), has always been a day of mourning and of fasting inspired by compassion (a "grieving fast"). At a very early date, the words of Jesus about the coming time when the disciples would fast because the bridegroom was taken from them (Mt 9.15; Mk 2.20; Lk 5.34-35) were applied to the days of his death and repose in the tomb. This grief-inspired fast was so much a part of the early Church's consciousness in the West that for a time it was also celebrated on every Friday and Saturday.

The oldest witnesses to a fast on Good Friday and Holy Saturday are from the second century (the apocryphal *Gospel according to the Hebrews* and Irenaeus of Lyons). The reference is to a "complete fast in which no food and drink at all were taken. At Easter Christians were thus obliged to spend forty hours or even two full days without eating or drinking. This interpretation is confirmed by the Church Order of Hippolytus which by way of exception allows sick persons and pregnant women to have bread and water."[27] Pope Innocent I at the beginning of the fifth century accounts for the fast with the view that the apostles themselves had already observed a grief-inspired fast during this "biduum."[28] Given this venerable tradition, it is understandable that the modern Church should still observe Good Friday as a day of fast and abstinence.

Although the first Christian centuries did not have a special Good Friday liturgy, various forms of noneucharistic liturgy did develop in the fourth century. Egeria, a pilgrim in about 400, reports from Jerusalem that the Christians of the city gathered in the morning at Golgotha to venerate the cross of Christ, which the Empress Helena had discovered in 320. They gathered again in the early afternoon for a liturgy of the word during which the story of the passion was read.[29] Here at Jerusalem we see the effort being made to achieve accuracy in details of time and place for the commemoration of the Christ-event in the liturgy, and in this way to impress that event more deeply on the minds of the faithful. In this respect the Holy Week liturgy of Jerusalem became a model for the West.

In the beginning, people in the West were satisfied with a liturgy of the word, as Augustine attests for North Africa. In this liturgy the passion narrative and the psalms relating to the sufferings of Christ played an important role. If local churches possessed a relic of the holy cross, as we know the Church of Rome did as early as the fourth century (a gift from Empress Helena), a ceremony of veneration of the cross developed quite soon.

We possess a more detailed knowledge of the course of the Good Friday service as celebrated in seventh-century Rome. The pope, barefoot, carried the relic of the cross in procession from the Lateran Basilica to the Church of the Holy Cross in Jerusalem, which Empress Helena had built. There the relic of the cross was venerated not only by the clergy but by the whole community; during the veneration two Old Testament passages and the passion narrative of John were read. The solemn prayer of the faithful originally terminated this liturgy, until the communion of the faithful was introduced in the seventh century.

This Roman liturgy was taken over by the Franks in the eighth century and developed further in the direction of greater dramatization. Around the middle of the tenth century some Benedictine monks of St. Alban's in Mainz recorded this fuller Good Friday liturgy in the so-called Romano-German Pontifical, which is also known as the Mainz Pontifical. Still in the tenth century, this new liturgical book made its way to Rome, which at that time was at a low point of its history, and exercised a normative influence on the liturgy there.

70

In the course of the Middle Ages the initially very simple celebration of communion for the faithful was developed into the *Missa praesanctificatorum* (Mass with the previously consecrated gifts), by adding many parts of a eucharistic celebration, though not, of course, the decisive element, namely, the eucharistic prayer. The fact that during the Middle Ages the faithful rarely received communion meant that finally only the priest communicated on Good Friday. The Tridentine Missal of 1570 turned this custom into a regulation that lasted for almost four hundred years. In popular idiom the Good Friday liturgy was a "ruined" or "distracted" liturgy.

The new Order of 1955 retained the traditional threefold division of the Good Friday service into liturgy of the word, veneration of the cross, and celebration of communion. It dropped a number of rites and rubrics, especially in the celebration of communion; among these was the prohibition against the faithful receiving communion. The revised Missal of 1970 took over this reform in its essentials.

This last statement also holds for the time of the celebration. From antiquity until into the High Middle Ages the ceremony took place at 3 PM, the hour of Christ's death. In the late Middle Ages, as the practice of fasting was affected by increasing laxity, the prescription that the liturgy should not be celebrated until after the office of none (= 3 PM) continued to be observed, but in a purely formalistic way, since none and, with it, the Good Friday liturgy were pushed ahead to the morning. This practice was accepted in the Missal of 1570, after Pius V, four years earlier, had forbidden all Masses in the afternoon and evening for very dubious reasons.

The reform decree of 1955 saw this anticipation as harmful to the "liturgical sense" of the faithful, and therefore went back to the original hour of celebration; the regulation read as follows: "On Good Friday the liturgy is celebrated in the afternoon and specifically at about three o'clock. If pastoral reasons make it advisable, a later hour—but not later than six o'clock—may be chosen." The new Missal has taken over this regulation but without setting a time limit for a postponement of the celebration on pastoral grounds. Provision is here being made especially for countries in which Good Friday is not a holiday and the faithful must work during the day.

In the following paragraphs I shall describe the Good Friday liturgy according to the new Missal of 1970 and its English version, the Sacramentary, of 1974. The liturgy is now celebrated in red vestments instead of black. Red is the color of the martyrs, who have Christ as their prototype and model and who see in Christ's obedience unto death the source of their own self-sacrifice and triumph.

THE LITURGY OF THE WORD

The priest and his attendants advance to the altar, which is completely bare, and either prostrate themselves at full length on the floor (Latin: *prostratio*) or else kneel; they remain for a while in silent prayer. Prostration is a gesture taken into the liturgy from the ceremonial of the imperial court at Constantinople, although it is also to be found in the Old Testament. The fact that an ancient tradition with such strong symbolic force should have survived to our own day in the Good Friday liturgy is a confirmation of the "law of the retention of what is ancient in the more sacred seasons of the liturgical year," which A. Baumstark formulated.[30]

After the prostration, the priest goes to his chair and there says one of the two prayers provided in the Sacramentary. The first reading is the fourth Servant Song (Is 52.13–53.12) which from time immemorial has been understood as depicting the redemptive suffering of Christ. Psalm 31, the responsorial psalm, is not only a lament but also expresses trust in the "faithful God." The second reading is a hymn of praise to the "great high priest" who has "become the source of eternal salvation to all who obey him" (Heb 4.14-16; 5.7-9). The second intermediate song (Phil 2.8-9), which introduces the gospel, is from the classical passage on the paschal mystery of Christ; it speaks not only of the obedience of Jesus unto death but also of his exaltation.

The account of the passion according to John (18.1–19.42) is to be read in the same manner as the passion narrative on Palm Sunday, i.e., without candles or incense, without any greeting of the people or signing of the book. A deacon reads the gospel, if a deacon is present; otherwise the priest does it. But the passion can also be read by laypersons, each taking a different role, "with the part of Christ, if possible, reserved to the priest" (rubric for Palm Sunday), since he represents Christ in the liturgy. After the reading of the passion there may be a short homily.

The solemn intercessions are early Christian material that has continued in existence right down to our time, even though the intercessions (or general intercessions, or prayer of the faithful) which had been a regular part of every eucharistic celebration in early Rome had for centuries been forgotten and were reintroduced only by Vatican II. Specifically, there are ten prayer intentions; they have a basic structure that has now been applied to the intercessions reintroduced as a regular part of every Mass. The intentions are, broadly speaking, "for holy Church, for the civil authorities, for those oppressed by various needs, for all mankind, and for the salvation of the entire world" (CL, no. 53; Flannery, p. 18). More particularly, prayers are offered for holy Church, the pope, all states of life in the Church, catechumens, Christian unity, the Jews, all who do not believe in Christ, all who do not believe in God, rulers, those in every kind of need.

If we compare these intercessions with those in use earlier, we discern a great conciseness and also a more considerate formulation in the prayers for Jews and for those who used to be called "heretics" and "schismatics." From among these intercessions the priest may choose those "which are more appropriate to local circumstances." "In case of serious public need, the local Ordinary may permit or decree the addition of a special intention" (rubrics).

In each intercession the priest first says or sings an "introduction in which each intention is stated" and then, after a pause for silent prayer, says or sings the oration. The traditional custom may be retained according to which, after the introduction, the faithful kneel when the deacon says, "Let us kneel," and stand again when he says, "Let us stand."

The second main part of the Good Friday liturgy is the veneration of the cross.

First, the cross is solemnly exhibited to the faithful (elevation of the cross). There are two ways of conducting this ceremony; "pastoral demands will determine which of the two forms is more effective and should be chosen" (rubric). In the first (traditional) form, a veiled cross is carried to the altar by one of the celebrants, accompanied by two ministers with lighted candles. At the altar it is given to the priest, who uncovers it in three stages, each time intoning (formerly in successively higher tones) the "invitation at the elevation of the cross," that is, the *Ecce lignum crucis*, "This is the wood of the cross, on which hung the Savior of the world." The community answers with "Come, let us worship," and then kneels in silent prayer. The unveiled cross is now placed at the entry to the sanctuary or in some other suitable spot in view of the community, or else it is held by two ministers. Then the veneration begins.

In the second form of elevation, the priest goes with his attendants to the door of the church, takes the unveiled cross, and advances in procession to the sanctuary. On the way he halts three times and each time sings the invitation for the elevation. The rest is as in the first form.

At the veneration of the cross the clergy and faithful come forward to the cross and venerate it with a genuflection or a kiss or some other sign. Meanwhile the time-honored and deeply moving chants for the veneration of the cross are sung by community or choir. Among these is the antiphon "We worship you, Lord" (now placed first in the Sacramentary), the Reproaches (Lamentations), and the sixth-century hymn, *Pange, lingua, gloriosi proelium certaminis* ("Sing, my tongue, the Savior's story"). When done in Gregorian chant, the antiphon just cited rivets attention both by its text and by its melody, for in both the joy of Easter already breaks through: "We worship you, Lord, we venerate your cross, we praise your resurrection. Through the cross you brought joy into the world." The Gregorian melody at its beginning has strong echoes of the Te Deum.[3]

THE CELEBRATION OF COMMUNION

After the veneration of the cross a cloth is laid on the altar, and then the Sacramentary and a corporal. The Blessed Sacrament is brought to the altar from the place of reservation, and the priest adores it with a genflection. The Our Father, embolism, and acclamation of the people follow. After a short preparatory prayer, the priest elevates a host and says as usual: "This is the Lamb of God . . ."; he then receives the Lord's body and distributes it to the community. The vessel with the remaining hosts is taken elsewhere or placed in the tabernacle. After a pause for silent meditation, the concluding prayer and the prayer over the people are said. The concluding prayer gives thanks for the new life the Father has bestowed on us "by the triumphant death and resurrection" of his Son, and thus once again brings out the unity of the paschal mystery. The prayer over the people, which the priest says with hands extended toward the congregation, likewise mentions the death and resurrection together and prays God on behalf of the people: "Grant them pardon; bring them comfort. May their faith grow stronger and their eternal salvation be assured."

c/ The Celebration of the Easter Vigil

In the early Church Holy Saturday, being the day of Christ's repose in the tomb, had no liturgy of its own. It was a day of strict grief-inspired fasting that focused the thoughts of the faithful very sharply on the death of Christ and his repose in the tomb. As I mentioned earlier, the first part of the Easter Vigil was likewise marked by mourning and fasting. Only after midnight, in the celebration of baptism and the eucharist, did mourning change to joy.

Many people today find it impossible to understand how, until 1951, the Roman liturgy could have transferred this "mother of all vigils" to early Holy Saturday morning and thus have largely blunted its rich symbolic power. How (they ask themselves) could the intensely festive Easter Vigil have become a clerical liturgy attended by only a few of the faithful and celebrated during the time of Christ's repose in the tomb? The question calls for a short historical overview.[32]

As late as the end of the fourth century the Easter Vigil seems to have occupied the entire night, so that no further liturgy was celebrated on Easter day. Yet we soon find warnings being issued here and there not to end the celebration before midnight. Toward the end of the sixth century it is already becoming clear that the Vigil Mass was indeed ending before midnight and that Easter Sunday now had its own Mass. Around the middle of the eighth century the Vigil Mass had been moved so far forward that it could begin when the first star had become visible. A ninth-century liturgical source (the Einsiedeln *Ordo*) names the hour of none (around three o'clock) as the time for beginning the Vigil Mass; this meant that the parts of the Vigil celebration which precede the Mass were beginning around noon. In other words, the time prescribed in the Middle Ages for celebrating Mass on fastdays had been reached; such Masses were to begin only "after none," that is, around 3 PM.

As fasting regulations were increasingly relaxed in the fourteenth century, Church law allowed none to be read in the morning hours and the fastday Mass to begin immediately. This arrangement was applied to the Vigil Mass as well. But this means that the preceding parts of the Vigil liturgy were pushed back even further, to early morning. In the Missal of Pius V (1570) this arrangement was not only permitted but made obligatory, after the same Pope had forbidden all afternoon and evening Masses in his Bull *Sanctissimus* of 1566.

As a result of all this—and to the wonder of the older folk among us—the Easter candle was lit and carried to the altar, to the accompaniment of the threefold *Lumen Christi*, at an hour when bright sunshine was already filling the church; the solemn Easter alleluia was sung and the Easter message was proclaimed in the liturgy of the word and the preface, but the people leaving the church knew that the fast did not end until noon! This liturgical "experience," which caused great discomfort to the more liturgically attuned, was worlds apart from the experience of people in the early centuries, as described by an expert in liturgical history: "The great antitheses of night and dawn, fasting and eucharistic meal, mourning and festive joy provided an awesome experience of the contrast between death and life, decease and resurrection, Satan and Kyrios, old eon and new eon."[33]

All the greater, then, was the joy that many felt when, in a decree of the Congregation of Rites, February 9, 1951, Pius XII allowed the Vigil service to be celebrated in the night before Easter (initially this was allowed as a one year's experiment), after a few episcopal conferences and other bodies had asked for this change a short time before. At the same time, the rite was made more concise, and some parts of it were revised. What was initially allowed as an experiment soon became general law in the new Holy Week Order of November 16, 1955. The Roman Catholic liturgy had rediscovered a lost treasure.

As the result of experience over a number of years, the Roman Missal of 1970 was able to improve the Easter Vigil celebration even further and to give it a central place in the Easter triduum. The *General Norms for the Liturgical Year* that accompany the Missal describe the Vigil thus: "During it [the Easter Vigil] the Church keeps watch, awaiting the resurrection of Christ and celebrating it in the sacraments. The entire celebration of this Vigil should take place at night, beginning after nightfall and ending with dawn" (no. 21).

The liturgy of Easter night comprises (a) the service of light; (b) the liturgy of the word; (c) the celebration of baptism; and (d) the celebration of the eucharist.

THE SERVICE OF LIGHT
For this service the priest and his assistants, wearing white vestments, come with the Easter candle to a wood fire in front of the church; there the community likewise assembles as far as possible. When a service in front of the church is not feasible, a suitable arrangement may be made at the church door. After the greeting and a short introduction the priest blesses the fire and asks God to inflame us with a desire for eternal light.

The old Roman liturgy did not have such a blessing of fire; the blessing is "rather of Frankish origin and seems intended from the beginning as a sacramental of the Church that would replace the fires lit in spring by the pagans in honor of Wotan or some other heathen divinity, in order to assure good crops."[34] The same heathen origin probably explains some other pagan customs that have persisted in many places down to the present, "as, for example, when small crosses are made from wood that has caught fire, and are stuck in the fields or the ashes of the burnt wood are scattered on the pastures" (ibid.). The custom still in use of striking this fire from stone if possible seems likewise to go back to ideas of the ancient Germans and of antiquity. In this custom the Middle Ages saw an allusion to Christ "the cornerstone, who after being laid low by the blows of the cross poured out his Holy Spirit on us."[35]

The Easter candle surely had its earliest basis in the custom, practiced from the beginning at Rome and elsewhere, of lighting up the night of Easter with numerous candles. These were regarded as symbolizing Christ who had been raised up from the night of death. There were originally two Easter candles, man high in size, but they were reduced to one, for which the Gallic liturgy provided a special blessing and to which the Gallic and Frankish delight in allegory added further elements of symbolism. It would take us too far afield in a book like this to trace the historical development of all the details, and I must therefore be content to describe the rite as we now have it.

The celebrant is free to decide whether and to what extent he will make use of these various symbols for the service of light. They involve him in cutting a cross into the Easter candle with a stylus and saying as he does so: "Christ yesterday and today, the beginning and the end." Then he incises the first and, under it, the last letter of the Greek alphabet, saying "Alpha and Omega." Finally, as he incises the four numbers of the current year in the four angles between the crossbars, he says: "All time belongs to him and all the ages; to him be glory and power through every age for ever. Amen." At the ends of the crossbars and at the point where the two meet he now inserts four grains of incense, each enclosed in a red nail of wax. This gesture is accompanied by the words "(1) By his holy (2) and glorious wounds (3) may Christ our Lord (4) guard us (5) and keep us. Amen."[36]

78

The priest now lights the Easter candle and says: "May the light of Christ, rising in glory, dispel the darkness of our hearts and minds." The deacon or priest elevates the Easter candle thus adorned and sings: *Lumen Christi*, "Christ our light," and all answer: "Thanks be to God."

All now form a procession and follow the deacon as he advances into the church with the Easter candle. At the entrance to the church (or in the middle of the Church if the blessing of the fire took place at the door), the Easter candle is elevated a second time and the *Lumen Christi* is repeated. At this point, all in the congregation light their candles from the Easter candle. In front of the altar the Easter candle is elevated a third time, and the *Lumen Christi* is sung once more. Then all the lights in the church are lit.

The procession behind the Easter candle is impressive and rich in symbolism. We spontaneously recall the words of Christ in John 8.12: "I am the light of the world; he who follows me will not walk in darkness, but will have the light of life." The Easter candle as it advances before us also reminds us of the pillar of fire in which Yahweh went before the Israelites in the night as they were leaving slavery, and showed them the way to freedom (cf. Ex 13.21).

The Easter candle is set on a stand in the sanctuary and incensed. There follows the Easter proclamation *(praeconium paschale)*, also called the *Exsultet* from the first word of the Latin text. During the singing of it the faithful stand, holding their lighted candles in their hand. This hymn of praise by an unknown writer draws upon the thought of Ambrose and Augustine, but in part it also makes use of still older texts. Most important among these is "the oldest known hymn of praise to the night of Easter," which dates from the first half of the fourth century. It occurs in the Easter homilies of Asterius the Sophist[37] and is dependent in its turn on the Jewish theology and liturgy of Passover.[38] The early Christian rite of lighting the lamps and praising the light, which took place each evening and was modeled on practices in the culture of Judaism and the ancient world, may also have influenced the Easter proclamation.[39]

The present form of the *Exsultet* probably arose in the world of the Gallic liturgy at the beginning of the seventh century.[40] The hymn can now be used in a longer or shorter form and, if the episcopal conference approves, may be accompanied by acclamations of the people. It begins with a summons to jubilation that is directed to the choirs of angels, to the earth that is radiant with "shining splendor," and to "Mother Church" on whom "the risen Savior shines." The text then takes the form of a preface which with lyric fervor celebrates Christ's redemptive act and sings of the Easter night in which he arose from the dead.

Attention then turns to the act by which God delivered "the people of Israel" from slavery in Egypt and led them to freedom through the waves of the Red Sea. This saving act of God becomes a symbol of the paschal mystery of Christ, which the text seeks to praise in ever new phrases and images, until finally it breaks out into astonished exclamations: "Father . . . how boundless your merciful love! . . . O happy fault, O necessary sin of Adam, which gained for us so great a redeemer! Most blessed of all nights. . . ." Finally with moving words the hymn addresses the Easter candle itself as symbol of the invisible Lord "who came back from the dead, and shed his peaceful light on all mankind."

Since this *Exsultet* is a high point in the entire proclamation of Easter, the question has been asked, with good reason, whether it would not be more suitably sung after the liturgy of the word and before the celebration of baptism.

THE LITURGY OF THE WORD
There are nine scripture readings in all, two of them (epistle and gospel) from the New Testament. For pastoral reasons the number of Old Testament readings can be reduced to as few as two, but one must always be the story of the crossing of the Red Sea because this prefigures the paschal mystery. Each of the seven Old Testament readings is followed by a responsorial psalm and a prayer.

The candles on the altar are lit after the prayer for the seventh reading, and the priest then intones the Gloria, during which the church bells are rung. After the prayer of the feast ("Lord God, you have brightened this night with the radiance of the risen Christ . . .") the epistle, Romans 6.3-11, is read; it speaks of our sharing in the life and destiny of Christ in virtue of our baptism.

After the reading, all stand, and for the first time after the long and somber weeks of Lent, the alleluia is heard once again. Many will regret that the priest does not sing it three times as formerly, each time on a higher note, with the people repeating it three times after him. But even when sung only once, the unusual and rich melody is deeply moving to anyone who in faith celebrates the passion and resurrection of Christ. "This alleluia rises with a slow movement; it rises above the grave of Adam, and it has the blood of Christ on its wings. It is the marriage song of the paschal night, which will grow slowly brighter as it meets the day of resurrection. But these are only words. The first alleluia of the paschal night is a mystery, un-utterable like all mysteries. As this alleluia is, so is the whole life of Christians: a gentle, quiet song of joy which meets the rise of day in the midst of the suffering night of time."[41]

The responsorial psalm, Psalm 118, becomes a festive hymn of thanksgiving for the salvific event of the resurrection: "O give thanks to the Lord for he is good; his steadfast love endures for ever!" The gospel is different in each year of the three-year cycle, so that passages on the resurrection are read from all of the synoptic gospels. The celebration of baptism follows upon the homily.

THE CELEBRATION OF BAPTISM
The celebrants go to the baptismal font, provided the font can be seen by the people (this is the most desirable location for the font); "otherwise a vessel of water is placed in the sanctuary" (rubric). Since the night of Easter has from time immemorial been the preferred time for baptism in the Church, it is still desirable that the sacrament actually be conferred at this point. If it is, the candidates are called forward and presented to the community. After a short introduction an abbreviated litany of the saints is sung, with the names of the patron saints of the church, the locality and the individual candidates being in-

serted. During the blessing of the baptismal water the priest dips the Easter candle into it either once or three times, saying: "We ask you, Father, with your Son to send the Holy Spirit upon the waters of this font."

After the renunciation of Satan and the baptismal profession of faith baptism is conferred. If the candidates are adults, they also receive confirmation from the baptizing priest, unless a bishop is present.

If no baptism is conferred, there is no blessing of baptismal water but simply a general blessing of water (holy water, Easter water). Since the restoration of the Easter Vigil in 1951, a renewal of baptismal promises, i.e., a renunciation and a profession of faith, is provided at this point, the faithful answering the priest's questions with "I do." Then the congregation is sprinkled with the blessed water, while the antiphon *Vidi aquam* ("I saw water . . .")[42] or some other baptismal song is sung. The sprinkling of the congregation with blessed water is an ancient form of reminder of their baptism; such a rite lives on in the Sunday Asperges.[43] This part of the Easter night liturgy closes with the general intercessions.

THE CELEBRATION OF THE EUCHARIST

At the preparation of the gifts it is recommended that newly baptized adults or young people bring the bread and wine to the altar. The preface is a hymn of praise and gratitude to Jesus Christ, our sacrificed Easter Lamb: "He is the true Lamb who took away the sins of the world. By dying he destroyed our death, by rising he restored our life." If the first eucharistic prayer is used, there are special inserts for Easter which are added from the Easter Vigil to the second Sunday of Easter and in which there is not only a recall of the Easter event of salvation but also an intercession for "those born into the new life of water and the Holy Spirit, with all their sins forgiven." The introduction to the kiss of peace might well contain a reminder of the greeting of peace which Jesus gave his disciples on the evening of his resurrection day. The solemn tripartite final blessing and the dismissal with its double alleluia conclude the liturgy of Easter night.

d/Easter Sunday

As we saw in the historical overview given earlier, Easter Sunday originally had no liturgy of its own, since the service during Easter night extended into the early morning. Now that the Easter Vigil has been restored to its place during the night, we must regard the eucharist celebrated during it as the true Mass for the feast, even if it be celebrated before midnight. Nonetheless those who have taken part in the Vigil Mass may receive communion again at a second Easter Mass; the same rule holds for celebration of Mass by priests. The fear in many countries that the Mass during the day on Easter would be celebrated before an empty church has proved unfounded.

The Mass (the readings of which are the same in all three years of the new cycle) is filled with wonder and joy at the resurrection of the Lord. Thus the entrance antiphon has the Lord himself say: "I have risen: I am with you once more; you placed your hand on me to keep me safe. How great is the depth of your wisdom! Alleluia." The intermediate songs (responsorial psalm and the alleluia verse) especially are full of jubilation. The first is from Psalm 118, with "This is the day the Lord has made," as the response. The second song on this day is the Easter Sequence *Victimae paschali laudes* ("To the paschal victim") with its triumphant profession of Easter faith: "We know that Christ has indeed risen from the dead. Do you, conqueror and king, have mercy on us. Amen. Alleluia."

In the first reading (Acts 10.34a, 37-43) Peter bears witness to the paschal mystery of Christ. For the second reading a choice of two Easter texts is offered: Colossians 3.1-4 and 1 Corinthians 5.6b-8. In both we are exhorted to draw conclusions for moral conduct from our participation in the death and resurrection of Christ. The gospel is the story of the resurrection in John 20.1-9. The presidential prayers, in a spirit of joy at Christ's resurrection, ask: "Let our celebration today raise us up and renew our lives by the Spirit that is within us" (opening prayer), and "Father of love, watch over your Church and bring us to the glory of the resurrection" (prayer after communion).

Since in most parishes many who attend this Mass have not

participated in the foregoing liturgies of the Easter triduum, the homily should endeavor to bring home to them the unity of the redemptive paschal mystery, that is, of the passion and resurrection, as both the Easter preface and the communion antiphon do. In the homily reference should also be made to the Easter Vigil; its importance as the climax of the entire liturgical year should be explained. Efforts to repeat some parts of the Vigil at "High Mass" on Easter Sunday may easily work to the disadvantage of the restored Vigil. In many parishes a good many parishioners already attend vespers on Easter. This office provides a meaningful close to the Easter triduum.

3 / THE EASTER SEASON OR *PENTEKOSTE*

In the Jewish festal calendar we can already see a reflection of the experience that it takes a certain amount of time for moments of deep festivity to run their course. There is further confirmation of this in the early Christian practice of celebrating the paschal mystery of Christ with thanksgiving and joy not only during the three days of the Easter triduum but also during the following seven weeks or fifty days. From the first half of the second century we already have a literary testimony to this in the apocryphal *Epistula apostolorum* (Letter of the Apostles).[44] A few decades later there are many more such testimonies.[45] The Council of Elvira rejects attempts to turn the period of fifty days (*Pentekostē* in Greek, *Quinquagesima* in Latin) into a forty-day period (Latin: *Quadragesima*).[46]

There is an example of such a festal period of fifty days in the Jewish calendar, in which the "feast of Weeks" (= Pentecost) was celebrated fifty days after the feast of Unleavened Bread (see above, Chapter II, section 2,b). According to Acts 2.1 ff. on this day occurred the visible outpouring of the Holy Spirit, which must be regarded as the real fruit of the paschal mystery. According to John 20.22 Christ had already filled his disciples with the Holy Spirit on Easter.

Liturgically, this fifty-day was characterized by joyous thanksgiving that found expression, among other ways, in frequent alleluias and a prohibition against fasting and against kneeling for prayer.[47] The new *General Norms for the Liturgical*

Year thus have a basis in very ancient tradition when they state that "the fifty days from Easter Sunday to Pentecost are celebrated as one feastday, sometimes called 'the great Sunday' " (no. 22). This fact receives symbolic expression in the requirement that the Easter candle, as an image of the risen Lord, should remain in the sanctuary during these fifty days and should be lit during the liturgy even on weekdays.[48]

At an earlier time it was customary to extinguish the candle and remove it after the gospel on Ascension Thursday; this could easily be misunderstood to mean that after his ascension the glorified Christ is no longer present in his community. The revised liturgy provides that once the Easter season is over the Easter candle is to have a place of honor in the baptistery or beside the font.[49] At baptisms the candles of the newly baptized are to be lit from the Easter candle. At funeral Masses the lighted Easter candle should be set in a prominent place, possibly next to the coffin.[50]

The first eight days of the Easter season make up the octave of Easter. By comparison with the "great octave" of seven weeks this one might be called a little octave, but without any intention of detracting from its importance. Its beginnings as a period marked by special liturgical celebration go back at least to the early part of the fourth century, perhaps even to the second half of the third, as can be inferred from the recently discovered homilies of Asterius the Sophist on the psalms.[51] On one occasion Asterius calls the octave day the "second 'eighth day.' "[52]

The liturgy of this octave derived its tone not only from the paschal mystery but also from the attention paid to the newly baptized. At the daily celebration of the eucharist these neophytes were introduced more fully to the mysteries of faith and especially to the sacraments of initiation which they had received during the Easter Vigil. The Easter homilies of Asterius are probably the earliest known example of such "mystagogical catecheses," although the best-known examples are surely the five mystagogical catecheses of Bishop Cyril (John?) of Jerusalem in the second half of the fourth century and the Ambrosian writings *De mysteriis* and *De sacramentis*.[53] According to Augustine the Easter octave represents an *ecclesiae consensus*, or unanimous practice of the Church, that is as ancient as Lent.[54] The faithful had to refrain from work and take part in the daily liturgy.

At one time this week was called "white week," i.e., week in white garments; in the East it was also called "week of renewal." Originally it ended on Sunday, which was therefore called "Sunday in white garments" *(dominica in albis)*. From the seventh century on the neophytes set aside their white garments on Saturday; this was due to the fact that the Vigil Mass had by now been moved back to Holy Saturday.

The entrance antiphons of the Easter octave, which in the later Roman liturgy were sung by the choir during the entrance procession of the white-clad neophytes, were chosen for their application to the latter: they proclaimed the salvation in which the newly baptized now shared. Thus, on Monday, "The Lord brought you a land flowing with milk and honey, so that his law would always be given honor among you, alleluia"; on Tuesday, "If men desire wisdom, she will give them the water of knowledge to drink; they will never waver from the truth; they will stand firm for ever"; on Wednesday, "Come, you whom my Father has blessed; inherit the kingdom prepared for you . . ."; on Thursday, "Your people praised your great victory, O Lord . . ."; on Friday, "The Lord led his people out of slavery . . ."; on Saturday, "The Lord led his people to freedom and they shouted with joy and gladness; alleluia"; and, finally, on White Sunday, "Like newborn children you should thirst for milk, on which your spirit can grow to strength, alleluia."

In the seventh century there arose the custom of the *Pascha annotinum* (literally: "one-year-old Pasch," from *annus*; "year") or anniversary commemoration of baptism. "Parents and godparents bring to Church the children baptized at Easter of the previous year, in order to celebrate the anniversary of their baptism in gratitude to God. They are joined by the entire community which thus has an additional annual memorial celebration of their own baptism."[55] Since the actual anniversary day might come before the current Easter due to the annually shifting date of Easter, the Monday after White Sunday was finally chosen as the memorial day. However, once infant baptism came to be administered immediately after birth (beginning of the second millennium), the custom of the *Pascha annotinum* gradually disappeared.

The still widespread custom of having children make their first communion on White Sunday came in only during the eighteenth century. Of course, first communion can just as well be made on any other day. It makes sense, however, to link the eucharist, as sacrament of initiation, with Easter and to celebrate it as being not only a private event but a matter of concern to the whole community. However, ways must be sought and found of avoiding a great deal of external pomp that distracts children rather than helps them.

In order to bring out the unity of the Easter season more clearly, "the Sundays of the Easter season are henceforth to be called Sundays *of* Easter and not Sundays *after* Easter. Thus White Sunday becomes the second Sunday of Easter."[56] Pentecost is now the eighth Sunday of the Easter season and marks the end of the great Easter octave or fifty days. The liturgy of these Sundays may not be replaced even by that of a solemnity; the same is true of the Sundays of the Easter penitential season (Lent) and the Sundays of Advent.

The liturgy of these Sundays bears the strong impress of the paschal mystery as a single entity, i.e., the suffering, death and resurrection of Christ. This unity embraces not only the resurrection but the ascension and the sending of the Spirit as well. The first readings are always from the Acts of the Apostles with its accounts of the life, growth and witness of the primitive Church. The second readings, which change through the three-year cycle, are from 1 Peter, 1 John and Revelation because "these texts seem most appropriate to the spirit of the Easter season, a spirit of joyful faith and confident hope."[57] The gospels of the second and third Sundays of Easter report appearances of the risen Christ. In order not to interrupt this theme the gospel of the Good Shepherd has been moved from the third to the fourth Sunday of Easter. On the following three Sundays the pericopes are from the discourses and prayers of the Lord at the Last Supper ("farewell discourses" and "high priestly prayer" of Jesus according to John). There are five prefaces available for the Easter season, of which only the first is meant for specific days (Easter Vigil, Easter Sunday, octave of Easter).

The weekdays of the Easter season in the second to sixth weeks have their own opening prayers, but the remaining parts of the Proper are contained in two week-long series that are used alternately. The reading is always from Acts; the gospel (except during the octave of Easter in which all the evangelists are represented) is a semicontinuous reading of the gospel of John, specifically from chapters 3, 6, 10, and 14–17. The solemn final blessing for the Easter season may be used every day.

It has already been noted that the early Church regarded the whole fifty-day period as a single festal period which focused on the unitary theme of Christ's passage through death to glory. A breakdown into separate aspects and a fading of the unitary vision came only later on. The change can be seen in connection with the feast of Christ's ascension. According to the account of Egeria the pilgrim (to take an example), at the end of the fourth century the Christians of Jerusalem were still celebrating the ascension and the sending of the Spirit together on the fiftieth day as the completion of Christ's saving act. Meanwhile, however, the other Churches were, in the fourth century, already celebrating a separate feast of the ascension on the fortieth day after Easter. In addition to a fundamental esteem for the "sacred" number 40, the chief influence here was the remark in Acts 1.3: "appearing to them during forty days and speaking of the kingdom of God," and the subsequent account of the ascension in vv. 9-11. Augustine, a number of whose sermons for this day have survived, already observes that this feast "is celebrated all over the world."[58]

Today the feast of the ascension of Christ has the rank of a solemnity. The festal Mass emphasizes both the return of Christ (entrance antiphon) and his abiding presence in the community (communion antiphon). The opening prayer sees in the ascension an exaltation of the human race as well as of Christ. With the grace of God we are to "rise with him to the joys of heaven" (prayer over the gifts). The two readings (Acts 1.1-11; Eph 1.17-23) are the same every year but the gospel has a three-year cycle: the accounts of the ascension in Matthew, Mark and Luke. The festal mystery also finds expression in the two prefaces and the inserts for the first eucharistic prayer. In places where the ascension of Christ is not a holy day of obligation, it is celebrated on the following Sunday.

"The weekdays after the Ascension to Saturday before Pentecost inclusive are a preparation for the coming of the Holy Spirit."[59] They have their own Mass formularies "which recall the promises of Christ relating to the outpouring of the Holy Spirit."[60] In this way the Pentecost novena which had become part of popular devotion is given a place in the official liturgy. The Church thus joins the disciples of Jesus, who after Pentecost "with one accord devoted themselves to prayer, together with the women and Mary the mother of Jesus, and with his brethren" (Acts 1.14).

Pentecost, the fiftieth day after Easter, is to be regarded as the crowning close to the Easter season. That is how the Eastern Churches have always thought of it in their liturgies. In the Roman liturgy, on the other hand, we see the same tendency at work that we have discerned in connection with other feasts: the tendency to make this day an independent entity and thus a more or less isolated feast of the sending of the Holy Spirit. Accordingly, it was given an octave; this, however (a sign of liturgical confusion), had to include the summer ember days (i.e., days of penance), since the ember days had acquired this position in the calendar at a much earlier time.

In many countries, a second and even a third day of celebration were added to Pentecost (as happened with Christmas and Easter), and people spoke of a special Pentecost cycle of feasts. Not least because of studies in liturgical history (especially those already mentioned of Odo Casel) which showed "the close connection between the gift of the Holy Spirit and the resurrection and ascension of the Lord,"[61] the Congregation of Rites has endeavored in its *General Norms for the Liturgical Year and the Calendar* to link the feast of Pentecost more closely with Easter.

The Vigil Mass, which at an earlier time was, like the Easter Vigil, a date for baptism, may no longer be celebrated on the morning of the previous Saturday. It has been replaced by a new Mass for the preceding evening, and this is regarded as a first Mass of Pentecost. A choice of four Old Testament readings is given. The opening prayer of this Mass explicitly asserts the connection of Easter and Pentecost: "Almighty and ever-living God, you fulfilled the Easter promise by sending us your Holy Spirit." The old preface for Pentecost, which characteristically bore the title *De Spiritu Sancto* ("Of the Holy Spirit"), has been replaced by a new one in which the connection with Easter is brought out more clearly: "Today you sent the Holy Spirit on those marked to be your children by sharing the life of your only Son, and so you brought the paschal mystery to its completion. . . . The joy of the resurrection renews the whole world, while the choirs of heaven sing for ever to your glory."

This unified view of the one fifty-day season is unfortunately less clear in the inserts for the first eucharistic prayer. It is said only that "the Holy Spirit appeared to the apostles in the form of countless tongues."

The first reading for the feast, Acts 2.1-11, describes the Pentecostal event in Jerusalem. The coincidence of this event with the Jewish feast of Weeks or Pentecost, which was both a feast of thanksgiving for the wheat harvest and a memorial of the establishment of the covenant at Sinai (see above, chapter II, section 2,b), is an unmistakable sign that Christians are the new covenanted people and that the Church is the first fruits of Christ's paschal mystery. The second reading (1 Cor 12.3b-7, 12-13) brings out the meaning of the Holy Spirit as the life principle of Christ's body, the Church.

While the gospel in the old Mass formulary was a passage from the farewell discourses in which Christ speaks, among other things, of the sending the Spirit (Jn 14.23-31), the new pericope, which is the same for all three years of the cycle, describes, significantly enough, the appearance of the risen Jesus on Easter Sunday evening. At this time his disciples already receive the Holy Spirit (Jn 20.19-23).

A sublime song in praise of the Holy Spirit's activity is given to us in the Sequence *Veni, Sancte Spiritu,* which remains obligatory of the feast of Pentecost. It has also been called the "Golden Sequence" and was composed by Stephen Langton, archbishop of Canterbury († 1228).[62]

The red color used in the vestments for Pentecost may be regarded as a holdover from the time when the feast was treated as an isolated entity. Innocent III had already interpreted the color as an allusion to the tongues of fire at the descent of the Holy Spirit.[63] But it would surely be more meaningful for the entire great octave of Easter to show the same color as the principal feast itself.

4 / THE EASTER PENITENTIAL PERIOD

a/The Historical Development

Mention has already been made in the section on Good Friday (chapter V, section 2,b) of the fact that the Christians of the second century were already preparing for the feast of Easter with a two-day, grief-inspired fast. In the third century this fast (though not as a "complete fast") was extended to all of Holy Week, as we learn from a letter of Dionysius of Alexandria.[64] The first Ecumenical Council of Nicaea already speaks of the *quadragesima paschae,* i.e., the forty-day period of preparation for Easter, as something obvious and familiar to all.[65]

The intention was to imitate Jesus who after his baptism in the Jordan fasted for forty days (Mt 4.2; Lk 4.1-2). The Church Fathers also saw in the practice an echo of the forty days Moses fasted on Sinai (Ex 34.28) and the forty days Elijah fasted on his journey to Mount Horeb (1 Kings 19.8), as well as of the forty years of Israel's sojourn in the wilderness; and so on.

The forty-day period originally began on the sixth Sunday before Easter and lasted until Holy Thursday when the solemn restoration of penitents to the community took place at Rome. There is disagreement about whether at one period in fourth-century Rome the fast was continued for only three weeks, as Socrates, the Greek historian of the Church, claims.[66]

Because there was no fasting on Sundays, an effort was made in the fifth century to increase the number of actual fastdays to forty. The goal was attained in two stages. First, Good Friday and Holy Saturday were separated from the Easter triduum and added to the preparatory fast, thus raising the number of fastdays to thirty-six. Many of the Fathers liked to point out that this was one-tenth of the number of days in the year.[67] Soon, however, the four weekdays before the first Sunday of Lent were added, changing the number once again to forty. Thus we have our Ash Wednesday as the beginning of Lent (= *caput ieiunii*, "beginning of the fast").

But not all were satisfied with this new arrangement. During the sixth century a special significance was attached to the three Sundays before Ash Wednesday; they were named (using round numbers) *Quinquagesima* (= the fiftieth), *Sexagesima* (= the sixtieth) and *Septuagesima* (= the seventieth). The heightened importance attributed to these Sundays was probably due in part to the fact that the stational liturgies on these days were celebrated in the famous churches of Rome's patron saints, Lawrence, Peter and Paul, and that the repeated attacks of the Goths and Lombards made the people ready for additional prayer and penance. A further influence in the establishment of this pre-Lent may have been the liturgical custom of the Byzantine Church, where Lent was begun on the eighth Sunday before Easter because in that Church there was no fasting on either Saturdays or Sundays and eight weeks were therefore needed for a forty-day period of fasting. In this Roman pre-Lent, however, no real fast was required, although the liturgy was characterized (later on) by violet vestments and the omission of the alleluia, Gloria and Te Deum. In the new organization of the liturgical year in 1969 this pre-Lent was dropped.

The Lenten fast meant that individuals took only a single daily meal; in accordance with ancient custom, this was eaten in the evening. Abstinence from meat and wine was added later on, as was abstinence from dairy products (milk, butter, cheese and eggs), in many countries, until the end of the Middle Ages and beyond.[68] From the High Middle Ages on, a growing relaxation may be observed in the practice of fasting; this was certainly connected with a higher esteem for the body in the philosophy and theology of the high scholastic period.

We moderns are amazed, and perhaps sceptical, when we read of the extent and severity of the fasting practiced in the early Church. As J. Schümmer shows, the practice was sustained by a wealth of intensely held beliefs. Those who came to the Christian faith as catechumens, whether from Judaism or from the pagan religions, were usually familiar with religiously motivated forms of abstinence from food. In addition, fasting for medical reasons, without any religious motivation, was not uncommon among the Greeks and Romans. [69] Moreover, the Christians of the time saw fasting as a source of fervor in prayer; as St. Nilus put it in a striking image, "the prayer of one who is fasting is like a young eagle that soars into the air, whereas the prayer of an immoderate eater is burdened by satiety and sinks earthward." [70]

Christians also saw in fasting a way of preparing for the reception of the Spirit, a powerful weapon in the fight against evil spirits, an appropriate preparation for such religious actions as the reception of baptism and the eucharist, and, finally, a way of being able to help the poor with money that would otherwise have been spent on food. When Tertullian reports the now famous words of the pagans, "See how they love another! They are even ready to die for one another," [71] we must bear in mind that to his contemporaries this readiness could not be more convincingly shown than by fasting in order to be able to feed a poor person. [72] Missionary reflection on the extensive fasting practiced in Judaism and the pagan religions (e.g., the mystery religions) may also have encouraged fasting in the early Church. [73] In all this, however, the Church was conscious of the prophet Isaiah's warning against fasting that becomes an external formality (Is 58.5 ff.), and she repeatedly drew attention to the corresponding admonitions of Jesus in the Sermon on the Mount (Mt 6.16-18).

As far as the content of Lent in the early Church is concerned, another important influence was the efforts made in connection with the reconciliation of penitents and the bringing of candidates for baptism to the reception of the sacraments of initiation during the Easter Vigil. Both of these ministries represented a response to the basic summons issued in Mark 1.15: "Repent, and believe in the Gospel." What the Church required of penitents and candidates by way of liturgical and ascetical effort was also done by the faithful in solidarity of spirit and, to some extent, in reality as well. An atmosphere of cooperation and reciprocity was thus established that benefited the entire community. This is not the place to describe the rites of penance and catechumenate in detail, especially since these differed widely depending on period and geographical location and, in addition, underwent a good deal of development.[74]

b/The New Organization of the Easter Penitential Period

When Lent was reorganized, the question arose whether the traditional description "season of fasting" does justice to the real meaning of this period of preparation. Many people thought the description an unsatisfactory one in an age when there are only two days of obligatory fasting (Ash Wednesday and Good Friday). In addition, the name seemed to distinguish this period in only a more or less negative way from other seasons of the liturgical year, whereas in fact this period of preparation for Easter has a richer meaning. Above and beyond works of abnegation, it calls for a greater openness to the word of God, a great zeal in attending the liturgy and performing works of charity, and a conversion (cf. Mk 1.15) in every area of life so as to obey the message of the gospel.

In our effort to grasp the full meaning of the Easter penitential period the new preface which Rome published in 1968 along with the new eucharistic prayers and which the new Missal now has as "preface for Lent I" will be a valuable aid and will prevent any one-sided interpretation. This preface focuses on the real meaning of this period of preparation and motivates our exertions during the weeks of Lent by drawing our attention to the Easter event: "Each year you give us this joyful season when we prepare to celebrate the paschal mystery with mind and heart renewed. You give us a spirit of loving reverence for you, our Father, and of willing service to our neighbor. As we recall the great events that gave us new life in Christ, you bring the image of your Son to perfection within us."

The two ecclesiastical institutions that have left an indelible mark on the liturgy of the forty-day season of Lent, namely, the practice of public penance and the catechumenal preparation of the candidates for baptism (the *competentes*), gradually disappeared in Christian countries. Consequently, much in the liturgy of Lent was largely unintelligible to later centuries. On the basis of a knowledge of the original meaning, Vatican II wrote directives for reform that are important enough to give here in full:

> The two elements which are especially characteristic of Lent—the recalling of baptism or the preparation for it, and penance—should be given greater emphasis in the liturgy and in liturgical catechesis. It is by means of them that the Church prepares the faithful for the celebration of Easter, while they hear God's word more frequently and devote more time to prayer.
>
> (a) More use is to be made of the baptismal features which are proper to the Lenten liturgy. Some of them which were part of an earlier tradition are to be restored where opportune.
>
> (b) The same may be said of the penitential elements. But catechesis, as well as pointing out the social consequences of sin, must impress on the minds of the faithful the distinctive character of penance as a detestation of sin because it is an offense against God. The role of the Church in penitential practices is not to be passed over, and the need to pray for sinners should be emphasized.
>
> During Lent, penance should be not only internal and individual but also external and social. The practice of penance should be encouraged in ways suited to the present day, to different regions, and to individual circumstances. It should be recommended by the authorities mentioned in Article 22 (CL, nos. 109-110; Flannery, pp. 30-31).

The reorganization of 1969 (GNLYC, nos. 27-31) endeavored to obey these instructions and to restore to the liturgy its noble simplicity and adapt it to the capacities of the faithful. To this end it seemed necessary to "omit things of less importance in order to emphasize those of greater importance."[75] Yet the authorities could not bring themselves to go back once more to the original beginning of Lent, i.e., the first Sunday of Lent, which marks the beginning of the forty-day period prior to the start of the Easter triduum. By way of justification the Roman commentary on the General Norms called attention to the fact that the rite of ashes on Ash Wednesday has made this day more popular among the faithful "than many other days of greater solemnity. It seems advisable for this reason to make no change here in our effort to restore to the sacred 'forty days' their full symbolic power."[76] Instead, the authorities settled for an Easter penitential period that "lasts from Ash Wednesday to the Mass of the Lord's Supper exclusive,"[77] or forty-four days if Sundays be included, thirty-eight if they are not.

The pre-Lent period is "abolished, since it had no special character of its own and in the divine Office made use of the parts for Ordinary Time. It was always extremely difficult to preach on it to the people (just what meaning do the words Septuagesima, Sexagesima and Quinquagesima have?); more particularly, the existence of this season robbed the penitential season of Lent of its novelty before it even began. The texts proper to these three Sundays are now used elsewhere in the Roman Missal; the Alleluia is sung until Ash Wednesday exclusive."[78]

What is this "novelty" that marks Lent? In the eucharistic liturgy, in addition to the themes of penance, baptism and the passion of Christ, the novelty consists in the use of purple vestments and the omission of the joyous Gloria and alleluia.

The Gloria—"an heirloom from the treasure of ancient Church hymns, a precious remnant of a literature now almost buried but once certainly very rich, a literature of songs for divine service written in the early Church in imitation of the biblical lyrics, especially the psalms"[79]—was not originally part of the liturgy of the Mass. In Rome it was used only in the papal Mass on especially festive occasions; later, it was also sung in pontifical Masses. Only toward the end of the eleventh century could the simple priest also use it, in Masses of a festive character. It was never permitted in the Masses of Lent.

Because of its melodic richness the alleluia (= praise the Lord), together with the accompanying verse of the second intermediate song (after the second reading), was already regarded in the early Church as a special ornament of the Roman liturgy. Although it was still being sung even in funeral services in late fourth-century Rome, it was banned from Lenten Masses from the fifth/sixth century on. The Greeks had retained the alleluia even during their penitential season; they made the omission of it in the Roman liturgy a matter of complaint and accusation at the time of the Great Schism (1054) and later.[80]

In Lent the alleluia is replaced as a second intermediate song by a text that used to be called the *tract*. It consisted of a series of psalm verses, with melodies that usually came down from an earlier period and were relatively simple because uninfluenced by the later artistic approach to song. For this reason they were regarded as especially appropriate to Lent. The new Missal takes greater account of the fact that the second intermediate song should prepare for the gospel and is meant as a kind of homage (acclamation) which we pay to the Lord who speaks to us in the gospel. This is why this song uses verses chiefly from the New Testament.

ASH WEDNESDAY
It had been decided at a very early time that the special penance for those guilty of a serious sin (a "capital sin") should start at the beginning of Lent; that is, originally on the Monday after the First Sunday, but later, on Ash Wednesday. Penitents donned a penitential garment and had ashes sprinkled on them. Then came the rite of expulsion from the Church, which took a quite dramatic form especially in Gaul. The wearing of a special penitential garment and the sprinkling with ashes as an expression of sorrow and repentance were already familiar to the Old Testament and pagan antiquity. Jesus himself uses this symbolism when he upbraids the Galilean cities of Chorazin and Bethsaida for their unwillingness to do penance: "If the mighty works done in you had been done in Tyre and Sidon, they would have repented long ago in sackcloth and ashes" (Mt 11.21). The early Church was also familiar with this practice (Tertullian, Cyprian, etc.).

Although the institution of public ecclesiastical penance disappeared toward the end of the first millennium, this rite of ashes was retained and applied now to all the faithful. At the Synod of Benevento (1091) Pope Urban II recommended this custom to all the churches. Clerics and laymen had the ashes sprinkled on their heads, while women had a sign of the cross made with ashes on their foreheads. A special prayer for the blessing of the ashes appears first in the eleventh century.[81] The rule that the ashes were to be obtained by burning the palm branches left over from the previous year occurs for the first time in the twelfth century.[82] The reasoning behind the view that the signing with ashes is "not only a reminder of death but also a promise of resurrection, or in other words an Easter rite in the full sense"[83] seems rather forced. For, from antiquity and the Old Testament down to the most recent Church documents the action is always seen as a symbol of transiency, sorrow and penance. The new Order for Lent retains the rule that Ash Wednesday is a day of universal fasting and that the ashes are to be distributed.[84]

In the new Missal the blessing of the ashes follows on the gospel and homily. After an invitation to prayer the priest reads one of two prayers which ask that we may spend the forty days of penance in the right frame of mind. In both prayers the real purpose of Lent emerges clearly: "May they keep this Lenten season in preparation for the joy of Easter"; "You do not want sinners to die but to live with the risen Christ."

The ashes, which according to the new Missal are still derived "from the branches blessed the preceding year for Passion Sunday" (rubric), are then sprinkled with holy water and distributed. In place of the traditional formula, which recalls the expulsion from Paradise: "Remember, man, you are dust and to dust you will return" (cf. Gen 3.19), the programmatic summons of Jesus in Mark 1.15 may be used: "Turn away from sin and be faithful to the gospel." During the distribution of the ashes, which concludes with the general intercessions, antiphons (with Psalm 51, one of the penitential psalms) or a responsory or some other appropriate song are sung. The rite of ashes can also take the form of a liturgy of the word apart from Mass.

The opening prayer of the Mass (which has no penitential rite) asks that "as we begin the discipline of Lent, [you would] make this season holy by our self-denial." This is a free rendition of a Latin prayer which, in the old Missal, concluded the blessing of the ashes and which asks (in Latin) that we may be strengthened for "Christian warfare." This strong image, which was very popular in the early Church and the Middle Ages and is already found in Job 7.1, is meant to bring home to us the fact that Christians are not called to an easy life but to battle against all the enemies of God, not least against their own self-centeredness.

The two readings (Joel 2.12-18, and 2 Cor 5.20–6.2) are forceful calls to penance and reconciliation. The alleluia is omitted until the Mass of the Easter Vigil and is replaced by a tract. The gospel passage, from the Sermon on the Mount (Mt 6.1-6, 16-18) warns against rendering our acts of almsgiving, prayer and fasting worthless by doing them for egocentric motives. The preface, the only one to speak explicitly of bodily fasting (i.e., in the Latin text; English: "through our observance of Lent") gives the classical reasons for fasting which show clearly that fasting serves a higher purpose.

THE SUNDAYS OF LENT

In keeping with the instructions of Vatican II (CL, nos. 109-10), the new liturgy endeavors to make greater use of the baptismal motifs proper to the Lenten liturgy and to take them, if occasion allows, from the older liturgy. This is true especially of texts that call for and lead to conversion and penance. This effort is brought to bear especially on the Sundays of Lent, since it is on these days that most of the community gathers for the liturgy. These Sundays give the revised liturgy of Lent its special character; each Sunday, for all that it has in common with the other Sundays, has its own unmistakable impress.

This differentiation is achieved chiefly by means of the gospel pericope, which gives the Sunday a special theme that is then supported by the other readings, the prayers, and the songs. The first, second and sixth Sundays also have a special preface which is related to the gospel. This is true of the third, fourth and fifth Sundays only in Year A of the cycle. However, on these last-named Sundays the gospel of Year A can also be read in Years B and C for pastoral reasons. This means that the corresponding special preface and gospel-related song-parts of the Mass for Year A will also be used. A shorter version is provided for a number of the gospel pericopes.

The first Sunday uses the pericope on the temptation of Jesus in the desert from Matthew, Mark or Luke depending on the year of the cycle. The corresponding preface emphasizes the forty-day fast of Jesus whereby he "makes this a holy season of self-denial." It extols his victory over "the devil's temptations" and offers thanks for the power given us in our turn "to rid ourselves of the hidden corruption of evil, and so to share his paschal meal in purity of heart, until we come to its fulfillment in the promised land of heaven." The other two readings, which also vary from year to year of the cycle, can without difficulty be related to the theme of the gospel.

The opening prayer, or prayer of the day, asks: "Father . . . help us to understand the meaning of your Son's death and resurrection, and teach us to reflect it in our lives." Thus the first Sunday of Lent contains the message of Christ's struggle (desert, fasting, hunger, temptation) but also of his victory over the powers hostile to God, as well as an anticipation of his glorification ("angels came and ministered to him"). It is an overture to the paschal mystery of Easter.

This introduction to the paschal mystery is even clearer in the gospel of the second Sunday of Lent. This is the passage on the transfiguration of Jesus. The full meaning of the event becomes really clear only when we see it in its context in the synoptic accounts. Jesus has foretold his suffering, death and resurrection to the disciples for the first time and thereby caused great consternation (Mt 16.21-23 par.). To this prediction he added the saying about the self-denial and acceptance of the cross that discipleship requires. The transfiguration on the mountain, which comes next in the story, is proof that the cross and death are not an end but a passage to glory. The special preface emphasizes this fundamental idea: "On your holy mountain he revealed himself in glory in the presence of his disciples. He had already prepared them for his approaching death. He wanted to teach them through the Law and the Prophets that the promised Christ had first to suffer and so come to the glory of his resurrection."

The Old Testament readings recount God's promises to Abraham and the covenant struck with him. The New Testament readings appeal with confident faith to the redemption accomplished by Jesus Christ "who will change our lowly body to be like his glorious body, by the power which enables him even to subject all things to himself" (Phil 3.21, C). What is told of Christ in the gospel will be our lot as well, that is, participation in his pasch or passage through suffering to joy. In order that we may be able to hold fast to this Easter message amid our earthly darkness, the opening prayer bids us ask: "God our Father, help us to hear your Son. Enlighten us with your word, that we may find the way to your glory."

The first two Sundays of Lent thus already point clearly to the Easter mystery by showing us the way and the goal for our earthly life and praying that we may travel this way as followers of Christ. On the next three Sundays in Year A of the cycle the baptismal motif, based on the gospel, dominates the entire Mass.

The third Sunday of Lent in Year A uses the passage on the meeting of Jesus with the Samaritan woman at Jacob's well (Jn 4.5-42). Through this encounter Jesus leads the woman and many of her countrymen to faith in him as Messiah and brings them to confess that "this is indeed the Savior of the world." He gives human beings a "living water." Whoever drinks of it "will never thirst; the water that I shall give him will become in him a spring of water welling up to eternal life." The preface extols especially the fact that Jesus gives the grace of faith in order to awaken in believing hearts the fire of life.

The Old Testament reading (Ex 17.3-17) likewise turns our attention to the mystery of baptism as it recounts how Moses, at God's command, strikes water from the rock. "And the Rock was Christ" (1 Cor 10.4): in this way, as everyone knows, does Paul link the Old Testament event to the Christ-event of baptism. But as the New Testament reading (Rom 5.1-2, 5-8) shows, baptism as a Christ-event is based on the sacrificial death of

Jesus who "shows his love for us in that while we were yet sinners [he] died for us."

The entrance antiphon (no. 2), the second intermediate song and the communion antiphon pick up the theme of the liberating water of baptism, while the opening prayer asks that we who are conscious of our sinfulness may "overcome our sins by prayer, fasting and works of mercy." The prayer over the gifts adds the petition that God would give us strength "to forgive one another."

While the third Sunday of Lent in Year A is essentially colored by the theme of baptism and is therefore especially suited to serve both as a preparation for baptism and as a reminder and renewal of the sacrament for the community as a whole, the gospel in Year B is the account of the cleansing of the temple, in which Jesus makes a clear reference to his death and resurrection (Jn 2.13-25). In the gospel for Year C (Lk 13.1-9) Jesus takes two "items from the newspaper" and makes appropriate comment on them with the words: "Unless you repent you will all likewise perish." The accompanying parable of the fruitless fig tree that is given a further chance of survival points in the same direction. The theme of the third Sunday in Year C is thus deliverance through conversion.

The fourth Sunday of Lent in Year A is also stamped with the theme of baptism. Jesus heals a man born blind by touching his eyes with a paste of earth and spittle and bidding him wash in the pool of Siloam. In this way he brings the man to faith in the "Son of man" (Jn 9.1-41). The connection of this pericope with baptism will be fully grasped only if we know that the early Church called baptism an "enlightenment" (Greek: *phōtismos*) and spoke of the candidates for baptism as "those being enlightened." The preface of this Mass brings out the connection as follows: "He came among us as a man, to lead mankind from darkness into the light of faith. Through Adam's fall we were born as slaves of sin, but now through baptism in Christ we are reborn as your adopted children."

The story of the anointing of David the shepherd as king of Israel, which is told in the Old Testament reading (1 Sam 16), can also be interpreted from the vantage point of baptism inasmuch as baptism too is a freely given call from God; it is a gift of the Spirit and brings participation in the royal priesthood of Christ. The New Testament reading (Eph 5.8-14) has even clearer reference to the gospel, for it begins: "Once you were darkness, but now you are light in the Lord; walk as children of light." It closes with a verse from a very early Christian hymn to Christ, "a baptismal hymn using the imagery of morning": "Awake, O sleeper, and rise from the dead, and Christ shall give you light." This motif of light is also heard in the second intermediate song and in the concluding prayer. The entrance antiphon is a summons to joy ("Laetare" Sunday); the opening prayer and the prayer over the gifts also speak of joy in anticipation of the feast of Easter.

The note of joy that is struck on this Sunday is connected by many liturgiologists with the catechumenal rite known as the "opening of the ears," which took place on the following Wednesday.[85] The rose-colored vestments which are usually worn on this Sunday in place of the more somber purple and which are first mentioned in the sixteenth century probably originated in the papal custom of blessing the "Golden Rose" on this day. This blessing "is connected, not with the preparation for baptism, but probably with a popular Roman custom of at least tenth-century origin, by which the victory of spring over winter was celebrated by the wearing of flowers. From the eleventh century, the Pope presented, instead of the natural bloom, an artificial costly rose, first to his officials, and later to eminent personages outside Rome."[86]

The gospel of Year B (Jn 3.14-21 the conversation with Nicodemus) speaks at length not only of the paschal mystery but of the symbolism of light. The New Testament reading (Eph 2.4-10) goes to the very heart of the Christian faith when it proclaims our participation in the paschal mystery of Christ: "God, who is rich in mercy, out of the great love with which he loved us, even when we were dead through our trespasses, made us alive together with Christ (by grace you have been saved), and raised us up with him, and made us sit in the heavenly places in Christ Jesus."

The gospel for Year C is the parable of the lost son (Lk 15.1-3, 11-32), which is a great hymn in praise of God the Father's merciful love. The theme has already been enunciated in the second intermediate song, which is, of course, in principle oriented to the gospel. It also echoes in the communion antiphon. The New Testament reading (2 Cor 5.17-21) speaks of reconciliation with God, which means new creation for those who are baptized; the passage ends with the appeal: "Be reconciled to God."

The fifth Sunday of Lent in Year A receives a special accent from the gospel of the raising of Lazarus (Jn 11.1-45). Jesus presents himself as "the resurrection and the life": "He who believes in me, though he die, yet shall he live, and whoever lives and believes in me shall never die." This is in all truth a new and even a revolutionary message, not only for the candidates for baptism but for all human beings, destined as they are to die. The two preceding readings also speak of God's life-giving Spirit, who opens the graves and leads the dead to the promised land (Ezek 37.12b-14). "If the Spirit of God who raised Jesus from the dead dwells in you, he who raised Christ Jesus from the dead will give life to your mortal bodies also through this Spirit who dwells in you" (Rom 8.8-11). Thus the liturgy of this Sunday too takes us to the heart of the Christian message of salvation. It is already an Easter message, as can be seen from the special preface for this Sunday: "In his love for us all, Christ Jesus gives us the sacraments to lift us up to everlasting life."

The striking pericopes for Year B convey the same liberating message of the paschal mystery. According to the gospel (Jn 12.20-33) Jesus is the grain of wheat that falls into the earth and dies in order to produce much fruit. "Now is my soul troubled. . . ." But "I, when I am lifted up from the earth, will draw all men to myself." The evangelist adds: "He said this to show by what death he was to die." In the second reading, the Letter to the Hebrews expresses the same thought: "Although he was a Son, he learned obedience through what he suffered; and being made perfect he became the source of eternal salvation to all who obey him" (Heb 5.7-9). This is the new covenant God had made with the human race after the old covenant with

Israel had been so often broken: "I will forgive their iniquity, and I will remember their sin no more" (first reading: Jer 31.31-34).

In the gospel for Year C Jesus grants the adulteress a new beginning by preventing her being stoned and by forgiving her sins. God grants the same new beginning to all of his people when he calls them in the first reading (Is 43.16-21): "Remember not the former things, nor consider the things of old. Behold, I am doing a new thing." It is worth sowing in tears to reap with joy (first intermediate song). The path is marked out for us because the goal is clear: "that I may know him and the power of his resurrection, and may share his sufferings, becoming like him in his death, that if possible I may attain the resurrection from the dead. . . . I press on to the goal for the prize of the upward call of God in Christ Jesus" (second reading: Phil 3.8-14).

Thus the Propers for the Masses of the third, fourth and fifth Sundays of Lent present in an impressively rich way both the message of salvation and guidance for the way. On the one hand, they represent an immediate preparation of the candidates for the reception of the sacraments of initiation. On the other hand, they are also calculated to renew the faith and love of the community and to fill them with gratitude for their calling.

Before the reorganization of Lent Passiontide began the fifth Sunday of Lent. The designation "Passiontide" was meant to indicate that from this Sunday on the texts of the Mass would lay greater emphasis on the suffering of Christ. This remains true in the revised liturgy, especially as the Easter triduum draws closer. On the other hand, we may not overlook the fact that the entire season of Lent speaks of the Lord's passage through suffering and death to resurrection. The decision to eliminate the name "Passiontide" is explained in the Commentary on the *General Norms for the Liturgical Year and the Calendar* as based on the desire "to preserve the internal unity of Lent. The Sunday now known as the First Sunday of the Passion will henceforth be the Fifth Sunday of Lent, as in the Ambrosian Rite."[87]

With the Sunday hitherto called the "First Sunday of the Passion" there was associated the custom of veiling crosses, statues and pictures in the church. This custom probably goes back to the "hunger cloth" or Lenten veil which, from the eleventh century on, was suspended in front of the altar at the beginning of Lent in order to hide it from the congregation. A possible reason for this original custom was the fact that there were public sinners present among the faithful. In point of fact, as part of the penitential rite these people were excluded from the church at the beginning of Lent, but, since all knew themselves to be sinners (as, for example, the extension of the rite of ashes to all the faithful shows), the community (it was thought) should be, and wished to be, deprived of the sight of the altar. At times, reference was made to a "fast of the eyes." Later on, the hunger cloths became smaller and had pictures of Christ's passion on them.

The veiling of crosses, statues and pictures, which came in somewhat later than the veiling of the altar, is perhaps based on the notion of a "fast of the eyes." At the end of the thirteenth century Bishop William Durandus of Mende (Southern France) explains this custom by the fact that Christ veiled his divinity during his passion. Durandus saw this explanation as implied in this Sunday's gospel, the concluding sentence of which read: "But Jesus hid himself and left the temple."[88] Prior to Vatican II the editors of the Schott Missal saw the veiling of crosses and so on as intended "to remind us of the Redeemer's humiliation and thus to imprint the image of the crucified Christ more deeply on our hearts."[89]

A certain hesitation can be seen in the revision of the Lenten liturgy. The commentary on the *General Norms* of 1969 says: "Crosses and the images of the saints are not to be covered henceforth, except in regions where the episcopal conferences judge it profitable to maintain this custom; during the forty days of Lent the devotion of the faithful should be directed to the passion of Christ."[90] But in a rubric at the end of the Mass formulary for Saturday in the fourth week of Lent, the new Roman Missal of 1970 (followed by the English-language Missal) says only that the practice may be observed if the episcopal conference so decides.

106

PALM SUNDAY

A very important place in this forty-day period belongs to the
sixth Sunday of Lent, "Palm Sunday of the Passion of Christ,"
as the full title runs in the Roman Missal. The title already
shows that the liturgy of the day will unite two commemorations: that of the entrance of Jesus into Jerusalem and that of his
passion.

The diary of Egeria the pilgrim tells us that at the beginning of
the fifth century the Christians of Jerusalem used to gather in
the early afternoon on the Mount of Olives for a lengthy liturgy
of the word. Then, toward evening, they would go in procession into Jerusalem, carrying palm branches or olive branches.[91]
This rite was soon esteemed and imitated in other Churches of
the East. As for its spread in the West, the name Palm Sunday
occurs in Spain and Gaul around 600,[92] but there is no procession with the palms. In these countries, "the sixth Sunday of
Lent was devoted to the giving of the symbol and the anointing
of catechumens. For this reason the gospel for the Mass of the
day was taken from John 12 which tells of the anointing at
Bethany (vv. 1-11). But the passage continued on to the story of
the entrance into Jerusalem (vv. 12-16). For this reason the Sunday soon acquired the name of Palm Sunday, although there
was as yet no special ceremony in commemoration of the
event."[93]

The custom of blessing the "palm branches" is attested around
the middle of the eighth century (Bobbio Sacramentary). "Since
palm and olive branches were obtainable only in southern
countries the custom was early introduced of blessing the green
and blossoming branches of other trees, including beech
branches; in Germany it was usually branches of willows that
already had their catkins."[94]

In the oldest Greek and Latin liturgical texts the palm branches
served only as a symbol of life, hope and victory, but popular
belief soon attributed great power and even magical effectiveness to them. To understand this we must recall that among the
pagan Greeks and Romans the branches of certain trees were
regarded as having apotropaic power, i.e., they could ward off
evil spirits and protect house, farm and pasture from harm done

107

by such spirits.[95] "This popular belief lived on among peoples converted to Christianity, who were also heirs to the cultures of antiquity. Another factor was the high esteem popular Christian belief had for everything closely connected with Christian worship. It was therefore considered justifiable to ascribe a curative power to palm branches, or the other branches substituted for these, once they had been carried in solemn procession, amid prayers and songs in honor of the Savior. . . . As a result, the branches that had been carried in procession were used to ward off all evil from homes and their residents, even before the formula of blessing came to include mention of such effects. The formula did not give rise to the practice; rather a long-standing practice among the people had led to the introduction of appropriate phrases into the formula. The custom thus acquired ecclesiastical legitimacy, as it were, and the expected effect was now attributed not to the palms as such but to the liturgical blessing spoken over them."[96]

Trust in the apotropaic power of blessed palm branches led eventually to many exaggerated notions and objectionable practices, some of which survived into the present century. For example, people ate the buds and shoots of blessed branches in order to ward off sicknesses; they planted palm branches in the form of crosses in the fields, or burned them there, in order to ward off storms, lightning and hail; they fastened the branches to crucifixes in their homes, in order to protect the residents from any adversity; and they saw the palms as effective defenses against vermin among the livestock, against harmful insects on vegetables, and against the foxes that threatened the poultry.[97] In all this, there was evidently no understanding of or instruction in the meaning and purpose of the Church's blessings, which are a form of intercession for God's help against the many threats to human existence and salvation. Blessed or consecrated objects are symbols; they express and stimulate faith, hope and love, and do not possess magical power.

At the end of the eighth century there is an increasing number of witnesses to a *procession with the palms*. The hymn *Gloria, laus et honor* ("All glory, laud and honor"), which Bishop Theodulf of Orleans had composed for the purpose, soon became a fixed part of the ceremony. In the Middle Ages the procession became increasingly dramatic and theatrical. "The presence of Christ in this procession was symbolized either by a cross or by the Book of Gospels. In Germany the so-called *Palmesel* was often used. This was a wooden ass on wheels, bearing on its back a figure of the Savior."[98]

The medieval custom, which later was gradually dropped, of gathering at a church outside the city walls for the blessing of the palms and of then going in procession to the principal church of the city was in a sense revived in the new Holy Week Order of 1955. It is suggested in the new Missal as well.

The new Missal provides various forms for the "Commemoration of the Lord's Entrance into Jerusalem." In the first form (The Procession) the congregation assembles at a secondary church or in some other suitable place. After an opening antiphon the priest, dressed in chasuble or cope, greets the community and gives an introduction to the meaning of the procession with the palms. He should make it clear that the procession is not intended to be a historically faithful representation of the entrance of Jesus but is rather a public profession of a discipleship inspired by faith and grateful love. Then one of the two available prayers is said in blessing the branches. "Today we honor Christ our triumphant King by carrying these branches." After the branches have been sprinkled with holy water, the passage on the entrance of Jesus is read from one of the four gospels and a brief homily may be given.

Now the procession forms behind a suitably decorated cross that is accompanied by ministers carrying censer and lighted candles. Various songs should be sung, e.g., the antiphon *Pueri Hebraeorum* ("The children of Jerusalem . . .") with Psalms 24 and 47, and the above-mentioned hymn by Theodulf of Orleans, or other suitable songs. After entering the church and paying homage to the altar, the priest reads the prayer of the day; the other introductory rites of the Mass are omitted.

In the second form (The Solemn Entrance), the commemoration is limited to a solemn entrance within the church before the principal Mass. The branches are blessed in a suitable place outside the sanctuary, and the gospel of the entrance into Jerusalem is proclaimed. Then the priest and his assistants and a group of the faithful advance to the altar in the order described above.

The third form (The Simple Entrance) combines the commemoration of Jesus' entrance into Jerusalem with the usual entrance procession for Mass, during which the entrance antiphon of the day or another song with the same theme is sung. The introductory rites of Mass are as usual. It is recommended, however, that "there should be a bible service on the theme of the Lord's messianic entrance and passion, either on Saturday evening or on Sunday at a convenient time" (rubric).

Like the Propers of the other Sundays of Lent, the Mass of Palm Sunday receives its stamp from the gospel pericope. It consists of the passion narrative from Matthew, Mark or Luke (three-year cycle), with the option of using an abbreviated version for pastoral reasons. The theme of the redemptive suffering of Jesus also dominates the other parts of the Proper, except for the entrance antiphon, which voices the jubilation felt at the messianic entrance of Jesus into Jerusalem. The Old Testament reading is from the third Servant Song (Is 50.4-7); it speaks of the obedience of the "Servant of God" amid his suffering, and leads into the responsorial psalm (verses from Psalm 22), with "My God, my God, why have you abandoned me?" as the antiphon.

The New Testament reading (Phil 2.6-11) already shows the exaltation of Jesus as resulting from his obedience amid suffering unto death, "even death on a cross." The key verse in this passage (v. 8) serves as the second intermediate song (it serves the same function on Good Friday). In a spirit of joy that already anticipates Easter, the preface describes the paschal mystery of Christ with marvelous terseness and lapidary brevity: "Though he was sinless, he suffered willingly for sinners. Though innocent, he accepted death to save the guilty. By his dying he destroyed our sins. By rising he has raised us up to holiness of life." The opening and concluding prayers also refer to the central saving action of Jesus and ask that we may have the profit of them, while the prayer over the gifts asks: "May the suffering and death of Jesus, your only Son, make us pleasing to you" and "may this perfect sacrifice win us your mercy and love."

THE WEEKDAYS OF THE EASTER PENITENTIAL SEASON

Not only Ash Wednesday and the Sundays of Lent but the weekdays as well are characterized by the two great themes of conversion and baptism. Thus they play a part in carrying out the overall theme of Lent: preparation for Easter. Each day has its own Proper of the Mass. The scriptural pericopes are the same every year, with reading and gospel forming a thematic unit.

From the beginning of the fourth week of Lent the gospel consists of a semicontinuous reading of the gospel of John. The readings about the Samaritan woman (Jn 4.5-42), the healing of the man born blind (Jn 9.1-41) and the raising of Lazarus (Jn 11.1-45), which are read on the third, fourth and fifth Sundays of Lent in Year A, also provide the gospel readings for optional Masses that can be celebrated on all the weekdays of the third, fourth and fifth weeks respectively, especially in Years B and C. If a weekday reading is omitted because of another celebration on that day, "the priest, considering the entire week's readings, may omit less important selections from the weekday lectionary or combine them with other readings when this will give a unified presentation of a specific theme."[99]

Evidently, the four prefaces for Lent, which are read on weekdays until the fifth Sunday, and the prefaces of the passion, which are read during the fifth week and Holy Week, also contribute in an important way to bringing home the meaning and purpose of Lent.

Like Palm Sunday the following days of Holy Week are dominated by the theme of Christ's suffering. The old custom of reading the passion according to Mark on Tuesday and the passion according to Luke on Wednesday has been dropped; these are now read on Palm Sunday in the three-year cycle. The readings for the first three days of Holy Week are from the first three Servant Songs of the prophet Isaiah, while the gospel pericopes report incidents from the last days before the Lord's passion. No other celebration may replace the liturgy of these days.

Holy Thursday, the evening of which is already part of the Easter triduum, has the Chrism Mass in the morning. This is the Mass at which "the bishop, in the company of his presbytery, blesses the sacred oils and consecrates the chrism."[100]

The blessing of the chrism, oil of catechumens, and oil of the sick is an extremely ancient tradition. Hippolytus speaks of it in his Church Order (the *Apostolic Tradition*) at the beginning of the third century.[101] In the West these blessings came to be celebrated on Holy Thursday. This was because baptism and confirmation were to be given during the Easter Vigil, and both the oil of catechumens and the chrism are used in these services.

In the Roman liturgy Holy Thursday was also the day for the reconciliation of public sinners in order that they might celebrate Easter with the community. At one time—though hardly in Rome itself—there were three Masses on this day: for the blessing of the holy oils, for the reconciliation of penitents, and in commemoration of the Last Supper of Jesus.[102] Later on, all three purposes were combined in a single Mass. As we saw earlier, the institution of public penance gradually disappeared. Until the reorganization of the Holy Week liturgy this single Mass was celebrated in the morning.[103]

The Chrism Mass in the new Missal is normally to be celebrated in the morning, in accordance with tradition; this is now prescribed in the new Rite of Blessing the Oils and Consecrating the Chrism, of December 3, 1970 (no. 9). If, however, it is difficult for the clergy and people to assemble at this time, the blessing may be transferred to an earlier day, but as close to Easter as possible (no. 10). The bishop concelebrates this Mass with his college of priests, normally in the cathedral. According to the new rite this Mass makes it clear that the bishop possesses the fullness of priesthood and that "the life in Christ of his faithful is in some way derived and dependent upon the bishop" (no. 1). As the introduction to this Mass says, it "manifests the communion of the priests with their bishop. It is thus desirable that, if possible, all the priests take part in it and receive communion under both kinds. To show the unity of the presbyterium, the priests who concelebrate with the bishops should come from different parts of the diocese."

The real theme of the Mass is the high priesthood of Christ, for which he was anointed by the Holy Spirit (first reading: Is 61.1-3a, 6a, 8b-9; gospel: Lk 4.16-21) and in which he gave his disciples a share (second reading: Rev 1.5-8, and the entrance antiphon which is taken from the same passage). The preface is one of praise and gratitude for the high priesthood of Christ, in which the entire people of God shares through the common priesthood, as do those whom he chose "to share his sacred ministry by the laying on of hands." The succeeding sentences of the preface are a striking synthesis of the tasks to which the recipients of the ordained priesthood are called: "He appoints them to renew in his name the sacrifice of our redemption as they set before your family his paschal meal. He calls them to lead your holy people in love, nourish them by your word, and strengthen them through the sacraments. Father, they are to give their lives in your service and for the salvation of your people as they strive to grow in the likeness of Christ and honor you by their courageous witness of faith and love."

In accordance with the Latin tradition the blessing of the oils takes place in this order: the oil of the sick is blessed before the final doxology of the eucharistic prayer; the oil of catechumens is blessed and the chrism is consecrated after the closing prayer (but for pastoral reasons the entire rite can be done at the end of the liturgy of the word). [104]

To the Chrism Mass can be joined a renewal of commitment to priestly service. Where this is customary, it is done right after the homily. "In his homily the bishop should urge the priests to be faithful in fulfilling their office in the Church and should invite them to renew publicly their priestly promises." [105]

Notes

1. For example, the *Epistula Apostolorum* (written between 130 and 140), Melito of Sardis († before 190), and Apollonius of Hierapolis († ca. 170). Cf. Casel, pp. 4-19.

2. *Historia ecclesiastica* V, 23-25 (E. Schwarz [5th ed., 1952], pp. 209-14).

3. On the state of the sources cf. Righetti 2:208-9.

4. Cf. J. Blinzler, *The Trial of Jesus*, tr. from the third German ed. by I. and F. McHugh (Westminster, Md., 1959); also has further bibliography.

5. Cf., among others, O. Heiming, "Gedanken zur Kalenderreform," in *Liturgie und Mönchtum* (Laacher Hefte, 2nd series) 9 (1951), 37.

6. Cf., among others, L. Meesen, "Oecuménisme et réforme du calendrier," MD, no. 81 (1965), 120.

7. In attempts at ecumenical unity, it would be better, however, not to make the historical date a prime factor, since this date is disputed.

8. Luther, *On the Councils and the Church* (1539), tr. by C. M. Jacobs, rev. by E. W. Gritsch, in *Luther's Works* (American Edition) 41 (Philadelphia, 1966), pp. 63-64.

9. W. Zeller, "Chronologie," *Evangelisches Kirchenlexikon* 1 (2nd ed.; Göttingen, 1961), 792.

10. Cf. the report of a discussion in the Faith and Order Commission of World Council of Churches, March 20, 1970, in *Ecumenical Review* 23 (1972), 179.

11. Cf. the recommendation of the Policy Reference Committee II: Relationships, Document No. CR1, in D. M. Paton (ed.), *Breaking Barriers: Nairobi 1975* (Grand Rapids, Mich., 1976), p. 193.

12. CommALI, cap. I, sect. IV (p. 64).

13. *De ratione temporum* I, 15 (PL 90:357).

14. Cf. H. Bächtold-Stäubli, *Handwörterbuch des deutschen Aberglaubens* 6 (Berlin–Leipzig, 1914), 1311-16.

15. *Sacramentarium* 42 (PL 172:769).

16. B. Fischer, "Ostern I. Liturgisch," LTK 7 (1962), 1277, who refers to J. Knobloch in *Die Sprache* 5 (Vienna, 1959), 27-45.

17. Casel, p. 53.

18. Augustine, *Epist.* 55, 24 (CSEL 34/2:195).

19. *Liber officialis* I, 12, 33 and IV, 21, 7-8, in J. M. Hanssens (ed.), *Amalarii episcopi opera liturgica omnia* 2 (Rome, 1948), pp. 79 and 470.

20. Eisenhofer-Lechner, p. 193.

21. *Decreta authentica Congreg. S. Rituum,* 3 (Rome, 1900), p. 124, no. 3535.

22. Canon 3 (PL 84:556-57).

23. Cf. Th. Schäfer, *Die Fusswaschung im monastichen Brauchtum und in der lateinischen Liturgie* (Beuron, 1956).

24. Citations in J. A. Jungmann, "Die Andacht der vierzig Stunden und das Heilige Grab," LJ 2 (1952), 184-98.

25. Ibid., p. 198.

26. In Latin, the day is called *Feria VI in Parasceve* ("Friday of Preparation," an ancient name, cf. Mk 15.42) or *Feria VI in Passione et Morte Domini* ("Friday of the Lord's Passion and Death"; this is the name in the OHS); the new Roman Missal omits the *et Morte* ("and Death").

27. Schümmer, p. 74.

28. Documentation for this and the following assertions may be found in, e.g., G. Römer, "Die Liturgie des Karfreitags," ZKT 77 (1955), 39-93; E. Lengeling, "Die feierliche 'Actio liturgica' am Tag des 'Leidens und Todes des Herrn,'" *Anima* 11 (1956), 444-64; and not least in Schmidt's outstanding collection of material.

29. Chapter 37 (pp. 110-13).

30. See the essay of the same title in JL 7 (1927), 1-23.

31. Details in A. Baumstark, "Der Orient und die Gesänge des Adoratio crucis," JL 2 (1922), 4-7.

32. On the essentials cf. J. A. Jungmann, "Die Vorverlegung der Ostervigil seit dem christlichen Altertum," LJ 1 (1950), 48-54, and A. Stuiber, "Von der Pascha-Nachtwache zum Karsamttagsgottesdienst," *Katechetische Blätter* 75 (1950), 98-109.

33. Stuiber, ibid., p. 99.

34. Eisenhofer 1:536.

35. Durandus, *Rationale divinorum officiorum* VI, 80, n. 1 (J. Beleth, ed., Naples, 1859, p. 543).

36. For this rite involving the grains of incense—a rite that arose out of a misunderstanding of the Latin word *incensus* (= candle)—cf. O. Casel, "Der österliche Lichtgesang der Kirche," *Liturgische Zeitschrift* 4 (1931-32), 187-91; also Eisenhofer 1:536-37.

37. Auf der Maur, p. 113.

38. Ibid., pp. 112-16.

39. Cf., among others, F. J. Dölger, "Lumen Christi. Untersuchungen zum abendlichen Licht-Segen in Antike und Christentum," AC 5 (1936), 1-43; O. Casel, "Der österliche Lichtgesang" (n. 121), pp. 179-80.

40. Cf. B. Fischer, "Ambrosius der Verfasser des österlichen Exultet?" AL 2 (1952), 61-74; K. Gamber, "Älteste Eucharistiegebete der lateinischen Osterliturgie," in *Paschatis Sollemnia*, pp. 159-78; Casel, ibid., pp. 179-91.

41. A. Löhr, *The Mass Through the Year* 2: *Holy Week to the Last Sunday after Pentecost*, tr. by I. T. Hale (Westminster, Md., 1959), p. 64.

42. The text of the *Vidi aquam* is based on the prophet Ezekiel's vision of the temple (47.1 ff.), which speaks of the redemptive water that flows from the right side of the temple; in this the Fathers of the Church saw a reference to the pierced side of the redeemer. B. Fischer offers a homiletic exposition in Gd 12 (1978), 56.

43. The text of the Asperges is in the Sacramentary, Appendix on the Rite of Blessing and Sprinkling Holy Water.

44. Cf. Casel, pp. 4-5.

45. E.g., Irenaeus, Origen, Hippolytus and Tertullian. Documentation in Casel, pp. 15 ff.

46. Canon 43 (Mansi 2:13). Originally, these names (whose first meaning is "fiftieth" and "fortieth") referred to the final day of the period but were later understood as referring to the entire period up to and including the final day of it.

47. Cf. Council of Nicaea, canon 20 (Kirch, p. 243).

48. The Easter candle remains in the sanctuary throughout the entire Easter season as it has been extended in the revised Roman Calendar (no. 23). Furthermore, not limited to the celebration of the eucharist, it should be used at all liturgical services until and including the solemnity of Pentecost.

49. H. Reifenberg, Gd 7 (1973), 92, has a noteworthy suggestion for developing this practice along the lines of liturgical symbolism.

50. *Rite of Funerals*, nos. 37-38.

51. Auf der Maur, p. 23: "Asterius is the first to tell us clearly and in detail of the developed Easter octave by providing a homily for each day. The fully developed Easter octave is not the creation of the late fourth century but, if we take Asterius as our witness, already exists in

a complete form in the first half of the fourth century. A daily sermon during this week seems to be taken for granted, thus indicating that Asterius was not introducing a novelty but following an already established tradition that may date back into the third century."

52. Ibid., p. 22.

53. Cyril of Jerusalem, *Catecheses* 19-23 (PG 33:1065-1128); the two works of Ambrose: CSEL 73:87-116 and 13-85.

54. *Epist.* 55, 32 (CSEL 34/2:207).

55. B. Fischer, "Formen gemeinschaftlicher Tauferinnerung im Abendland," LJ 9 (1959), 91.

56. CommALI, cap. L, sect. I. 2. A. 3 (p. 56).

57. Lect: Introd, chap. II, sect. IV. 1 (p. xxxv).

58. *Sermo* 179, 1 (PL 39:2084).

59. GNLYC, no. 26.

60. CommALI, cap. I, sect. I. 2. A. 3 (p. 57).

61. Ibid., p. 56.

62. Cf. Righetti 2:240.

63. *De sacro altaris mysterio* I, 65 (PL 217:299 ff.).

64. *Epist. ad Basilidem* (PG 10:1273).

65. Canon 5 [3] (Kirch, p. 241).

66. *Historia ecclesiastica* V, 22 (PG 67:632). For the entire range of problems cf. J. A. Jungmann, "Die Quadragesima in den Forschungen von Antoine Chavasse," AL 5/1 (1957), 89 ff.

67. Thus Gregory I, *Homilia 16 in evangelia* 5 (PL 76:1137), and Cassian, *Collationes* 21, 25-27 (CSEL 13/2:600-603).

68. Cf. Kellner, pp. 77-78.

69. Schümmer, pp. 208-9.

70. Ibid., pp. 112-13.

71. *Apologeticum* 39, 7 (CCL 1:151).

72. Schümmer, p. 222.

73. Ibid., pp. 223-24.

74. On the rites of penance the reader may consult J. A. Jungmann, *Die lateinischen Bussriten* (Innsbruck, 1932), and K. Rahner, "Frühe Bussgeschichte in Einzeluntersuchungen," in his *Schriften zur*

Theologie XI (Zürich, 1973). For questions regarding the baptismal catechumenate cf. A. Stenzel, *Die Taufe. Eine genetische Erklärung der Taufliturgie* (Innsbruck, 1958).

75. CommALI, cap. I, sect. I. 2. B (p. 57).

76. Ibid., cap. I, sect. I. 2. B. 1 (p. 58).

77. GNLYC, no. 28.

78. CommALI, cap. I, sect. I. 2. B. 1 (p. 58).

79. Jungmann 1:346.

80. Details ibid., 1:431, n. 67.

81. Franz 1:463.

82. Documentation in Eisenhofer 1:497.

83. A. Kirchgässner, "Ostern als Neujahrsfest," in *Paschatis Solemnia*, p. 56.

84. Cf. GNLYC, no. 29.

85. Eisenhofer 1:500.

86. Eisenhofer-Lechner, p. 92.

87. CommALI, cap. I, sect. I. 2. B. 1 (p. 58).

88. *Rationale divinorum officiorum* I, 3, n. 34 (Beleth, pp. 28-29).

89. Freiburg, 1958; Introduction to the First Sunday of the Passion.

90. CommALI, cap. I, sect. I. 2. B. 1 (p. 58).

91. Chapter 31 (pp. 104-5).

92. E.g., Isidore of Seville († 636), *De ecclesiastic officiis* I, 28 (PL 82:251).

93. A. Chavasse, "Le cycle paschal," in Martimort, p. 711.

94. Franz 1:487, n. 5.

95. Details ibid., 1:481.

96. Ibid.

97. Ibid., 1:505-6.

98. Eisenhofer-Lechner, p. 187.

99. Lect:Introd, chap. I, sect. VII d (p. xxx).

100. CommALI, cap. I, sect. I. 2. B. 1 (p. 59).

101. *Traditio Apostolica* 5, ed. B. Botte, *La Tradition apostolique de saint Hippolyte* (LQF 39; Münster, 1963), p. 18.

102. Cf. the Gelasian Sacramentary, ed. H. A. Wilson (Oxford, 1894), pp. 63-74.

103. On the complicated and to some extent obscure historical development of the Holy Thursday liturgy cf. P. H. Schmidt, "Geist und Geschichte des Gründonnerstags," LJ 3 (1953), 234-52; also Schmidt 2:715-47.

104. Cf. the Rite of the Blessing of Oils and of Consecrating the Chrism, nos. 11-12.

105. Rubric for the Holy Thursday Chrism Mass.

Christmas and the Christmas Cycle

In the first three centuries of the Church's life there was no feast
except the Sunday celebration of the paschal mystery and the
annual celebration of the same which we now call "Easter." The
situation changed at the beginning of the fourth century. At
this time the tendency arose of explicating, as it were, the festal
content of the one annual feast, presenting the saving action of
Christ in a historico-representational manner, and celebrating
the various aspects of it. As we saw in connection with the
Easter cycle, this meant, for example, that from the one Easter
Vigil were derived prior commemorations of the Lord's suffering and death on Good Friday, his institution of the eucharist
on Holy Thursday evening, and his entrance into Jerusalem on
Palm Sunday. In the time after Easter the same tendency led to
the Ascension and the sending of the Spirit being celebrated as
increasingly independent feasts.

It is not surprising, therefore that the first stage of the one Christ-event, namely his incarnation and birth, should likewise become the object of festal commemoration in both East and West.

1 / THE ORIGIN OF THE FEAST OF CHRISTMAS

Blank spots and areas on the map, unexplored regions, have in the past always aroused the urge to explore. The same is true for the question of the origin of Christmas and of Epiphany which is closely connected with Christmas. This origin is still quite obscure, although for almost a hundred years now many scholars have devoted considerable effort and ingenuity to determining the genesis of these feasts and the motives for them. [1]

One fact that is certain is that the birthday of Christ on December 25 was already being celebrated in 336 AD in the liturgy of the city of Rome. This is indicated by a calendar that lists the anniversaries of the deaths of the bishops of Rome *(Depositio episcoporum)* and the Roman martyrs *(Depositio martyrum)*; the calendar is ascribed to Furius Dionysius Filocalus and dates from the year 354. [2] There is a good deal of evidence that the feast of the Epiphany, which came to be celebrated on January 6 in the East, entered the Roman liturgy only after the feast of December 25 had been established, whereas it had been adopted in Milan, Gaul and Spain before the Roman feast of Christmas was taken over in those parts.

Scholars form two camps when it comes to the reasons for the introduction of a Roman feast of Christ's birth on December 25. According to the apologetics and history of religious hypothesis the impulse for this feast came from the pagan feast of the "Unconquered Sun-God" *Natale Solis Invicti)*, which the Roman emperor Aurelian established throughout the empire in 274 in honor of the Syrian sun-god of Emesa and which he ordered to be celebrated on December 25, the day of the winter solstice. The emperor's hope was that the feast would help to unite and strengthen his vast empire.

In order to immunize Christians against the attraction of this pagan feast, the Church of Rome (according to this hypothesis) established a feast of Christ's birth to be celebrated on the same day. In so doing, she could point out that the Old Testament scriptures had already described the expected redeemer as "the sun of righteousness" (Mal 4.2 [3.20]). In the New Testament Christ describes himself as "the light of the world" (Jn 8.12), while according to the Prologue of John he is "the true light that enlightens every man" (1.9) and has now come into the world.

Our present feast of Christmas, then, is dependent only for its date, and not for its content, on the Roman feast of the sun-god; the decisive impulse for the establishment of the Christian feast comes from the pagan feast. Christians could now make the triumphant claim to their pagan fellow citizens that they, the Christians, were celebrating the feast of the true Sun which alone can give light and salvation to the world.

The calculation hypothesis[3] starts with the fact that as early as the third century Christian theologians were endeavoring to calculate the date of Christ's birth, which is not mentioned in the gospels. The Christ-as-sun symbolism that was so deep-rooted in the Christian consciousness caused them to pay special attention to the equinoxes and solstices. One opinion was that John the Baptist was conceived at the autumn equinox and born at the summer solstice. But since according to Luke 1.26 Christ was conceived six months after John, he was conceived at the spring equinox (March 25) and was therefore born on December 25.

In this coincidence of the beginning of the sun's new career with the beginning of Jesus' earthly life people saw (it is argued) an enchanting work of divine providence. "Anyone who has entered into the mentality of third- and fourth-century Christians will have no difficulty understanding how the symbolic power of Christ's birth on the day of the winter solstice could exalt all hearts. Here indeed was the 'hand of God'! Here was his own seal made evident in the midst of human calculations! What more fitting choice could divine providence have made than a day so freighted with symbolism? . . . I do not hesitate to say that the triumphant radiance of this symbolic date contains the real mystery of the triumphant entry into the world which the feast of Christmas represents."[4] Even though these efforts to calculate the date of Christ's birth strike us today as very aprioristic and questionable, yet (says the hypothesis) it is this calculation and conviction, and not any attention to the pagan feast of the Unconquered Sun, that really account for the celebration of Christ's birth on December 25.

A comparison and evaluation of the arguments for each of these two hypotheses suggests that the attempts to calculate the date of Christ's birth may very well have created a background and a readiness for matching Aurelian's feast of the sun-god with a feast of Christ's birth. Only success could be expected for such a new feast, once people were already persuaded that the historical date of Christ's birth was December 25. At the same time, however, the history of religions hypothesis can claim that the real and decisive impulse came immediately from the introduction of the "birthday of the Unconquered Sun."

There was little centralization in the Church of that time, and yet the new feast had spread with astonishing rapidity throughout the West and in many of the Eastern Churches before the fourth century was over. The reason is probably that the struggle against the Arian heresy focused greater attention on the person, and not simply the work, of the God-man, and that a feast of Christ's birth would give a suitable liturgical expression to the profession of faith drawn up at Nicaea, the Council which condemned the Arian heresy in 325. In most of the Eastern liturgies "the form of the feast was based on that of the Epiphany. As far as content was concerned, only the mystery of the birth was, in principle, separated out from the complex of ideas proper to the feast of the Manifestation. In fact, however, duplications of ideas arose here and there, even in the Roman liturgy."[5]

The original content of the feast of Christmas is the incarnation of the God-man, his "manifestation in the flesh," including both conception and birth. For this reason it is understandable that when the feast of the Annunciation of the Lord (March 25) was introduced in the seventh century it was not accepted as

124

a holy day of obligation, especially since it stood within the shadow of the approaching feast of Easter and of Holy Week.

2 / THE LITURGY OF CHRISTMAS

In the Roman tradition, which can be traced back to the sixth century, every priest can celebrate three Masses on Christmas. Even the new Missal of 1970 has kept this unusual custom. The Missal has Masses for midnight (Latin: *Missa in nocte*), at dawn (Latin: *Missa in aurora*), and during the day (Latin: *Missa in die*). The medieval mystics saw in this practice an allusion to the "threefold birth" of the Lord:

> The first and supreme birth takes place when the heavenly Father bears his only-begotten Son as one with himself in essence yet as also a distinct person. The second birth, which we commemorate today, results from the maternal fruitfulness which the chaste Virgin exercised in perfect purity. The third birth is this: that God is truly but spiritually born every day and at every hour in a good soul, as a result of grace and love. We celebrate these three births by means of the three holy Masses.[6]

This is an ingenious and pious interpretation, but the historical origin of the three Masses is much more prosaic. In the fourth century the first and only Mass was the festal Mass which the pope celebrated in St. Peter's at the usual hour, i.e., around nine o'clock. In the fifth century the midnight Mass in the Basilica of St. Mary Major was added. After the Council of Ephesus (431), which declared the divine maternity of Mary to be a dogma, the basilica was erected, as a church of Mary, under Pope Sixtus III (432–440), to replace the old Basilica of Liborius on the Esquiline. A little later, a subterranean chapel was built under the new basilica, as a replica of the cave at Bethlehem in which Christ was born. After the night Office the pope celebrated the "Midnight Mass" in this chapel, then took part in lauds, and finally went off to rest.[7] This nocturnal celebration of Mass was probably inspired and encouraged by a custom of the Christians of Jerusalem. During the night before Epiphany the Jerusalem Christians would celebrate a Mass in the church which Emperor Constantine had built over the cave of Christ's birth at Bethlehem; then they would return in procession to Jerusalem and celebrate another eucharist in the morning.

Around the middle of the sixth century a third Mass was added; it was celebrated in the church of St. Anastasia near the Palatine. This church was dedicated to Anastasia of Sirmium, a martyr highly regarded in the East; after the Byzantine Greeks had conquered Rome, they made this their imperial church. Because the festal commemoration of this saint fell on December 25 in the East, the pope personally celebrated this Mass, probably out of respect for the Byzantine governor, but the saint herself was not explicitly mentioned in the Proper of the Mass.

The three Christmas Masses were entered in the papal sacramentaries and were taken over elsewhere, once these sacramentaries made their way abroad. Apart from the fact that an Old Testament reading has been added to the Christmas Masses in the new Missal, the Propers are essentially the same as before.

The Midnight Mass receives its special stamp primarily from the gospel, which recounts the birth of Christ at Bethlehem (Lk 2.1-14). The passage ends with the song of the angels, which also begins the Gloria of the Mass and in fact gave this hymn its name. The Gloria has a special tonality on this day. The Old Testament reading (Is 9.2-4, 6-7) speaks of the messianic hope that has been fulfilled on this day: "The people who walked in darkness have seen a great light. . . . For to us a child is born, to us a son is given; and the government will be upon his shoulder, and his name will be called 'Wonderful Counselor, Mighty God, Everlasting Father, Prince of Peace'! "The second reading (Tit 2.11-14) embraces in a single sweep this first appearance of "the grace of God" and its final appearance for which Christians must now prepare by living "sober, upright, and godly lives in this world." The alleluia verse sings jubilantly of "good news and great joy to all the world: Today is born our Savior, Christ the Lord."

The symbolism of light finds expression in the opening prayer: "You make this holy night radiant with the splendor of Jesus

Christ our light," and again in the first of the three Christmas prefaces, which speaks of "a new and radiant vision of your glory."

The prayer over the gifts speaks (in the Latin original) of the "holy exchange" in which "we are made like your Son, in whom our human nature is united with his divine being." This idea of the exchange, so dear to the Fathers of the Church, is picked up again in the opening prayer of the Mass during the Day: "Your Son shared our weakness [literally: our humanity]: may we share his glory [literally: his divinity]." Above all, however, it finds classical expression in the third preface for Christmas, which may be used in the Masses of Christmas day and during the octave: "Your eternal Word has taken upon himself our human weakness, giving our mortal nature immortal value."

The entrance antiphon, Psalm 2.7 ("The Lord said to me . . ."), which is the same as the old Introit, may be replaced by another verse in which direct reference is made to the mystery of the incarnation ("Let us all rejoice in the Lord . . ."). Special reverence is shown to this mystery in all the Christmas Masses, inasmuch as the congregation kneels when the words of the Creed about the conception and birth of Jesus are spoken.

The gospel (Lk 2.15-20) of the Mass at Dawn tells in a simple but moving way of the shepherds' meeting with the child in the manger. The symbolism of light is emphasized even more strongly than in the Midnight Mass: "A light will shine on us this day . . ." (entrance antiphon and refrain for the responsorial psalm); "We are filled with the new light by the coming of your Word among us. May the light of faith shine in our words and actions" (opening prayer); "Light dawns for the righteous, and joy for the upright of heart" (responsorial psalm, Ps 97.11). "Faith and joy" (concluding prayer) run like a leitmotif through the entire liturgy of the Mass.

The Mass during the Day uses the Prologue of the Fourth Gospel (1.1-18) to proclaim the mystery of the incarnation as seen in Johannine theology: "In the beginning was the Word, and the Word was with God, and the Word was God. . . . In him was life, and the life was the light of men. The light shines in the darkness, and the darkness has not overcome it. . . . The true light that enlightens every man was coming into the world. . . . And the Word became flesh and dwelt among us." This incarnation brings the greatest possible fulfillment of the prophet's words about the messenger of peace "who publishes peace, who brings good tidings of good, who publishes salvation" (first reading, Is 52.7-10). After the many and varied oracles of the prophets the Father has now spoken his definitive revelation in Christ. For the Son "reflects the glory of God and bears the very stamp of his nature, upholding the universe by his word of power. When he had made purification for sins, he sat down at the right hand of the Majesty on high" (second reading, Heb 1.1-6).

These and other texts make it clear that Christmas too is celebrated as a feast of our redemption, even though the focus of attention is on the incarnation and the "marvelous exchange," and not on the passion and resurrection. But the paschal mystery itself also finds expression in the Christmas liturgy as the citation from the second reading of the Mass during the Day shows and as the second reading of the Midnight Mass makes even clearer: "Jesus Christ . . . gave himself for us to redeem us from all iniquity and to purify for himself a people of his own who are zealous for good deeds" (Tit 2.14).

In view of this content which Christmas and Easter have in common, the suggestion has been made that "we would do better to divide the year into an 'Easter celebration of redemption' and a 'Christmas celebration of redemption.' "[8] In this context the well-known sentence from the Roman Martyrology for December 25 should be recalled: "Jesus Christ, eternal God and Son of the eternal Father, willed by his holy coming to consecrate the world," i.e., to sanctify and redeem it. Thus the Christmas liturgy is concerned with the exalted Lord who in his incarnation "emptied" himself of his equality with God, lived a human life in "the form of a servant," and humbled himself in obedience unto death on the cross, in order that he might then be exalted as "Lord" (Phil 2.6-11).

Because the life of the Virgin Mary is inseparable from the mystery of Jesus' humanity, her name is mentioned not only in the creed but in the inserts for the eucharistic prayer as well. Above all, as we shall see, the octave-day of Christmas is devoted especially to commemoration of her.

Another part of the festal liturgy for Christmas is the Vigil Mass that is celebrated on the evening of the twenty-fourth. The morning Mass of the twenty-fourth is still regarded as an Advent Mass. Such vigil Masses occur elsewhere only in connection with Pentecost, the solemnities of the birth of John the Baptist and of the apostles Peter and Paul, and the solemnity of Mary's assumption into heaven.[9] "Regarding the celebration of vigils, it is to be observed that the medieval idea of a vigil, namely a day of penance before a feast, has been entirely removed from the reformed liturgy. Except in the case of the Easter Vigil, which is to be celebrated during that holiest of nights, the name 'Vigil Mass' means henceforth a Mass that can be celebrated as a festal Mass on the evening before a solemnity, either before or after First Vespers."[10]

The texts of the new Vigil Mass of Christmas are only partially the same as those of the old Vigil Mass that used to be celebrated in purple vestments on the morning of the twenty-fourth. Two texts from the old Mass have been retained: the entrance antiphon with its confident expectation of salvation (Ex 16.6-7: "Today you will know that the Lord is coming to save us, and in the morning you will see his glory"), and the opening prayer, which skillfully connects expectation of Christ's first coming with his return at the end of time.

The first reading (Is 62.1-5) describes in glowing colors the glory of the new Jerusalem as God's beloved bride. In the second reading (Acts 13.16-17, 22-25) Paul during a mission sermon cites a saying of John the Precursor: "What do you suppose that I am? I am not he. No, but after me one is coming, the sandals of whose feet I am not worthy to untie." The gospel (Mt 1.1-25) gives the genealogy of Jesus and the message of the angel to Joseph: "That which is conceived in her is of the Holy Spirit; she will bear a son, and you shall call his name Jesus, for he will save his people from their sins." Because the Mass is already part of the feast, the regulations concerning the creed and the inserts in the eucharistic prayer for Christmas Masses apply here as well.

3 / ADVENT AS A SEASON OF PREPARATION FOR CHRISTMAS

Like Easter, Christmas acquired a period of preparation, to which the name Advent (coming) was given. Little research has as yet been done into many phases of the historical development; these phases did not follow the same pattern in the various Churches. Popular piety and custom, which concentrated so strongly on Christmas, have given Advent a special place in Christian consciousness.

a/The Historical Development of Advent

The first traces of a season of preparation for Christmas are found not in the Roman liturgy but in Spain and especially in Gaul. It is significant here that in these countries, which had close links with the Eastern Church, the feast of the Epiphany on January 6 was the original feast of Christ's birth and, for a time, an important day for baptism (this was not the case at Rome).

If we prescind from some uncertain reports from the second half of the fourth century that speak of "three weeks of intense religious activity,"[11] the oldest witness to an Advent as a time of preparation is the regulations on fasting issued by Bishop Perpetuus of Tours († 490). These call for three days of fasting per week during the period from the feast of St. Martin (November 11) to Christmas. Jungmann has shown that this regulation was based on an earlier "St. Martin's Lent" which lasted from the saint's feast to Epiphany, that is, for 56 days or 8 weeks. But since in that region, which at the time had close ties with Byzantium and Jerusalem, there was no fasting on Saturdays or Sundays, the period contained only forty fastdays. The real motive behind such a Lent was the fact that Epiphany was a day for baptism, and there was a desire to show no less respect for this occasion by way of preparation for it than was shown for

Easter as a day of baptism. [12] Just which Churches observed
such a Lent, and during what period of history, is uncertain,
since the sources are too scanty. Above all, however, all that we
have been saying does not tell us anything as yet about the
actual liturgy of Advent.

The first traces of such a liturgy can be detected in the middle of
the fifth century in Ravenna, which was heavily influenced by
the East. Expectation of Christ's birth is the central theme of
this liturgy. In Rome, the beginnings of an Advent liturgy become visible for the first time in the middle of the sixth century,
in connection with the winter *ember days,* the Masses of which
make use of Advent themes. [13] A new and significant direction
is taken under Gregory the Great (590–604); whose Sacramentary (for the city of Rome) contains four Sunday Masses and
three ember day Masses that have the impress of Advent on
them. Here it can be seen that the original focus of Advent was
not so much on expectation of the final coming (the parousia) as
on the incarnation of Christ and on preparation for its liturgical
celebration. [14] For the incarnation as a historical event marks the
beginning of our salvation and ensures its completion in the
return of Christ. [15]

In other parts of the Church, especially in Gaul, there were,
however, notable shifts of emphasis in this regard, with the
eschatological dimension of Advent being sharply accented.
This was probably due to the influence of Irish missionaries
(e.g., Columbanus, 530–615), who laid heavy stress on the
coming of the Lord for judgment and on the need of doing penance before the final judgment, and who in their preaching on
penance turned Advent into a penitential season. [16] Thus in the
Gallic liturgies and others the Gloria and alleluia were dropped
from the Mass and the Te Deum from the Office, and purple
vestments were used.

Something of this penitential character was transmitted from
Gaul to the Roman liturgy of Advent in the twelfth century; for
example, the omission of the Gloria and the wearing of purple
vestments. But in Rome Advent was not regarded as properly a
penitential season, as can be seen from the fact that the joyous
alleluia was retained. It is interesting to see the reason given in

the Commentary on the *General Norms for the Liturgical Year* for the omission of the Gloria: "It is not omitted for the same reason as it is omitted in Lent, but in order that on the night of Christmas the angels' song may ring out once again in all its newness."[17] There has been no obligatory Advent fast since the 1917/1918 Code of Canon Law was promulgated.

As for the length of the Advent season, the Roman solution (four Sundays of Advent) won out only after hesitations, although King Pepin and his son Charlemagne had decreed it for the Frankish kingdom. For a lengthy period Advent might last four, five or six weeks depending on the diocese. Even today the liturgy of Milan has six Sundays of Advent. Only in the course of the tenth and eleventh centuries does the Roman position seem to have been accepted throughout the Franko-Gallic world.

If December 25 fell on a Sunday, many Churches began Advent on November 26 in order to be able to celebrate four Sundays of Advent and a Vigil of Christmas. Finally, however, the rule prevailed that Advent should begin in this case only on December 3, but the liturgy of the fourth Sunday was to yield to that of the Vigil.[18] The rule that Advent should begin on November 27 at the earliest and December 3 at the latest has been retained in the reformed liturgy: "Advent begins with first evening prayer of the Sunday which falls on or closest to November 30 and ends before the first evening prayer of Christmas."[19] The liturgy of the fourth Sunday, however, can no longer be suppressed if it falls on December 24.

b/The Liturgy of Advent

The new *General Norms for the Liturgical Year* makes a very important statement about the meaning of the Advent period of preparation and thereby sets up guidelines for the liturgical celebration: "The season of Advent has a twofold character. It is a time of preparation for Christmas when the first coming of God's Son to men is recalled. It is also a season when minds are directed by this memorial to Christ's second coming at the end of time. It is thus a season of joyful and spiritual expectation" (no. 39).

This passage expresses the basic ethos that has always been in control throughout the history of the Roman liturgy: Advent is not primarily a season of penance in preparation for the judgment of the returning Lord, but a festive commemoration of the incarnation and, on the basis of the incarnation, a devout and joyous expectation of the parousia. Croce, in his historical investigation of Advent, rightly speaks of a basic law governing all liturgy: "The events of salvation can be the object of liturgical celebration only to the extent that they are already a historical reality. For this reason we can celebrate the birth, death and resurrection of Jesus Christ; we can also celebrate the action of Jesus in the Church, as it has revealed itself with power on Pentecost and in the life of every saint. But his coming for judgment and the definitive redemption of his Church cannot yet be the object of celebration in the proper sense, for it has not yet taken place; it can only be awaited."[20]

We must not see a contradiction to the above quoted explanation of Advent when the Commentary on the *General Norms* speaks of the weekdays from December 17 to December 24 inclusive as more directly oriented to the Lord's birth,[21] while it speaks of the period from the first Sunday of Advent to December 16 as having an eschatological emphasis "since it [the liturgy] urges souls to look for the second coming of Christ."[22] There is no contradiction because even in the eschatologically oriented period the first coming of Christ is not forgotten, but rather both aspects are present.

The Proper of the Mass for each Sunday of Advent is the same in all three years of the cycle, except for the scripture readings and the first intermediate song (responsorial psalm), while the alleluia verse differs in one case. The keynote for each Mass is struck by the gospel, which more or less sets the theme for all the other texts.

The Advent liturgy has been enriched in a significant way by the provision of two Advent prefaces. The Missal of Pius V did not have even one Advent preface; in 1968 two Advent prefaces were published along with the new eucharistic prayers, and these have been taken over into the Roman Missal. The first of the two prefaces is used from the first Sunday to December 16, the second from December 17 to December 24.

On the first Sunday of Advent the gospel speaks of the Lord's return and urges watchfulness (Mt 24.37-44; Mk 13.33-37; Lk 21.25-28, 34-36). The Old Testament readings for the three-year cycle are taken from Book of Isaiah. They describe the messianic kingdom of peace in which God will gather all peoples (A), call for the Messiah to come (B), and promise the messianic "Branch of David" (C). The New Testament readings, taken from various letters of Paul, warn the hearers to wake from sleep and cast off the works of darkness, "for salvation is nearer to us now . . . the night is far gone, the day is at hand" (Rom 13.11-14 = A); they express the Apostle's confidence that "you are not lacking in any spiritual gift, as you wait for the revealing of our Lord Jesus Christ" (1 Cor 1.3-9 = B); they ask for growth in love "so that he [the Lord] may establish your hearts unblamable in holiness . . . at the coming of our Lord Jesus with all his saints" (1 Thess 3.12-4.2 = C). The Mass texts for this Sunday of Advent thus focus with special intensity on the second coming of Christ.

The gospel for the second Sunday of Advent gives the call for penance by John, precursor of Christ and preparer of his way, as this call is reported in the three Synoptics: "Repent, for the kingdom of heaven is at hand" (Mt 3.1-12 = A); "preaching a baptism of repentance for the forgiveness of sins" (Mk 1.1-8, and Lk 3.1-6 = B and C). The Old Testament reading in Year A promises the "shoot from the stump of Jesse" and depicts his messianic rule in glowing colors (Is 11.1-10). In Years B and C the return of God's people from exile becomes an inspiring metaphor of the coming of complete salvation in the messianic kingdom (Is 40.1-5, 9-11; Bar 5.1-9). In the New Testament readings Christ is proclaimed as universal Savior (Rom 15.4-9 = A), who will bring "new heavens and a new earth" (2 Pet 3.8-14 = B). On this day of Christ we must be "pure and blameless . . . filled with the fruits of righteousness which come through Jesus Christ" (Phil 1.4-6, 8-11 = C).

The opening prayer picks up these ideas and exhortations: "Remove the things that hinder us from receiving Christ with joy, so that we may share his wisdom and become one with him." Promise, exhortation, and joyous expectation characterize this Sunday and are all brought together in the entrance antiphon that serves to introduce the theme of the day: "People of Zion, the Lord will come to save all nations, and your hearts will exult to hear his majestic voice" (cf. Is 30.19, 30).

The third Sunday is familiar to many of the faithful as "Gaudete" Sunday. *Gaudete* ("rejoice") is the first word of the entrance antiphon, which is taken from the second reading of Year C and urges us to Advent joy: "Rejoice in the Lord always; again I say, Rejoice! The Lord is near" (Phil 4.4-5). An especially striking aspect of the Mass is the use of rose-colored vestments. They replace the sober purple of penance and are a sign of anticipatory Christmas joy. This usage probably came from assimilation to the fourth Sunday of Lent, "Laetare" Sunday, which also strikes a note of joy.

The gospel brings the person of the Baptist before us once again. In Year A he is in prison and sends his disciples to ask Jesus "Are you he who is to come, or shall we look for another?" Jesus points to "what you hear and see" and specifically to the messianic miracles which Isaiah had foretold (cf. first Sunday). Jesus then pays a notable tribute to John himself and calls him the promised messenger who was to prepare the way for the Messiah (Mt 11.2-11).

The New Testament reading from the Letter of James urges his readers to be patient until the Lord comes and exhorts them: "Establish your hearts, for the coming of the Lord is at hand" (5.7-10). Although this Sunday only infrequently falls within the period of more proximate preparation for Christmas (i.e., December 17–24), the opening prayer is filled with expectation of the feast of Christ's birth: "May we, your people, who look forward to the birthday of Christ experience the joy of salvation and celebrate that feast with love and thanksgiving." The closing prayer, taken over from the old Missal, has a similar petition: "Prepare us for the birthday of our Savior."

In the gospel of Year B John calls himself "the voice of one crying in the wilderness" and preparing the way for the Messiah. Of the latter he says: "Among you stands one whom you do not know" (Jn 1.6-8, 19-28). The Old Testament reading from

Isaiah also speaks of the Messiah (Is 61.1-2a, 10-11), while the New Testament reading summons us to holiness in preparation for the coming of the Lord Jesus Christ (1 Thess 5.16-24). Note should be taken of the responsorial psalm, which consists of most of the verses of the Magnificat.

The gospel of Year C again sets John the Baptist before us, this time as he gives various groups advice on how to live and turns their attention away from himself to the coming Redeemer: "He who is mightier than I is coming . . . he will baptize you with the Holy Spirit and with fire" (Lk 3.10-18). The first and second readings are similar in that both urge us to rejoice at the proximate coming of the Lord (Zeph 3.14-18a and Phil 4.4-7; the entrance antiphon is from this second passage). Gaudete Sunday, then, is characterized by anticipatory joy and expectation, which must, however, find expression in a readiness to live according to the Spirit of Christ.

With the fourth Sunday we are in the period of proximate preparation for the feast of the Lord's birth. The Propers of the Mass are therefore concerned with the events that immediately precede the Lord's birth or with texts that refer to these events. Thus the gospel of Year A speaks of Joseph's doubts and of the angel's message that he should take Mary to wife because the child she is expecting is from the Holy Spirit and will "save his people from their sins" (Mt 1.18-24). In Years B and C the gospel readings are of the annunciation of the Lord (Lk 1.26-38) and Mary's visit to her cousin Elizabeth, on which occasion she is called blessed because of her faith; she then sings her own hymn of gratitude, the Magnificat (Lk 1.39-47).

The opening prayer starts with the annunciation but then moves from the incarnation to the paschal mystery: "As you revealed to us by an angel the coming of your Son as man, so lead us through his suffering and death to the glory of his resurrection." The prayer over the gifts also mentions the annunciation and the incarnation of Jesus in Mary's womb. Reference is likewise made to the Mother of the Lord in the first reading of Year A, in which God himself, through the prophet Isaiah, gives King Ahaz the "sign of Immanuel" (Is 7.10-14). In the first reading of Year B God proclaims, through the prophet Nathan, that the kingdom of David will stand for ever (2 Sam 7.1-5, 8b-11, 16). In Year C the prophet Micah foretells the coming of the Messiah from Bethlehem Ephrathah: in the strength of the Lord he will feed the flock made up of the returning exiles, "and there shall be peace" (Mic 5.1-4a).

The New Testament reading in Year A is the first verses of the Letter to the Romans, where Paul speaks of his vocation to preach the gospel, "the gospel concerning his son" (Rom 1.1-7). The last verses of the same letter, i.e., the concluding doxology, forms the corresponding reading in Year B (Rom 16.25-27), while Year C's reading is the passage from the Letter to the Hebrews on the words Christ speaks as he comes into the world: " 'A body hast thou prepared for me. . . . Lo, I have come to do thy will, O God'. . . . And by that will we have been sanctified through the offering of the body of Jesus Christ once for all" (Heb 10.5-10). In this pre-Christmas reading, as in the opening prayer, the connection of the incarnation with the paschal mystery and redemption is once again made clear.

The closing prayer for all Masses of the Fourth Sunday again directs our gaze to the imminent feast when it bids us pray: "As Christmas draws near make us grow in faith and love to celebrate the coming of Christ our Savior."

The liturgy for the weekdays of Advent has been substantially enriched. Before the reform there were no Mass formularies for the weekdays of Advent; now every day in the second phase of Advent (December 17–24) has its own Proper. For the weekdays of the first phase there is a weekly series which is repeated; thus, e.g., each Monday of this period has the same Proper, except for the opening prayer and the scripture readings which are different for each day. The presidential prayers of this first phase of Advent bring out both the eschatological and the Christmas dimensions of the season.

The lectionary provides readings from Isaiah for the first nine weekdays, and these in turn determine the choice of gospel. Thursday of the second week begins a series of gospel pericopes on John the Baptist, with complementary texts in the other reading. "The gospels of the last week before Christmas are from Matthew (Chapter 1) and Luke (Chapter 1), the events which immediately prepared for the Lord's birth. Selections for the first reading are from different books of the Old Testament which have important messianic prophecies and a relationship to the gospel texts."[23]

The weekdays of this week before Christmas have been especially enriched by using as alleluia verses the famous O-Antiphons from the Liturgy of the Hours, where they serve as antiphons for the Magnificat from December 17 to December 24. They are "a very unique work of art and a special ornament of the pre-Christmas liturgy. Even personages in the Bible loved to juxtapose words and sentences from the treasury of the scriptures and thus create ever new compositions which are filled with the Spirit of the word of God. . . . This type of composition has never fallen into disuse in the Church and has created a poetry that fills the liturgy with its splendor. One of the most important examples of such poetry is the O-Antiphons. . . . The composer (or composers) had a superior, indeed a magnificent, command of the Bible's wealth of motifs."[24] Each O-Antiphon combines a laudatory invocation of the expected Messiah with a petition for his coming as Savior. In Latin they begin with the vocative *O* (whence the name); here is how each begins in the new Missal:

1. Come, Wisdom of our God Most High *(O Sapientia)*.
2. Come, Leader of ancient Israel *(O Adonai)*.
3. Come, Flower of Jesse's stem *(O radix Jesse)*.
4. Come, Key of David *(O clavis David)*.
5. Come, Radiant Dawn *(O Oriens)*.
6. Come, King of all nations *(O Rex gentium)*.
7. Come, Emmanuel *(O Emmanuel)*.[25]

The "*Rorate* Masses," which used to be often celebrated on the weekdays of Advent in German-speaking countries and were well attended, were originally votive Masses in honor of the Mother of God on the Saturdays of Advent. These can still be celebrated on the weekdays of Advent, but only until December 16 inclusive.[26]

4 / THE OCTAVE OF CHRISTMAS

Apart from Easter only Christmas has an octave or liturgical week of feasts. This is surely a sign of the high esteem the Church has for this feast even in our day.

The octave day coincides with the first day of the civil year. Since the middle of the second century BC the Roman consuls had begun their term of office on this first day of January; then, when the Roman calendar was reorganized in 46 BC, Gaius Julius Caesar shifted the beginning of the new year from March 1 to January 1.

Within Christianity this day has undergone some changes of meaning. Because pagans made the beginning of the new year a feast in honor of Janus, the god who faces in two directions, and celebrated it with boisterous joy, superstitious practices and gross orgies, the Church tried to immunize the faithful by instituting penitential liturgies and calling upon Christians to fast. There was a special Mass formulary *Ad prohibendum ab idolis* ("For protection against idolatry"). We may take the following words from one of Augustine's sermons as representative of many statements by the Fathers: "Let them give new year's gifts: you should give alms. Let them sing boisterous songs: you should open your hearts to the word of God. Let them rush to the theater: you should rush to church. Let them get drunk: you should fast."[27] The Second Council of Tours (567) prescribed that penitential devotions were to be held on the first three days of January as a way of eliminating pagan practices, and the Fourth Council of Toledo (633) ordered a strict fast modeled on the Lenten fast. Echoes of this penitential practice remained in the Tridentine Missal down to our own time, inasmuch as the prayer over the gifts and the concluding prayer of the January 1 Mass came from the old penitential Mass.[28]

The Church of Rome then used another tactic that had been effective in similar situations: she made January 1 a feast of Mary and specifically the Anniversary *(Natale)* of the Mother of God. In so doing, Rome was probably influenced by the Church of Constantinople in which devotion to Mary and feasts of Mary had become popular at a much earlier date. When the two Byzantine feasts of Mary—the Annunciation and the

Assumption—were taken over in Rome at the beginning of the seventh century, the *Natale S. Mariae* was overshadowed once again and yielded to an octave-day celebration of Christmas.

During the sixth century the feast of the Circumcision of the Lord came to be celebrated on January 1 in Spain and especially in Gaul, with Luke 2.21 providing the basis for the feast and choice of day. Only in the thirteenth/fourteenth century do we also find this feast at Rome where, until the recent reform, it was celebrated under the title "Circumcision of the Lord and Octave of Christmas" and was oriented toward Mary and Christmas. The *General Norms* of 1969 returned to the original Roman view of the day when it ordained that "January 1, the octave day of Christmas, is the solemnity of Mary, Mother of God. It also recalls the conferral of the name of Jesus."[29] A commemoration of Mary is also celebrated in the Eastern rites, on December 26 in the Byzantine, West Syrian and East Syrian rites and on January 16 in the Coptic rite.

The new calendar has dispensed with a separate feast of the Name of Jesus. The origins of this feast go back to the fifteenth century when John of Capistrano and Bernardine of Siena worked to spread the cult of the holy name of Jesus. In 1721 Pope Innocent XIII assigned the feast to the second Sunday after Epiphany; in 1913 Pius X assigned it to the Sunday between the first and sixth of January or to January 2 if no Sunday occurred during this period.

The Proper of the Mass (the same in all years of the cycle) for this new and at the same time very ancient feast focuses primarily on the divine motherhood of Mary whom "we proclaim . . . to be the Mother of Christ and the mother of the Church" (concluding prayer). The gospel (Lk 2.16-21) says of her that she kept all these Christmas events and pondered them in her heart; the pericope also mentions the circumcision of Jesus and the giving of his name to him. The second reading (Gal 4.4-7) looks at the coming of God's Son, "born of woman" "when the time had fully come," from the viewpoint of "those who were under the law, so that we might receive adoption as sons." On the other hand, the giving of the name Jesus is apparently in the forefront of attention in the first reading (Num 6.22-27) since after the institution of the blessing of Aaron the text says: "So shall they put my name upon the people of Israel, and I will bless them."

It has been thought regrettable—and with good reason—that the liturgy of this day takes no account of the fact that January 1 is also the beginning of the civil year.[30] Since almost all the nations of the human family attribute special significance to the day, the liturgy should not pass over it in silence. In this context heed should be given to a statement of Cardinal Montini, later Pope Paul VI, who said during the debates of Vatican II: "The liturgy was instituted for human beings, not human beings for the liturgy."[31]

In its section of "Masses for Various Public Needs" the new Missal does have, in first place, a Mass for the "Beginning of the Civil Year," in which the presidential prayers in particular mention the beginning of the new year and ask God's blessing on it ("May this new year which we dedicate to you bring us abundant prosperity and growth in holy living"). However, the introductory rubric says laconically: "This Mass may not be celebrated on January 1, the solemnity of Mary the Mother of God." Behind this statement lies an anxious fidelity to the general rubrical principle that no votive Masses may be celebrated on solemnities. A reexamination and change of this decision seems both sensible and urgent. "In the Constitution on the Church in the Modern World (Art. 1), the Church has said that nothing human fails to find an echo in her heart. Since, then, human beings today often face the future with concern and at times even resignation, is it not the Church's duty to offer them, in a liturgy for which a positive basis already exists, direction and help that will enable them to cope, in faith, with past, present and future?"[32]

Even the oldest liturgical calendars already have a series of saints' feasts directly following on Christmas. The Middle Ages saw these saints as a cortege of honor accompanying the Christ-child, and gave them the name *Comites Christi* ("Companions of Christ").[33] In the Roman liturgy these companions are Stephen the first martyr on December 26, John the Apostle and Evangelist on December 27, and the children whom Herod slew in Bethlehem on December 28 (cf. Mt 2.13-18). These three were regarded as representing the three possible forms of martyrdom: voluntary and executed (Stephen), voluntary but not executed (John), and executed but not voluntary (Holy Innocents).[34]

The feast of St. Stephen dates from the fourth century in the East; in the West it is known from the beginning of the fifth. His cult received a strong stimulus when Lucian, a priest, found his relics in Jerusalem in 415; pieces of these made their way to many countries and churches. Churches and chapels in honor of this "Archdeacon" (i.e., first deacon; cf. Acts 6.5) were built in many places. In medieval Rome alone there were supposed to have been thirty-four.[35]

The first reading of the Mass describes his ministry and martyrdom (Acts 6.8-10; 7.54-60); in the gospel Jesus tells the disciples of the persecutions they will endure for his sake. The opening prayer describes the saint as a model of love for enemies, the concluding prayer as a model of fearless witness to the faith. In medieval times there were many popular customs connected with his feast day.[36]

The feast of John the Apostle and Evangelist also goes back to the fourth century in the East; it was originally accompanied by a commemoration of his brother, James the Greater. On the basis chiefly of what Irenaeus says, "the tradition was formed that the Apostle John carried on his ministry in Ephesus, was banished during the reign of Domitian to the island of Patmos where he wrote the Apocalypse, then returned to Ephesus where he composed his gospel and died at an advanced age (in the reign of Trajan)."[37] His cult was favored in the Middle Ages by the legends that, in order to convert a pagan priest, he drank a cup of poisoned wine and was not harmed by it, and that he was thrown into a cauldron of boiling oil outside the Latin Gate of Rome, again without suffering injury.

The presidential prayers of the festal Mass point out that John has made known to us in a special way the mystery of the eternal and incarnate Word. The reading (1 Jn 1.1-4) presents him to us as a witness who both saw and heard and whose testimony demands credence. The gospel describes his experience at the empty tomb on Easter morning: "he saw and believed" (Jn 20.2-8).

From the early Middle Ages down to our own day the custom of blessing and distributing "St. John's wine" has been observed. It is connected with the pagan custom (among Greeks, Romans, Germans) of partaking of a drink in honor of a god. Once Christianity had been introduced, the custom became one of drinking to the honor of certain saints, e.g., Michael, Stephen, John the Baptist, Martin of Tours among others. The drink in loving memory of John acquired special significance and lasting popularity once an official blessing of St. John's wine had been instituted. The blessing in turn was certainly connected with the legend of the drinking of the poisoned wine.[38]

The feast of the Holy Innocents on December 28 seems to be a Western creation. The first mention of it occurs in the calendar of the North African city of Carthage for 505,[39] after many Fathers of the Church had extolled the martyrdom of these children. The connection with the events of Christmas certainly influenced the choice of a date for the feast. Although it was a feast of martyrs, it acquired a sorrowful character under the influence of the Gallic liturgy, being celebrated in purple vestments and without Gloria or Te Deum. Only in the Code of Rubrics, *Ratio et via*, of July 25, 1960, was it assimilated to the other feasts of martyrs.

In the Mass the gospel (Mt 2.13-18) tells of the flight into Egypt and the slaying of the children of Bethlehem. The reading, however, is from the First Letter of John, which is begun on the previous day and read continuously until the end of the Christmas season (i.e., January 12 at the latest).

On September 29 is the optional memorial of Thomas Becket of Canterbury, bishop and martyr († 1170), and on December 31 that of Pope Sylvester I († 335).

The feast of the Holy Family is celebrated on the Sunday within the octave of Christmas. If Christmas and its octave day fall on a Sunday, this feast is celebrated on December 31. The feast is a quite recent one and is to be regarded as either a devotion-feast or an idea-feast. The cult of the Holy Family of Jesus, Mary and Joseph spread around the world in the nineteenth century, with Canada as the main source of influence, and was promoted especially by Leo XIII. The family of Nazareth was regarded as a model and source of help for the beleaguered Christian family. From 1893 on a feast of the Holy Family could be celebrated on the third Sunday after Epiphany if dioceses and religious orders requested it. After Pius X had temporarily suppressed the feast (1911), it was reintroduced in the Missal of 1920 *(editio typica)*, but now on the first Sunday after Epiphany.

The Mass for the feast focuses its attention on the "splendid example" (Latin text) of the Holy Family and asks for the grace that our families too "may live as the holy family, united in respect and love" (opening prayer) and that "we may constantly imitate the example of the Holy Family and so attain to their eternal company after the trials of this life" (Latin text of concluding prayer). The Old Testament reading (Sir 3.2-6, 12-14) speaks of the attitude children should have toward their parents, and the New Testament reading (Col 3.12-21) of the Christian way of life that must be followed by families as well as by individuals. The gospel for Year A recounts the flight of the Holy Family to Egypt and their return to Nazareth (Mt 2.13-15, 19-23); in Year B it describes the events that take place when the Child Jesus is presented in the temple (Lk 2.22-40); in Year C it tells of the pilgrimage of Mary and Joseph with the twelve-year-old Jesus to the feast of Passover in Jerusalem (Lk 2.41-52). Instead of a special preface one of the three Christmas prefaces is used, as befits a feast celebrated within the octave.

5 / EPIPHANY

The solemnity of the Epiphany of the Lord (Greek: *epiphaneia* or *theophaneia*, "appearance *or* manifestation of God") is the original feast of Christ's birth in the East. In antiquity an "epiphany" meant either a visible manifestation of a god or the solemn visit of a ruler, who was venerated as a god, to the cities of his realm. The oldest traces of a feast of the Epiphany are from Alexandria in Egypt where Clement, an ecclesiastical writer at the beginning of the third century, says that the followers of Basilides, who were gnostics, celebrated a feast of the baptism of Jesus, which event they regarded as being the real moment of the Son of God's birth into the world.[40] It is probable that "the feast of the Epiphany" was introduced "into the Great

Church in reaction to the gnostic feast"[41] and became familiar to the Churches of the East as the feast of Christ's birth.

There is in fact much to be said for the view that the choice of January 6 in the East, like the choice of December 25 in the West, was influenced by a pagan feast. For during the night of January 5–6 the pagans of Alexandria celebrated the birthday of the god Aion (god of time and eternity); in a solemn ceremony water was drawn from the Nile and stored away.[42] At an early date the commemoration of Jesus' baptism was associated with this feast of his birth, and the day became an important date for baptism in the East. Likewise associated with this feast was the commemoration of the first miracle of Jesus at the wedding feast in Cana, where he changed water into wine and thus once again revealed his glory (cf. Jn 2.11). The commemoration of this miracle of the wine on this day was probably suggested by pagan notions that on the night of January 6 many springs yielded wine instead of water.[43] In response to this fantasy, Christians could say that Jesus had actually worked such a change.

In the second half of the fourth century East and West took over each other's birthday feast of Jesus. While the East celebrated on December 25 not only the birth of Jesus but also the coming of the Magi and reserved January 6 for the commemoration of Jesus' baptism and his miracle at Cana and for the conferral of baptism, the West on January 6 celebrated the Epiphany of the redeemer in connection with the coming of the wise men, the baptism of Jesus and the wedding feast at Cana. The antiphon for the Magnificat at second vespers links the three events in a succinct manner, while the antiphon for the Benedictus integrates all three into the image of Christ's wedding with his Church: "Today the Bridegroom claims his bride, the Church, since Christ has washed her sins away in Jordan's waters; the Magi hasten with their gifts to the royal wedding; and the wedding guests rejoice, for Christ has changed water into wine, alleluia." J. A. Jungmann puts the thematic difference between the two feasts in this way: "The mystery of the Incarnation is the proper subject of them both; but at Christmas we consider chiefly the coming down of the Son of God who became one of the poor children of men, while on the Epiphany we direct our attention to this Child's divine dignity which already is beginning to manifest itself in the world."[44]

Epiphany is also known as the feast of the Three Holy Kings or as Three Kings' Day. This emphasis obscures the fact that the feast is not a saint's feast but a feast of the Lord. Moreover, as everyone knows, the gospel account says nothing about kings or about the Magi being three in number. Origen is the first to speak of three Magi; he probably gets the number from the three gifts. The designation "kings" first occurs in Caesarius of Arles in the sixth century. The names Caspar, Melchior and Balthasar have been used since the ninth century.

Among the many customs associated with this day I may mention the medieval custom of the "star-singers," which has been revived by Catholic youth groups in our day. Since the end of the Middle Ages there has also been a blessing of homes on this day, using holy water and incense. The letters C, M and B are usually traced on the doors. A "blessing of chalk" in the Roman Ritual explains the letters are referring to the three kings and thus favors the widespread popular explanation.[45] According to other interpreters, however, the letters are the initials of the three words *Christus mansionem benedicat*, "May Christ bless the dwelling."[46]

The principal theme of the festal Mass is determined by the gospel which shows the "wise men from the East" being led by a star to seek the newborn "king of the Jews" and pay him homage (Mt 2.1-12). Here it is clear that Jesus is the messianic king of the entire world, whose intention it is to lead even the pagans to salvation. The coming of the Magi marks the first step in fulfilling the glowing promises which the prophet makes to the city of Jerusalem in the Old Testament reading (Is 60.1-6): "Arise, shine; for your light has come, and the glory of the Lord has risen upon you. . . . Nations shall come to your light, and kings to the brightness of your rising." The universality of God's salvation in the new Jerusalem which is the Church also finds expression in the second reading (Eph 3.2-3a, 5-6): it proclaims as a revelation in the Spirit that "the Gentiles are fellow heirs, members of the same body, and partakers of the promise in Christ Jesus through the gospel." The entrance antiphon treats this salvific manifestation of Christ as a leitmotif:

"The Lord and ruler is coming; kingship is his, and government and power."

The community of believers, for its part, identifies itself with the wise men from the East in the alleluia verse and communion antiphon, and professes that "we have seen his star in the east, and have come (with gifts) to adore the Lord." The preface too proclaims the message regarding the Savior of the world and the "light of all peoples": "Now that his glory has shone among us, you have renewed humanity in his immortal image." The connection with Christmas is especially clear in the insertions for the first eucharistic prayer, since they speak of the celebration of this most holy day "when your only Son, sharing your eternal glory, showed himself in a human body." I said earlier that Christmas, like Easter, is a feast of redemption. The same can be said, though from a different viewpoint, of the solemnity of Epiphany.

It has often, and correctly, been pointed out that this solemnity, which in the old calendar of feasts was of second rank, right behind Easter (a double of the first class with a privileged octave of the second class) is in fact the real feast of Christ the King in the liturgy. "Only an obscuring of the content of the liturgical feast of Epiphany and an intellectualization of liturgical theology could have led Pius XI in 1925 to introduce a second feast of Christ the King on the last Sunday of October. This move is typical of the development that modern piety has undergone; this development becomes clear from a comparison of the two feasts. The feast of Christ the King celebrates the general idea of Christ's kingship; it celebrates a title of honor, a name, a concept. On the other hand, it is essential to the liturgical feast of Epiphany that it brings before us, in a concrete way, a royal action of Christ, an event that is an essential part of the process of salvation. On the one hand, then, an idea; on the other, the reality of the mystery of Epiphany which contains in itself the entire mystery of redemption."[47]

The introduction to the Mass of Epiphany says that if January 6 is not a holy day of obligation, the feast is to be transferred to the Sunday between January 2 and January 8. If this Sunday should come after January 6, then the feast of the Lord's baptism is transferred that year to the following Monday.[48]

6 / THE FEAST OF THE BAPTISM OF JESUS

In the historical survey I pointed out that the baptism of Jesus and the wedding at Cana were originally part of the feast of Epiphany. In the Roman liturgy this emerges more clearly in the Liturgy of the Hours than in the festal Mass. In addition, until the most recent reorganization of the liturgical year, the commemoration of the baptism of Jesus was associated primarily with the octave day of Epiphany. The *General Norms* once again brings the commemoration a bit closer to Epiphany, since the "feast of the Baptism of the Lord" is now celebrated on the Sunday after Epiphany (cf. no. 38). The baptism is the subject of the gospel pericope for the second Sunday after Epiphany in Year A, while the passage on the wedding feast at Cana is used in Year C.

At the center of the Proper of the feast is the gospel of the baptism of Jesus, with the three synoptic accounts being read in the three years of the cycle. The Fathers of the Church assigned a very important place to this event in their theology of salvation. Its significance is to be seen, first, in the revelation of the divine sonship of Jesus that is given by the "voice from heaven": "This is my beloved Son, in whom I am well pleased" (Mt 3.17). The event is significant, in addition, because the Holy Spirit, in the form of a dove, descends on Jesus. In their theology the Fathers saw this descent as the real anointing and appointment of Jesus to his messianic office before his public life begins. At the same time (according to the Fathers), by receiving the baptism of John, Jesus professes his solidarity with the guilty human race and gives water the power to forgive sins.

The New Testament reading (Acts 10.34-38) expressly refers to the messianic anointing and mission of Jesus; here Peter says: "You know . . . the word which was proclaimed throughout all Judea . . . after the baptism which John preached: how God anointed Jesus of Nazareth with the Holy Spirit and with power; how he went about doing good and healing all. . . ." The Old Testament reading is taken from the first Servant Song (Is 42.1-4, 6-7) and, as traditionally interpreted, likewise refers to the anointing and mission of the Messiah: "Behold my servant, whom I uphold, my chosen, in whom my soul delights. I have put my Spirit upon him, he will bring forth justice to the nations. . . .' I have given you as a covenant to the people, a light to the nations.' " The preface very aptly sums up the content of the festal event as seen from the viewpoint of the theology of salvation: "You celebrated your new gift of baptism by signs and wonders at the Jordan. Your voice was heard from heaven to awaken faith in the presence among us of the Word made man. Your Spirit was seen as a dove, revealing Jesus as your servant, and anointing him with joy as the Christ, sent to bring to the poor the good news of salvation."

The feast of the Lord's baptism brings the Christmas cycle to a close. The period known as Ordinary Time now begins; in fact the week following this Sunday of the Lord's baptism is already the first of the 33/34 weeks of Ordinary Time.

7 / TWO CHRISTMAS FEASTS OUTSIDE THE CHRISTMAS CYCLE

There is a connection at the level of content between the mystery of the incarnation and its festal celebration, on the one hand, and, on the other, two feasts of the Lord which, as their previous names indicate—"Purification of the Blessed Virgin Mary" and "Annunciation of the Blessed Virgin Mary"—were usually thought of as feasts of Mary. The two are now known as "Presentation of the Lord" and "Annunciation of the Lord."

Presentation of the Lord (February 2)

The feast of the "Presentation of the Lord" on February 2, the fortieth day after Christmas, is concerned with the biblical events in the temple of Jerusalem which are reported in Luke 2.22-39 and in which Jesus, rather than his mother, is in fact the center of attention.

According to the Old Testament regulations for ritual purity (Lev 12.1-8), a woman was regarded as unclean for forty days after the birth of a male child, and for eighty after the birth of a female. Consequently, she had to bring the priest a lamb and a young pigeon or turtledove as a sin offering, or two turtledoves if she were poor. "He [the priest] shall . . . make atonement for her; then she shall be clean." In addition, a firstborn son was regarded as belonging to the Lord (Ex 13.2); he therefore had to be brought before the Lord (Ex 13.12) and redeemed with an offering of money (Num 18.16). In keeping with these regulations Mary and Joseph brought Jesus to the temple, and Mary offered the sacrifice that "purified" her and at the same time ransomed her firstborn.

As far as the origin of this feast is concerned, we may distinguish an eastern (Jerusalem) and a western (Rome) factor in its establishment. Egeria the pilgrim tells us that about the year 400 in Jerusalem a great feast was celebrated on the fortieth day after Epiphany (which at that time was the sole birthday feast of Jesus), that is, on February 14. There was a great procession to the church of the Resurrection, where priests and bishops explained the events of Luke 2.22-39 in their sermons. The festivities ended with a Mass.[49] Egeria gives no name for the feast, but it appears at about the middle of the fifth century as the "Feast of the Meeting" (Greek: *Hypapantē*), and there is already a candlelight procession connected with it.[50] The name of the feast is intended as a reminder that on this occasion Jesus entered his Father's temple for the first time and there met Simeon and Anna.

This feast may already have been known in Rome by the middle of the fifth century.[51] According to later witnesses a candlelight procession was connected with this fortieth day after Christmas; it was intended to replace an ancient pagan procession of expiation that was celebrated every five years at the beginning of February, in the form of a procession around the bounds of the city *(amburbale)*. The purple vestments prescribed for this Mass (as late as 1960) recall the original penitential character of the feast (in Rome). The candles carried in the Christian procession are a reminder that on this day Simeon called Jesus "a light for revelation to the gentiles" (Lk 2.32). A blessing of these candles was added before the year 1000 in Gaul.[52]

The blessing of candles and the carrying of them in procession led to the name "Candlemas" (i.e., Candle Mass), which gave little indication of the real theme of the feast. Similarly, "Purification of Mary," the official name until 1969, must be regarded as unfortunate and open to misunderstanding, since according to the teaching of the Church Mary is completely sinless. The historical Commentary on the new general Roman calendar (1969), which notes the changes that have been made, observes: *"Purification of the Blessed Virgin Mary*. The name of today's feast is changed to 'Presentation of the Lord,' thus making it clearer that the feast is a feast of the Lord."[53]

In the new Missal the blessing of candles before the festal Mass may take either of two forms. In the first, "the people gather in a chapel or other suitable place outside the church where the Mass will be celebrated. They carry unlighted candles." When the priest comes, wearing white vestments, the candles are lit and an antiphon is sung: "The Lord will come with mighty power and give light to the eyes of all who serve him, alleluia" (but some other suitable song may be sung instead). The priest greets the congregation and introduces them to the meaning of the festal liturgy. He then blesses the candles, using one of the two prayers provided. The first alludes to the revelation of Christ as "a light for revelation to the gentiles" that was given to the elderly Simeon: "Bless these candles and make them holy. May we who carry them to praise your glory walk in the path of goodness and come to the light that shines for ever." After the candles have been sprinkled with holy water, the people process singing to the church; they may sing the Canticle of Simeon or some other suitable song.

The second form of the blessing of candles is distinguished from the first only by the fact that instead of a procession there is only a solemn entrance of the priest and a representative group of the faithful. The starting point for this entrance is "a suitable place (either in front of the door or in the church itself) where most of the congregation can easily take part." There is the introduction, as above, and the blessing of the candles, followed by the solemn entrance and procession to the sanctuary. In this simplified form, as in the other, the faithful are to hold lighted candles in their hands.

The thematic focus of the Proper of the Mass is, of course, the events in the temple as described in the gospel pericope (Lk 2.22-40). A shortened version of this gospel may be read. The events are also proclaimed in summary form in the preface of the feast, where we read: "Today your Son, who shares your eternal splendor, was presented in the temple and revealed by the Spirit as the glory of Israel and the light of all peoples. Our hearts are joyful, for we have seen your salvation." The liturgy sees the appearance of Christ in the temple as the fulfillment of what the prophet Malachi announces in the Old Testament reading (3.1-4) as the coming of the Lord to his temple and as the much desired coming of his "messenger of the covenant" for judgment. The Lord's entrance into his sanctuary is therefore also the theme of the responsorial psalm (Ps 24.7-10).

The New Testament reading (Heb 2.14-18) sees the incarnation of Jesus as the presupposition of his redemptive activity: "Therefore he had to be made like his brethren in every respect, so that he might become a merciful and faithful high priest in the service of God, to make expiation for the sins of the people." The concluding prayer asks that we may be strengthened in our hope and attain to the fullness of redemption: "May this communion . . . prepare us to meet Christ when he comes to bring us into everlasting life." It is clear that the liturgy of the feast is not satisfied with pious contemplation of an idyllic scene but takes as its purview the entire mystery of salvation. It looks both to the beginning of the journey and to its end.

The Solemnity of the Annunciation of the Lord

In the East the origins of this feast go back to the period before the Ecumenical Council of Ephesus (431). At that time there already existed what was probably the earliest feast of Mary, entitled "Commemoration of the holy, ever-virgin mother of God." This was celebrated on December 26, or in immediate proximity to the birth of Christ.[54] In the West, too, there was a commemoration of the annunciation or incarnation as early as the fifth century; it was celebrated in Ravenna on the Sunday before Christmas, as we learn from Peter Chrysologus.[55]

A feast of the Annunciation on March 25, nine months before Christmas, is attested in the East by the middle of the sixth century[56]; in the West the earliest testimonies to such a feast day are from the seventh century.[57] We saw above, in the discussion of the origins of Christmas, that as early as the third century special significance was attached to the spring equinox, which was dated at that time on March 25. This day was regarded as the first day of creation, as the birthday of Christ or the day of his conception, and as the day of his death on the cross.[58] It is understandable, then, that once the commemoration of Christ's birthday had been assigned to December 25, March 25 should come to be thought of as the day when his life had begun in Mary's womb.

Because March 25 usually falls in the Easter penitential season, and the sobriety of this season seemed incompatible with the joy proper to the feast, the old date of December 18 was observed for a long time in Spain, while the Church of Milan celebrated it on the last Sunday of Advent.[59]

The name of the feast made it at times a feast of the Lord, at times a feast of Mary. Thus the *Liber pontificalis* speaks of "The Annunciation of the Lord"; and the names "Conception of Christ" and "Incarnation of Christ" were also in use. Other calendars, however, refer to it as "The Annunciation of Mary." In view of the significance of the event for the history of salvation the *General Norms* prefers the name "Annunciation of the Lord," but does not intend to detract from Mary's important role in this saving event; it also gives the feast the rank of a solemnity, after Pope Leo XIII (1895) had already made it a double of the first class. If the feast falls in Holy Week or (rarely) in Easter Week, it is celebrated on the Monday after the octave of Easter.

The gospel of the feast (Lk 1.26-38) tells of God's decision to make Mary the mother of his Son. This child "will be great, and will be called the Son of the Most High; and the Lord God will give to him the throne of his father David, and he will reign over the house of Jacob for ever; and of his kingdom there will be no end." Mary's self-sacrificing consent and the incarnation of God's Son which this consent makes possible mark the beginning of the messianic age, the mystery of Christ, the new covenant of God with the human race. This is a gift inspired by God's unfathomable graciousness. But the (subordinate) role of Mary as "handmaid of the Lord" may and must also be emphasized. In her the "sign of Immanuel," of which the Old Testament reading speaks (Is 7.10-14), is fulfilled.

The second reading (Heb 10.4-10) embraces in a single vision the mystery of the incarnation and the redemptive paschal mystery; it tells us that "when Christ came into the world" he said: "Sacrifices and offerings thou hast not desired, but a body hast thou prepared for me. . . . 'Lo, I have come to do thy will, O God.'" From this the Letter to the Hebrews concludes that "by that will we have been sanctified through the offering of the body of Jesus Christ once for all." The alleluia verse sings jubilantly of the festal mystery, using the words of St. John's Prologue: "The Word of God became man and lived among us; and we saw his glory." The preface of the feast thanks and praises God because "the Virgin Mary . . . bore your Son in purest love. In Christ, the eternal truth, your promise to Israel came true." With faith in the mystery of the incarnation (opening prayer), the Church asks that in that mystery she may see her own origin (prayer over the gifts); that God would give her a share in the divine life of his Son (opening prayer); and that "by the power of his resurrection may we come to eternal joy" (concluding prayer). As on Christmas, priest and congregation kneel in adoration during the Creed when the article on the conception and birth of Christ is proclaimed.

This brief look at the liturgy of the festal Mass (the themes of which are further developed in the Liturgy of the Hours) shows that this solemnity is indeed to be regarded primarily as a feast of the Lord and only secondarily as a feast of Mary. But we should not forget that Christmas, as originally understood, included as part of the mystery of that feast the mystery of the incarnation in the womb of Mary.

Notes

1. H. Frank, a Benedictine of Maria Laach, gives a good survey of these scholarly efforts in his "Frühgeschichte und Ursprung des römischen Weihnachtsfestes im Lichte neuerer Forschung," AL 2 (1952), 1-24, and in his article "Weihnachten I. Heortologie," LTK 10 (1965), 984-88.

2. Text and interpretation in Pascher, pp. 325-28.

3. This can be regarded as originating with the Frenchman L.

Duchesne, especially in his book *Christian Worship: Its Origin and Evolution*, tr. by M. L. McClure (London, 1903) [there is a later French ed., Paris, 1925]. More recently H. Engberding has accepted this hypothesis and attempted, not successfully, to put it on solid ground: "Der 25. Dezember als Tag der Feier der Geburt des Herrn," AL 2 (1952), 25-43.

4. Engberding, ibid., p. 42.

5. Frank (n. 191), in LTK 10:986.

6. John Tauler, *Predigten*, ed. by G. Hofmann (Freiburg–Basel–Vienna, 1961), p. 13.

7. Cf. Righetti 2:58-60.

8. R. Berger, "Ostern und Weihnachten: Zum Grundgefüge des Kirchenjahres," AL 7 (1963), 19.

9. Cf. CommALI, cap. I, sect. II. 1 (p. 60).

10. Ibid. The way was paved for this decision by the Instruction *Eucharisticum Mysterium* of the Congregation of Rites on the celebration and worship of the eucharist (May 25, 1967), no. 28.

11. Cited in Jungmann, "Advent," pp. 233-37; cf. the sceptical reaction of Croce, pp. 259-60, especially n. 13.

12. Cf. Jungmann, "Advent," pp. 237-49.

13. Cf. Croce, pp. 270-72.

14. Cf. ibid., pp. 272-78.

15. Cf. ibid., p. 275.

16. Cf. ibid., pp. 290-91.

17. CommALI, cap. I, sect. II. 2 (p. 61).

18. Cf. Croce, pp. 456-58.

19. GNLYC, no. 40.

20. Croce, p. 471.

21. Cf. GNLYC, no. 42.

22. CommALI, cap. I, sect. II. 2 (p. 61).

23. Lect:Introd, chap. II, sect. I, no. 2 (p. xxxiii).

24. Pascher, p. 366.

25. The alleluia verses are listed together in no. 202 of the Lectionary.

26. Cf. the GIRM, no. 333; and Lengeling, p. 447.

27. *Sermo* 198, 2 (PL 38:1025).

28. Cf. Righetti, 2:74-75.

29. GNLYC, nos. 35-36.

30. E.g., Schwarzenberger, "Die Liturgie ist für die Menschen da," Gd 4 (1970), 185-87; idem, "Die liturgische Feier des 1. Januar. Geschichte und pastoralliturgische Desiderata," LJ 20 (1970), 216-30.

31. Fourth General Meeting of the first session of Vatican Council II, October 22, 1962, in *Acta Synodalia* I/1 (Vatican City, 1970), p. 315.

32. Schwarzenberger, "Die liturgische Feier," p. 230.

33. Thus Durandus, *Rationale divinorum officiorum* VII, 42, 1 (Beleth, p. 711).

34. Ibid., VII, 42, 2. 6. 10.

35. Radó 2:1127.

36. K. Beith, "Stephanus III. Volksverehrung," LTK 9:1052.

37. R. Schnackenburg, "Johannes (Apostel und Evangelist)," LTK 5:1000.

38. Details in Franz 1:283-84; Eisenhofer 1:574-75.

39. PL 13:1228.

40. Stromata I, 21, 146, 1-2 (ed. O. Stählin, GCS 52 [Berlin, 1960[3]], p. 90). F. Nikolasch devotes an extensive study to this gnostic teaching in his "Zum Ursprung des Epiphaniefestes," EL 82 (1968), 393-429.

41. Nikolasch, ibid., p. 428.

42. Cf. K. Holl, "Der Ursprung des Epiphaniefestes," *Sitzungsberichte der Preussischen Akademie der Wissenchaften*, 1971, pp. 402-38.

43. Epiphanius of Salamis († 403), *Panarion haeresium* 51, 40, 1; ed. K. Holl, *Epiphanius* (Leipzig, 1922), p. 301.

44. J. A. Jungmann, *Public Worship: A Survey*, tr. by C. Howell (Collegeville, 1957), p. 208.

45. "Blessing of Chalk on Epiphany," in *The Roman Ritual* 3. *The Blessings*, tr. by P. T. Weller (Milwaukee, 1946), pp. 36-39.

46. Documentation in, e.g., Eisenhofer, 1:576; Pascher, pp. 421-22; Radó 2:1136-37.

47. W. Dürig, "Epiphanie," in *Erscheinung des Herrn* (Am Tisch des Wortes, Neue Reihe 118; Stuttgart, 1971), p. 12.

48. Cf. *Notitiae* 13 (1977), 477.

49. Chapter 26 (pp. 96-97). Cf.: "Everything is performed in the pre-scribed manner with the greatest solemnity, just as on Easter Sunday" (p. 97).

50. More detailed documentation in Radó 2:1140.

51. Cf. Radó, ibid., who thus interprets a remark of Pope Leo I.

52. Formulas of blessing from the 10th–12th centuries in Franz 1:445-58.

53. CommNC, cap. II (Variationes), for February 2 (p. 115).

54. Cf. Radó 2:1323, who appeals chiefly to M. Jugie and A. Baumstark.

55. *Sermones* 140-44 (PL 52:575-88).

56. According to a sermon of Bishop Abraham of Ephesus (PO 16:442-47).

57. According to the *Liber pontificalis* 80 (ed. Duchesne 1:376); further evidence in Righetti 2:300-1; Radó 2:1339-40.

58. Cf. H. Engberding (n. 193, above), p. 150; Pascher, pp. 330-31; Radó 2:1340.

59. More detailed documentation in Righetti 2:301-2.

Ordinary Time

In the section on the structure of the liturgical year (Chapter III, 4) I have already indicated that the "temporal cycle" does not consist solely of the two great cycles of feasts but that the 33/34 weeks between these cycles—"Ordinary Time" or "time in the yearly cycle" *(tempus per annum)*—are an essential part of it. [1]

1 / DIVISION AND SIGNIFICANCE OF ORDINARY TIME

As the Commentary on the new *General Norms* explains, this "time in the yearly cycle" was hitherto divided "into two parts, the extent of which differed from year to year depending on the date of Easter; it was divided into a time after Epiphany and a time after Pentecost. The texts for the Masses of the Sundays after Epiphany that were not read because Lent intervened were

used before the last Sunday after Pentecost."[2] For the period
between Epiphany and Septuagesima Sunday six Sundays with
a liturgy for Mass and Office were provided. If Easter came
especially early only the first two of these six Sundays might be
celebrated. The period after Pentecost, on the other hand, might
have as many as 28 Sundays. But there were only 24 liturgical
formularies for postpentecostal Sundays, and therefore the unused formularies for the post-Epiphany period were intercalated (as postponed Sundays) between the 23rd and 24th Sundays after Pentecost. This was certainly not an ideal solution.

The numbering of Sundays as postpentecostal occurs first in
Frankish liturgy books of the eighth century. Previously these
Sundays were counted in relation to various postpentecostal
feasts. For example, a book of gospels from the seventh century
(the Würzburg *Comes*), which represents the liturgy of the city
of Rome, has "two weeks after Pentecost, seven after Peter and
Paul *(post natale Apostolorum)*, five after Lawrence, and seven
after Cyprian (September 14). Instead of the feast of St. Cyprian
other sources (sacramentaries) choose the feast of Michael the
Archangel (September 29) as a dividing point and count up to
nine Sundays *post angeli.*"[3] Once the feast of the Trinity had
been introduced (below, section 3), there was also a counting of
weeks "after Trinity" *(post festum Ss. Trinitatis)*; this was taken
over by the Churches of the Reformation and is still customary
in them.[4]

In the new organization of 1969 the weeks after the Sunday of
the Lord's Baptism until Ash Wednesday and the Sundays from
Pentecost Monday to the beginning of Advent form a unit with
continuous numbering that gives 33/34 weeks of "Ordinary
Time." "Especially on the last Sundays, the mystery of Christ in
all its fullness is celebrated."[5] What Jounel wrote before the
reorganization of the liturgical year is still valid of these Sundays of Ordinary Time: "These Sundays . . . are Sundays in a
pure state. They have no secondary traits but simply embody
the very essence of the Christian Sunday or Lord's Day as presented to us in the tradition of the Church. Each of them is an
Easter, each a feast."[6] "Each Sunday has its own prayers, readings and songs. On the weekdays the prayers and songs may

be taken from any of the 34 Mass formularies, as the celebrant wishes,"[7] unless a feast or memorial of a saint takes precedence.

The new Lectionary for Mass gives important indications on how these Sundays are to be counted. The Sunday after Epiphany, on which the feast of the Lord's Baptism is celebrated, counts theoretically as the first Sunday of Ordinary Time; the liturgy proper to the first week begins, however, only on the Monday following this Sunday. After the Tuesday before Ash Wednesday there is an interruption of Ordinary Time, which begins again on the Monday after Pentecost. The latter, like the Sunday after Epiphany, is theoretically—but only theoretically—one of the 33/34 Sundays of Ordinary Time. It is to be noted that if a given year has only 33 Sundays, one week of Ordinary Time is omitted. If, for example, the week of Ash Wednesday is the 5th week, then the 7th week begins with the Monday after Pentecost. The purpose of this is to prevent the elimination of the 34th Sunday at the end of the liturgical year; its eschatological texts require that it be retained.[8]

2 / THE LECTIONARY FOR ORDINARY TIME

The Sundays and weekdays of Ordinary Time acquire their liturgical and theological complexion primarily from the readings assigned them in the new Lectionary. While the scriptural passages for the festal cycles with their special liturgical character are chosen with certain themes in mind, the principle followed in the readings of Ordinary Time is the semicontinuous reading of scripture; that is, a book of the Bible is read through, although for pastoral reasons certain parts are omitted: "Many liturgies, including the Roman liturgy, traditionally omit certain verses from biblical reading. One should not be too quick to do this because the style, purpose, or meaning of the scriptural text may easily be damaged. But, for pastoral reasons, it seemed best to continue this tradition, taking care that the essential meaning of the text remain unchanged. Otherwise some texts would be too lengthy or readings of greater spiritual value to the people would have to be entirely omitted, because of one or two verses of little general worth or involving truly difficult questions."[9]

The Sundays of Ordinary Time

The Old Testament readings are chosen with the theme of the gospel in mind. The aim in so doing was to prevent the introduction of too many themes, while at the same time trying to bring out the unity of the Old and New Testaments. In addition there was concern to choose readings that were quite short and easily understood, but also to make the more important texts of the Old Testament known to the faithful.

The New Testament readings are from the letters of Paul and the letter of James, now that the letters of Peter and John are read during the Easter and Christmas season. If we prescind from the fact that 1 Corinthians is read on the early Sundays of all three years and that the Letter to the Hebrews is divided between Years B and C, it can be said that every letter has "its own" Year for reading, as can be seen from the following table.

The Second Reading on the Sundays of Ordinary Time

SUNDAY	YEAR A	YEAR B	YEAR C
2	1 Corinthians 1-4	1 Corinthians 6-11	1 Corinthians 12-15
3	1 Corinthians 1-4	1 Corinthians 6-11	1 Corinthians 12-15
4	1 Corinthians 1-4	1 Corinthians 6-11	1 Corinthians 12-15
5	1 Corinthians 1-4	1 Corinthians 6-11	1 Corinthians 12-15
6	1 Corinthians 1-4	1 Corinthians 6-11	1 Corinthians 12-15
7	1 Corinthians 1-4	2 Corinthians	1 Corinthians 12-15
8	1 Corinthians 1-4	2 Corinthians	1 Corinthians 12-15
9	Romans	2 Corinthians	Galatians
10	Romans	2 Corinthians	Galatians
11	Romans	2 Corinthians	Galatians
12	Romans	2 Corinthians	Galatians
13	Romans	2 Corinthians	Galatians
14	Romans	2 Corinthians	Galatians
15	Romans	Ephesians	Colossians
16	Romans	Ephesians	Colossians
17	Romans	Ephesians	Colossians
18	Romans	Ephesians	Colossians
19	Romans	Ephesians	Hebrews 11-12
20	Romans	Ephesians	Hebrews 11-12
21	Romans	Ephesians	Hebrews 11-12
22	Romans	James	Hebrews 11-12
23	Romans	James	Philemon
24	Romans	James	1 Timothy

162

SUNDAY	YEAR *A*	YEAR *B*	YEAR C
25	Philippians	James	1 Timothy
26	Philippians	James	1 Timothy
27	Philippians	Hebrews 2-10	2 Timothy
28	Philippians	Hebrews 2-10	2 Timothy
29	1 Thessalonians	Hebrews 2-10	2 Timothy
30	1 Thessalonians	Hebrews 2-10	2 Timothy
31	1 Thessalonians	Hebrews 2-10	2 Thessalonians
32	1 Thessalonians	Hebrews 2-10	2 Thessalonians
33	1 Thessalonians	Hebrews 2-10	2 Thessalonians

The gospel pericopes are, by and large, taken from Matthew in Year A, Mark in Year B, and Luke in Year C, so that we may speak of a Matthean, Markan and Lukan year. The only exceptions are the second Sunday of Ordinary Time on which three pericopes from John are chosen that echo the feast of Epiphany, and Sundays 17–21 in Year B on which the sixth chapter of John, the "Discourse of the Bread of Life," is used: "This insertion is only natural, since the multiplication of the bread in John's Gospel parallels the same narrative in Mark."[10] On the 34th, and last, Sunday, the readings from the Old Testament culminate in the message about "Christ the King, prefigured by David and proclaimed in the humiliations he suffered by dying for us on the cross, who governs and guides his Church until his return at the end of time."[11]

The Weekdays of Ordinary Time

Unlike the Sundays the weekdays have only one reading in addition to the gospel. But whereas the gospel is the same every year, there are two annual cycles for the nongospel reading, with Series I being used in odd-numbered years and Series II in even-numbered years.

The first or nongospel reading alternates every few weeks between Old Testament and New Testament, depending on the length of the book being read. Because the Old Testament is so much more extensive, the readings from it must be limited to a selection of texts that are characteristic of a given book. The history of salvation up to the incarnation of Christ is an important criterion of selection. At times the religious significance of the historical accounts is brought out by following them with various passages from the sapiential writings. Only a few books of the Old Testament could not be included in the weekday lectionary of the Old Testament, such as the short books of the prophets Obadiah and Zephaniah, the Song of Solomon, the books of Esther and Judith. But even these are represented on some days of the two cycles of feasts.

The nonevangelical writings of the New Testament are all represented except for the Acts of the Apostles, a good deal of which is read during the Easter season. The other writings are not only read but are read extensively enough for their main contents to be represented. "However, passages having little pastoral relevance today have been omitted, such as those concerning the gift of tongues or the discipline of the early Church."[12] Because of the eschatological emphasis during the final weeks of Ordinary Time the readings during this period are taken from the Apocalypse and the Book of Daniel. Here again, a tabular arrangement will clarify the situation.

The First Reading for the Weekdays of Ordinary Time

WEEK	SERIES *I*	SERIES *II*
1	Hebrews	1 Samuel
2	Hebrews	1 Samuel
3	Hebrews	2 Samuel
4	Hebrews	2 Samuel; 1 Kings 1-16
5	Genesis 1-11	1 Kings 1-16
6	Genesis 1-11	James
7	Sirach	James
8	Sirach	1 Peter; Jude
9	Tobit	2 Peter; 2 Timothy
10	2 Corinthians	1 Kings 17-22
11	2 Corinthians	1 Kings 17-22; 2 Kings
12	Genesis 12-50	2 Kings; Lamentations
13	Genesis 12-50	Amos
14	Genesis 12-50	Hosea; Isaiah
15	Exodus	Isaiah; Micah
16	Exodus	Micah; Jeremiah
17	Exodus; Leviticus	Jeremiah
18	Numbers; Deuteronomy	Jeremiah; Nahum; Habakkuk
19	Deuteronomy; Joshua	Ezekiel

WEEK	SERIES *I*	SERIES *II*
20	Judges; Ruth	Ezekiel
21	1 Thessalonians	2 Thessalonians; 1 Corinthians
22	1 Thessalonians; Colossians	1 Corinthians
23	Colossians; 1 Timothy	1 Corinthians
24	1 Timothy	1 Corinthians
25	Ezra; Haggai; Zechariah	Proverbs; Ecclesiastes
26	Zechariah; Nehemiah; Baruch	Job
27	Jonah; Malachi, Joel	Galatians
28	Romans	Galatians; Ephesians
29	Romans	Ephesians
30	Romans	Ephesians
31	Romans	Ephesians; Philippians
32	Wisdom	Titus; Philemon; 2 and 3 John
33	1 and 2 Maccabees	Revelation
34	Daniel	Revelation

The gospel pericopes are from the three synoptic gospels in the form of a semicontinuous reading of them. In weeks 1–9 they are from Mark, the oldest and most concise of the gospels; in weeks 10–21, they are from Matthew and in weeks 22–34 from Luke. The first 12 chapters of Mark are read without omissions, except for two passages from chapter 6 that are read on weekdays outside of Ordinary Time. With Mark as a background a choice is then made of passages from Matthew and Luke, the aim being primarily to read everything from these gospels that is not found in Mark. But "all the elements which give the different gospels their distinctive style and which are necessary for an intelligent understanding of each gospel are read two or three times."[13]

If the occurrence of another celebration causes one or other weekday reading to be omitted, the celebrant should assure a meaningful connection of the entire week's readings by dividing them differently or by reading the omitted passage even if this means dropping something else of lesser importance.

If the memorial of a saint or a Mass for a special occasion is chosen, the celebrant should nonetheless try to assure a certain continuity in the weekday readings. "Generally it would be preferable to use the semicontinuous readings from the book assigned in the weekday lectionary to that liturgical season."[14] An exception is made for "appropriate readings," that is, those special readings chosen because they refer to the mystery proper to the saint or feast.

High hopes have been set on the new Lectionary. After Vatican II had directed that a richer fare was to be provided for the faithful at the table of God's word by seeing to it that "a more representative part of the sacred scriptures will be read to the people in the course of a prescribed number of years" (CL, no. 51; Flannery, p. 17), intensive work on a new lectionary was begun on a worldwide scale.[15] The resultant book was approved by Pope Paul VI in his Apostolic Constitution *Missale Romanum* of April 3, 1969, published by the Congregation for Divine Worship on May 25, 1969, and introduced to the people on the first Sunday of Advent in that same year. Pope Paul VI formulated the pastoral aims of this lectionary in the following striking manner:

> All this has been planned to develop among the faithful a greater hunger for the word of God. Under the guidance of the Holy Spirit, this word leads the people of the New Covenant to the perfect unity of the Church. We are fully confident that both priests and faithful will prepare their minds and hearts more devoutly for the Lord's Supper, meditating on the scriptures, nourished day by day with the words of our Lord. . . . Sacred scripture will then be a perpetual source of spiritual life, the chief instrument for handing down Christian doctrine, and the center of all theological study.[16]

3 / THE FEASTS OF THE LORD DURING ORDINARY TIME

Over the course of several centuries during the second millennium of the Christian era four solemnities have been introduced into Ordinary Time. Because of their dependence on the date of Easter these feasts are called "movable solemnities of Ordinary Time"; in view of their object they are also called "Solemnities of the Lord during the Season of the Year."[17] The four are the feasts of the Trinity, Corpus Christi, the Sacred Heart, and Christ the King.

Because all of these feasts had their origin in a piety characteristic of the age that gave them birth, and were regarded as special helps to the Church in her external and internal trials, they may be considered to be feasts of devotion. They may also be described as feasts of ideas inasmuch as in them a particular truth of the faith or a particular aspect of the mystery of Christ becomes the object of profession of faith and of hope and thanksgiving, and the "idea embodied in the feast" is seen as suggesting a pastoral program for renewing and strengthening the Church. As I mentioned earlier (Chapter III, 3) the original Roman liturgy knew no such feasts.

The Solemnity of the Trinity

As a result of the christological and trinitarian controversies of the fourth and fifth centuries, which arose especially from the heresy of Arius, the western countries of Spain and Gaul, which like the East felt the Arian threat, showed in their preaching and devotion a special emphasis on belief in the Trinity. There is already plenty of evidence for this in the seventh and eighth centuries. Our modern preface of the Trinity appears around the middle of the eighth century in the old Gelasian Sacramentary; around 800 the Mass of the Trinity is found as a votive Mass for Sundays, while Sunday generally showed an increasingly trinitarian emphasis.[18]

In Frankish and Gallic Benedictine monasteries a special feast of the Trinity was probably celebrated on the Sunday after Pentecost even before the year 1000. For a very long time Rome resisted such a feast. Pope Alexander II († 1077) is reported to have said that no particular day should be especially devoted to a feast of the Blessed Trinity, any more than to a feast of the Blessed Unity, since the commemoration of both is celebrated every Sunday and even daily.[19] Alexander III († 1181) made a similar statement about 100 years later. Nonetheless this feast continued to spread, and finally John XXII introduced it to the universal Church in 1334, during the exile in Avignon.

The location of this feast on the Sunday after Pentecost may be interpreted as a grateful look back at the now completed mystery of salvation, which, according to early theology, is accomplished by the Father through the Son in the Holy Spirit. Later on, this unity of the divine saving action was somewhat obscured by a greater emphasis on the appropriation of individual saving acts to one or other of the divine persons, as formulated, e.g., in the catechisms: "God the Father created us, God the Son redeemed us, God the Holy Spirit sanctified us."[20]

The festal Mass, which has different readings and responsorial psalms in each year of the three-year cycle, begins with praise of the triune God, "for he has shown that he loves us" (entrance antiphon). The opening prayer asks (in the Latin text) that "in a confession of true faith we may acknowledge the glory of the eternal Trinity and adore the Unity with its majestic power." The concluding prayer expresses a similar thought.

The gospel in Year A (Jn 3.16-18) tells of the saving love of the Father that attains its climactic expression in the self-sacrifice of his Son. The Old Testament reading (Ex 34.4b-6, 8-9) speaks of God as "a God merciful and gracious . . . and abounding in steadfast love and faithfulness." The second reading promises the presence of "the God of love and peace" and closes with a trinitarian blessing: "The grace of the Lord Jesus Christ and the love of God and the fellowship of the Holy Spirit be with you all" (2 Cor 13.11-13).

In Year B the gospel reports the words of Jesus at the close of Matthew's gospel as he sends his disciples forth and promises them his abiding presence. The decisive reason for choosing this passage was surely the baptismal command with its mention of the three divine persons. The Old Testament reading (Deut 4.32-34, 39-40) emphasizes the oneness of the covenant God who has rescued his people from Egypt in such a striking way. Under the new covenant God has given the baptized his Spirit who makes them children of the Father and sharers in the paschal mystery of Christ (second reading: Rom 8.14-17).

168

The gospel for Year C is from the farewell discourses of Jesus (Jn 16.12-15) and is remarkable for the way it brings out the mystery celebrated on this day: "All that the Father has is mine; therefore I said that he [the Spirit of truth] will take what is mine and declare it to you." In the Old Testament reading (Prov 8.22-31) we meet the personified Wisdom of God which even before creation "was beside him [God], like a master workman." Wisdom was there, "delighting in the sons of men." From the viewpoint of New Testament revelation this Old Testament passage is a veiled reference to the plurality of persons in God. The powerful sentences of the second reading (Rom 5.1-5) state the basic values of redemption: peace with God through Jesus Christ, access to God, and unshakable hope, "because God's love has been poured into our hearts through the Holy Spirit who has been given to us."

The readings thus contain a rich treasure of proclamation, and the community has good reason to praise the One and Triune God in the alleluia verse: "Glory to the Father, the Son and the Holy Spirit: to God who is, who was, and who is to come."

The Solemnity of the Body and Blood of Christ (Corpus Christi)

The origin of this feast, which is celebrated on the Thursday after Trinity Sunday, must be connected with the intense cult of the Blessed Sacrament that developed during the twelfth century. In that cult, special emphasis was placed on the real presence of "Christ whole and entire" in the consecrated bread. This eucharistic "movement" was accompanied by the profound desire of medieval men and women to *see*; this led to, among other things, the elevation of the host after the consecration, a practice first attested for Paris in 1220.[21]

In this situation a vision which Juliana of Liège, an Augustinian nun, received in 1209, played an important role in the establishment of a special feast. She saw the gleaming disc of the moon, but it had a dark spot on it; this, she was told, represented the lack of a feast of the eucharist in the annual cycle. At the urging of Juliana and her spiritual adviser, Bishop Robert of Liège introduced such a feast into his diocese for the first time in 1246. In 1264 Pope Urban IV, who had been archdeacon of Liège, extended the feast to the entire Church. In the Bull *Transiturus*, by which he established the feast, the pope gives the reasons for his action and, in the process, develops a gratifyingly rounded presentation of the eucharist as both sacrifice and meal.

Thomas Aquinas is said to have compiled or written the text for Office and Mass at the pope's request. On various grounds, however, questions are raised about his sole authorship of the Office with its splendid hymns.[22] The death of Urban IV in this same year did not help as far as the spread of the feast was concerned. Only in 1311–12 at the Council of Vienne did Pope Clement V once again press for its introduction; Pope John XXII published the Bull *Transiturus* in the Clementine Decretals.[23]

The traditional name for the feast has been *Festum Ss. Corporis Christi*, "Feast of the Most Holy Body of Christ," with the short Latin name *Corpus Christi* being used even in English. With a view to assuring a fuller understanding of the sacrament the new Roman Missal has expanded the name of the feast: *Ss.mi Corporis et Sanguinis Christi Solemnitas*, "Solemnity of the Most Holy Body and Blood of Christ," but the English has retained the traditional name of "Corpus Christi."

The new Latin name also makes clear that this feast includes the mystery of the "precious blood." In honor of the latter Pius IX introduced the "Feast of the Precious Blood" after his happy return from exile in 1849, and assigned it to July 1. The Commentary on the new *General Norms* rightly observes that "the Solemnity of the Most Holy Body of Christ is at the same time a celebration of the Most Precious Blood of our Lord Jesus Christ, as is clear from the text of the Mass and Office and from the Bull of Pope Urban IV in which he instituted that feast in 1264."[24]

It has been noted, with some justice, that the commemoration of the sacrament of the eucharist has already taken place on Holy Thursday, the day of its institution, and that Corpus Christi is therefore a duplication. However, we must bear in mind that Holy Thursday evening, which begins the sacred triduum, is part of Good Friday and that there is, consequently, little room for the unfettered expression of festal joy. It is therefore defensible and appropriate to have another occasion in Ordinary Time when faith can express its joyous thanksgiving for the eucharist as the precious fruit and operative presence of the paschal mystery. After all, the central paschal mystery itself in its entirety is celebrated as a feast not just once a year but every Sunday, and yet the objection of duplication has no place.

The Proper of the Mass shows the theological hand of St. Thomas Aquinas especially in the presidential prayers. In his theological Summa (Part III, Question 73, the body of Article 4) he analyzes the significance of the eucharist by relating it to past, present and future: with reference to the past it is a commemoration of Christ's passion and a real sacrifice; with reference to the present it is a sacrament of union with Christ and one another; and with reference to the future it is an anticipated "enjoyment of the divinity." This threefold significance is given in very similar words in the presidential prayers: "You gave us the eucharist as a memorial of your suffering and death" (opening prayer); "Lord, may the bread and wine we offer bring your Church the unity and peace they signify" (prayer over the gifts); "You give us your body and blood in the eucharist as a sign that even now we share your life. May we come to possess it fully in the kingdom" (concluding prayer).

These three aspects find their classical expression in the antiphon for the Magnificat at second vespers: "How holy this feast in which Christ is our food; his passion is recalled; grace fills our hearts; and we receive a pledge of the glory to come, alleluia." We are also given classical theology in the sequence that is sung after the second reading: the famous *Lauda, Sion, Salvatorem* ("Zion, praise your Savior" or, in a poetic translation, "Laud, O Zion, your salvation").

The gospel in Year A is from the great discourse in which Christ promises the eucharist (Jn 6.51-58). The "living bread which came down from heaven" is prefigured in the manna, the story of which is told in the first reading (Deut 8.2-3, 14-16a). The second reading (1 Cor 10.16-17) sets forth the eucharistic belief of the community at Corinth: the point of the eucharistic action is our participation in the body and blood of Christ and our coalescence into a single body.

The gospel for Year B (Mk 14.12-16, 22-26) describes the last supper of Jesus and his institution of the eucharistic mystery; it thus links Corpus Christi clearly with Holy Thursday. The blood of the new covenant that is shed for many is prefigured in the covenant blood with which Moses sprinkled the people of Israel (first reading: Ex 24.3-8). As "the mediator of a new covenant," Christ secures "an eternal redemption," "taking not the blood of goats and calves but his own blood." (second reading: Heb 9.11-15).

In the gospel for Year C (Lk 9.11b-17) the evangelist describes the miracle of the multiplication of the loaves in a way that makes it point ahead to the greater miracle of the eucharistic food: "Taking the five loaves and the two fish he looked up to heaven, and blessed and broke them, and gave them to the disciples"). The Old Testament reading (Gen 14.18-20) shows us the mysterious figure of Melchizedek, the priest-king who with his gifts of bread and wine became a prefiguration of Christ and his eucharistic sacrifice. The second reading (1 Cor 11.23-26) gives the earliest account (ca. 55 AD) of the institution of the eucharist and interprets it as a meal commemorating the sacrificial death of Christ: " 'Do this, as often as you drink it, in remembrance of me.' For as often as you eat this bread and drink the cup, you proclaim the Lord's death until he comes."

The saving event that is proclaimed and celebrated in the Mass of the feast is thus one of great depth and richness of content. By comparison, the subsequent Corpus Christi procession, though visually more impressive, must take second place. Here again let me begin with some historical background.

In his Bull *Transiturus*, which introduced the feast, Urban IV says nothing of a procession; the first evidence of it is for the period 1274–1279 at Cologne (St. Gereon).[25] Before the fourteenth century was over, it had been adopted with enthusiasm in most countries and carried out with great solemnity and splendor. The consecrated host was carried in the procession, initially without being visible, but later made visible to all in a precious vessel intended for the purpose (a monstrance). In

172

Germany the Corpus Christi procession soon took on the character of a procession through the fields and a rogation procession. There was a station (an assembling for prayer) at four outdoor altars; at these the beginnings of the four gospels were sung toward the four quarters of the heavens, and petitions were offered for ecclesial and civic needs. A blessing with the eucharistic sacrament followed.

Especially during the baroque period the Corpus Christi procession developed into "a triumphal procession of thanksgiving, a public display. The tableaus depicting the passion and its Old Testament prefigurations that had already accompanied the procession in the Middle Ages now developed into magnificent floats, depicting scenes that frequently had no clear connection with the eucharist (e.g., St. George slaying the dragon). The period of the Enlightenment, however, left only a few meager remnants of all this colorful activity."[26]

Rome does not regard the Corpus Christi procession as a liturgical act falling under Roman law and its sole supervision, but as one of the *pia exercitia* (exercises of devotion) that come under the bishop's supervision.[27]

During the past two decades many groups have become dissatisfied with the traditional form of the procession. There have been efforts, especially in the large cities, to develop new forms for it. For example, a festive Mass might be celebrated in a public square, with the various parishes coming in procession from their churches (this represents, to some extent, an imitation of the old Roman stational liturgies); in the one Mass all would experience the "sacrament of unity" as a source of community with Christ and one another.[28]

Now, after many efforts and experiments a growing number of people are calling for a retention or restoration of the procession with the Blessed Sacrament. An important influence here is the idea—not a new one certainly, but one that has received new emphasis from Vatican II—of the Church as the pilgrim people of God *(in statu viatoris)* who can overcome the many dangers of their journey only with the presence and help of the Lord. "Our contemporaries so often suffer from the randomness of existence. If the Corpus Christi procession were properly conducted in the spirit of the liturgy, it could, more than any other procession, be or become a way of making them aware, by means of a real symbol, that they are not alone as they make their way along the difficult mountain paths of life on earth but rather that in the communion of the Church, which has the eucharistic Lord with her, going before, beside and behind her, they are on the way to eternal union with the Christ of the parousia, when 'he comes on that day to be glorified in his saints, and to be marveled at in all who have believed' (2 Thess 1.10)."[29]

The Feast of the Sacred Heart of Jesus

This solemnity is celebrated on the third Friday after Pentecost, or the day that used to follow upon the octave of Corpus Christi. It is a typical feast of devotion, honoring the God-man for the love that is symbolized by his heart. The beginnings of such a devotion may be found in the Fathers, who appeal especially to passages in the gospel of John (e.g., 7.37; 19.34). These passages were also the point of departure for the medieval theologians: a few isolated figures in the twelfth century (Anselm of Canterbury, Bernard of Clairvaux), and then a large number in the thirteenth (e.g., Albert the Great, Bonaventure).

This cult received an especially strong impetus from the mystics of the thirteenth and fourteenth centuries, in the person of such individuals as Mechtild of Magdeburg, Gertrude of Helfta, and Henrich Seuse. Later on, the representatives of the *Devotio moderna* and the Jesuits of the sixteenth century promoted the Sacred Heart devotion with special zeal. In the seventeenth century the French Oratorians of Pierre Bérulle († 1629) and John Eudes († 1680) brought the devotion to new heights. John Eudes, with the permission of his bishop, was also the first to celebrate a feast in honor of the Heart of Jesus in the churches of his community (October 20, 1672). Between 1673 and 1675 Margaret Mary Alacoque, a Visitation nun at Paray-le-Monial, had a series of visions in which Christ bade her work for the introduction of a feast of the Sacred Heart on the Friday after the octave of Corpus Christi and for the practice of Fridays in honor of the Heart of Jesus and of holy hours.

Rome resisted for almost a hundred years, and only in 1765 did

Clement XIII allow the Polish bishops and the Roman Archcon-
fraternity of the Sacred Heart to celebrate such a feast. In 1856
Pius IX made the feast obligatory for the universal Church; in
1899 Leo XIII raised it to a higher rank and ordered that the
world should be consecrated to the Most Sacred Heart of Jesus
for the coming century.[30] Pius XI revised the liturgy of the feast
in 1927 and elevated it still further, to the same rank as Christmas, although it was not made a holy day of obligation. On the
first centenary (1956) of its introduction as a universal feast Pius
XII issued the Encyclical Letter *Haurietis aquas*.[31]

The chief opposition to devotion to the Sacred Heart came from
Jansenism and the theologians of the Enlightenment. Our century, too, brought more or less open reservations regarding it;
Pius XII discusses these in his encyclical. Many of the objections are based on misunderstandings and prove groundless
once the term "heart" is understood as a primordial word or
primordial concept, as explained by Karl Rahner: "For Scripture
and the teaching and practice of the Church assume, when they
speak of the heart of Jesus, the self-same total-human primordial word 'heart' as the innermost core of the body-soul totality
of the person. The object of the Sacred Heart devotion is consequently the Lord with respect to this his heart."[32]

The Mass for the feast in the new Missal is composed largely of
the texts which Pius XI personally chose in 1928, in collabora-
tion with the Benedictine abbot H. Quentin. Earlier formularies
had focused primarily on the passion of Christ and the mysti-
cism of the Song of Solomon. Pius XI laid greater emphasis on
the idea of expiation, as can be seen, for example, in the opening prayer and the prayer over the gifts.

The entrance antiphon sings with the psalmist (Ps 33.11, 19) of
the changeless "thoughts of his heart": "He will rescue them
from death and feed them in time of famine." A choice of two
opening prayers is given. The first (which is new) looks to "the
gifts of love we have received" and asks the Father to "open our
hearts to share his [Christ's] life and continue to bless us with
his love," while the second (the old prayer) asks that we may
"offer him living worship by love-filled service to our brothers
and sisters" (the Latin text has: "that we may offer him devoted

service and the worthy expiation we owe him"). The old concluding prayer (we have "tasted the sweetness of your loving heart") is replaced by the prayer: "May this sacrament fill us with love. Draw us closer to Christ your Son and help us to recognize him in others." New, too, is the preface which is notable for its close adherence to the scriptures and to the theology of the Fathers: "Lifted high on the cross, Christ gave his life for us, so much did he love us. From his wounded side flowed blood and water, the fountain of sacramental life in the Church. To his open heart the Savior invites all men, to draw water in joy from the springs of salvation."

The gospel in Year A (Mt. 11.25-30) contains the "cry of messianic jubilation" and the invitation to all in distress to seek and find rest in the heart of Jesus. The love of God had already been shown in the election and deliverance of Israel (first reading: Deut 7.6-11). But it has now been revealed even more fully in the fact that "God sent his only Son into the world, so that we might live through him. . . . God is love, and he who abides in love abides in God, and God abides in him" (second reading: 1 Jn 4.7-16).

The gospel in Year B (Jn 19.31-37) is taken from the old Mass of the feast; it tells how a soldier opened the Redeemer's side with a lance. The first reading (Hos 11.1, 3-4, 8c-9) speaks of Yahweh's fatherly affection for Israel. The New Testament reading (Eph 3.8-12, 14-19), which again is from the formulary of Pius XI, praises "the unsearchable riches of Christ" and his love "which surpasses knowledge."

In Year C the gospel (Lk 15.3-7) and first reading (Ezek 34.11-16) describe the Lord's love for us in the image of the Good Shepherd who goes after the straying sheep and brings them back. The New Testament reading (Rom 5.5b-11) is a hymn of praise to the merciful love of God, which has shown itself above all in the fact that "while we were yet sinners Christ died for us." The theme of the Good Shepherd also runs through the responsorial psalm (Ps 23) and the alleluia verse (Jn 10.14). We think spontaneously of Good Shepherd Sunday (the fourth Sunday of Easter) and realize that the themes of the feast of the Sacred Heart are found more than once in the liturgical year.

Other forms of devotion to the Sacred Heart are the Fridays in honor of the Sacred Heart, that is, the first Friday of each month, and the holy hour on the eve of first Friday. Leo XIII approved (1899) a special votive Mass for first Fridays. The two devotions, when properly explained and celebrated, have long since proved their pastoral value in many parishes.[33]

Solemnity of Christ the King (Christ the King Sunday)

The most recent of the feasts of ideas in honor of the Lord owes its origin to Pope Pius XI. In his Encyclical Letter *Quas primas* of December 11, 1925 he develops the idea that the most effective weapon against the destructive forces of the age is the acknowledgment of the kingship of Christ.[34] This recognition will bring "the signal benefits of true liberty, of calm order, of harmony, and of peace." For these results, "it is necessary that the royal dignity of Our Lord be recognized and accepted as widely as possible. To this end it seems to Us that nothing else would help so effectively as the institution of a special feast dedicated to Christ our King. The annual celebration of the sacred mysteries is more effective in informing people about the Faith and in bringing to them the joys of the spiritual life than the solemn pronouncements of the teaching Church. Documents are often read only by a few learned men; feasts move and teach all the faithful. The former speak but once; the latter every year and forever. The former bring a saving touch to the intellect; the latter influence not only the mind but the heart and man's whole nature."[35]

The external influence that led to the introduction of the feast in that particular year was the sixteenth centenary of the First Ecumenical Council of Nicaea, which taught the consubstantiality of Christ with the Father and thus provided the basis, as it were, for his kingly rule. The Pope appointed the last Sunday of October as the day of the feast. He chose this day chiefly in view of the coming feast of All Saints; the feast of Christ the King would thus exalt "before all men the glory of Him Who triumphs in His saints and in His elect."[36] On this Sunday a public consecration to the heart of the Redeemer was to take place.

Although the feast was greeted with enthusiasm, especially among men and young people, a number of reservations were also voiced. These had to do with the fact that the idea of this feast is already quite adequately, and indeed more organically, embodied in other seasons and feasts of the liturgical year, for example, Advent, Christmas, Epiphany, Easter, Ascension and, in fact, every Sunday, for Sunday, as its Greek and Latin names indicate, is, when properly understood, a feast of Christ the *Kyrios* or Lord. In 1941 J. A. Jungmann expressed this dissatisfaction in an essay in the history of ideas:

> And yet [i.e., despite the enthusiastic reception] a feeling of weariness may come over us as we view these interminable expansions of the liturgical picture of Christ. Constant new enterprises, constant new images, constant new climaxes, constant new phraseologies. Are these not a sign that at some point we have abandoned the firm foundation and that as we plunged ahead in our devotional zeal we began to slip and slide? Or is it rather that two thousand years ago we felt bound to set out on a long circuit, as it were, if we were to learn to see the riches of Christ from ever new vantage points—first in their concentrated beauty, but then in their individual reality as well, in their historical development, in their inner depth and outward dignity? The second of these two alternatives is probably the correct one. And it seems that the circle is finally closing and that the circuit is returning to its starting point.[37]

The ground seems better prepared today for this wish of Jungmann, and it must be regarded as a happy contribution to its fulfillment that the "Solemnity of Our Lord Jesus Christ, King of the Universe," as the full title of the feast runs in Latin, has now been shifted to the last Sunday of the liturgical year. This change locates the feast more squarely in that eschatological context that has always marked the final Sunday of the liturgical year. It is now clearer that the exalted Lord and King is the goal not only of the liturgical year but of our entire earthly pilgrimage: "Jesus Christ . . . the same yesterday and today and for ever" (Heb 13.8), "the Alpha and the Omega, the first and the last, the beginning and the end" (Rev 22.13).

If there must be a feast of Christ the King, then the final "Lord's Day" seems a more natural place for it than its former date. In fact, Pius XI based his choice of that earlier date on the consideration, among others, that "the close of the liturgical year is at hand" and the Christian mysteries have as it were reached their conclusion.[38] At the end of the liturgical year, then, stands the Lord of glory, "the goal of human history, the focal point of the desires of history and civilization, the center of mankind, the joy of all hearts, and the fulfillment of all aspirations. . . . Animated and drawn together in his Spirit we press onward toward the consummation of history which fully corresponds to the plan of his love: 'to unite all things in him, things in heaven and things on earth' (Eph 1:10)."[39]

The Mass of the feast is only slightly changed from the old formulary, although we must not overlook the fact that the richer biblical fare given in the three-year cycle of readings presents a fuller scriptural picture of Christ. The entrance antiphon (Rev 5.12; 1-6) expresses the message of the paschal mystery in concise form: The Lamb who was slain receives "glory and power for ever." His exaltation and establishment as Head of all creation allows us to pray with confidence: "You break the power of evil and make all things new. . . . May all in heaven and earth acclaim your glory and never cease to praise you" (opening prayer); "We offer you the sacrifice by which your Son reconciles mankind. May it bring unity and peace to the world" (prayer over the gifts). The preface praises Christ as the "eternal priest and universal king" who at the end of time will present to his Father "an eternal and universal kingdom: a kingdom of truth and life, a kingdom of holiness and grace, a kingdom of justice, love, and peace."

In Year A the gospel (Mt 25.31-46) stresses the fact that active love of neighbor will be a decisive criterion at the final judgment because Christ identifies himself with all who suffer: "As you did it to one of these my brethren, you did it to me." The Old Testament reading (Ezek 34.11-12, 15-17) describes God's concern for human beings with the image of a shepherd's solicitude (cf. the Feast of the Sacred Heart, Year C). The Christ who has been raised from the dead is the pledge of our own resurrection; he is the Lord who overcomes the final enemy, death (second reading: 1 Cor 15.20-26, 28).

In the gospel of Year B (Jn 18.33b-37) Christ affirms his royal dignity to Pilate and defines his rule against misconceptions of it. The liturgy regards Daniel's vision of the son of man to whom "dominion and glory and kingdom" are given as fulfilled in Christ (first reading: Dan 7.13-14). The second reading (Rev 1.5-8) contains an enthusiastic hymn to Christ. He is "the faithful witness, the first-born of the dead, and the ruler of kings on earth." In his paschal mystery he has "made us a kingdom, priests to his God and Father."

In Year C the gospel (Lk 23.35-43) makes it clear that even when humiliated and mocked, Christ remains a king and has the royal power to lead human beings into the glory of paradise. David, who is anointed king by all the tribes of Israel, prefigures Christ the universal king (first reading: 1 Sam 5.1-3). To him the human race owes its deliverance. The hymn to Christ in the letter to the Colossians proclaims his unique dignity (second reading: Col 1.12-20).

The Feasts of the Transfiguration of the Lord and the Triumph of the Cross

These feasts are distinguished from the preceding in a purely extrinsic way by the fact that they have a fixed month and day for their celebration. Both owe their existence to events in the history of the Church.

THE FEAST OF THE TRANFIGURATION OF THE LORD (AUGUST 6)

The basis of the festal liturgy is the accounts given in the three synoptic gospels; these are in substantial agreement about what happened (Mt 17.1-8; Mk 9.2-9; Lk 9.28b-36). According to the story, Jesus accompanied by Peter, James and John, climbed a high mountain and there was transfigured; Moses and Elijah appeared and spoke with him. Then there was a theophany, with a voice calling from a cloud: "This my beloved Son, with whom I am well pleased; listen to him" (Mt 17.5).

This event became the object of a liturgical feast as early as the fifth century in the East Syrian liturgy, and then eventually in the other Eastern Churches. In the Franco-Roman empire the feast appears for the first time in the tenth century but then spreads quickly. The keen interest felt at that time in the Holy Land and the various sites connected with the life of Jesus may have contributed to the spread of the feast. It was taken into the calendar of the universal Church in 1457 under Pope Calixtus III, in grateful commemoration of the victory which John of Capistrano and John Hunyadi had won over the Turks in the previous year.[40]

The Mass of the feast is the same each year except for the gospel, which is taken from the synoptics in a three-year cycle (see above). In its content the formulary is wholly centered on the event recorded in scripture. The second reading refers to it (2 Pet 1.16-19), while the Old Testament reading (Dan 7.9-10, 13-14) tells of the prophet's vision of "the Ancient of Days" on his fiery throne and the appearance of the "son of man." The special preface sees the significance of the festal event as residing in, among other things, the fact that Jesus "revealed his glory to the disciples, to strengthen them for the scandal of the cross" and that he gave the entire Church the hope that it "would one day share his glory." Our sharing in this glory of the Lord is also the object of the petitions in the presidential prayers.

THE FEAST OF THE TRIUMPH OF THE CROSS (SEPTEMBER 14)

The cross on which Jesus died was initially thought of simply as the material instrument of his execution. But even in apostolic times it became a symbol of his sacrificial death and even of Christ as such and of the Christian faith as a whole. Thus Paul can speak of the power of Christ's cross (1 Cor 1.17) and say that to those who are perishing the message of the cross is folly (v. 18) and that many "live as enemies of the cross of Christ" (Phil 3.18).

The first traces of a feast of veneration of the cross are found in the first half of the fourth century. According to the *Alexandrian Chronicle* (or *Chronicon Paschale*) empress Helena discovered the Lord's cross on September 14, 320. On September 13, 335 the churches of the Martyrium (or Church of the Cross) and of the Resurrection (Church of the Anastasis) were consecrated on Golgotha in Jerusalem. The next day, the cross that Helena had discovered was solemnly exposed for the veneration of the faithful. These events then became the basis of an annual commemoration; there is evidence for such a feast in Constantinople in the fifth century and in Rome by the end of the seventh century. It became customary on September 14 in those Churches (Jerusalem, Constantinople, Rome) which had a major relic of the cross to show this to the faithful in a solemn ceremony called the *Exaltatio* ("Lifting up") of the cross; it was this ceremony that gave the feast its name.

In the Gallic liturgy of the eighth century there was a feast of the cross on May 3, the date on which the emperor Heraclius in 628 rescued the relic of the cross which the Persians had captured, and brought it in triumphal procession to Jerusalem. This Gallic feast also made its way into the Roman calendar, but, by a distortion of historical fact, this feast of May 3 was called "Discovery of the Holy Cross," while the feast of September 14 was called "Exaltation of the Holy Cross" but was made to refer to the restoration of the cross by Heraclius. As early as 1741 Benedict XIV tried to eliminate this unfortunate duplication; finally the May 3 feast was removed from the Roman calendar by John XXIII (Code of Rubrics). This new arrangement has been taken over in the *General Norms* so that the feast of the cross on September 14 once again has its original meaning.[41]

The main themes of the festal Mass are the death of Christ on the cross and the redemption he won for us thereby. The entrance antiphon gives the leitmotiv for the celebration: "We should glory in the cross of our Lord Jesus Christ, for he is our salvation, our life and our resurrection; through him we are saved and made free" (cf. Gal 6.14). The special preface sees the cross as the antithesis of the tree of knowledge in the Garden of Eden: "You decreed that man should be saved through the wood of the cross. The tree of man's defeat became his tree of victory; where life was lost, there life has been restored through Christ our Lord."

The gospel (Jn 3.13-17) and the Old Testament reading (Num 21.4-9) consider the "bronze serpent" which Moses "lifted up" on a pole so that it might bring healing to those doomed to death, to be a prefiguration and likeness of the Lord who has been "lifted up" on the cross. The second reading (Phil 2.6-11) is the classical passage on the humiliation of Christ through his obedience "unto death on a cross" and on his subsequent glorification. To this reading the community responds with adoration and praise in the alleluia verse: "We adore you, O Christ, and we praise you, because by your cross you have redeemed the world." With this central mystery of the faith in view the presidential prayers ask for a share in the fruits of redemption (opening prayer), for the forgiveness of sins (prayer over the gifts), and for the glory of the resurrection. The themes of the feast are thus basically the same as those of the Good Friday liturgy.

The Feasts of the Dedication of Churches

At an early date in the history of the Church there were celebrations not only of the anniversaries of the dead, especially the martyrs, but also of the anniversaries of the election and consecration of bishops and popes and the consecration of churches. People spoke of the *natale* (or *dies natalis*), "birthday," of a church or basilica. There were not only pagan precedents for such anniversaries but an Old Testament precedent as well: the annual celebration, instituted by Judas Maccabaeus, of the rededication of the temple in 165 BC (cf. above, pp. 14-15). We owe our oldest description of such a Christian feast of the dedication of a church to Egeria the pilgrim who around the year 400 describes the dedication of the Martyrium and Anastasis churches in Jerusalem.[42] The practice of these annual commemorations probably reached Rome and the remainder of the West by the fifth century. If a church were dedicated to a particular saint, the day of its dedication often became, later on, the feast day of that saint.[43]

Originally these feasts of the dedication of churches were celebrated only locally. But there were certain exceptions that are still acknowledged today: the feasts of the dedication of the

Lateran Basilica, the Basilicas of Peter and Paul, and St. Mary Major.

The dedication of the Lateran Basilica is celebrated as a feast on November 9. Emperor Constantine had given the great Lateran palace and its surrounding grounds to the Church of Rome; then in 324 he had a basilica built there in honor of the Redeemer. At the beginning of the tenth century the basilica was also dedicated to John the Baptist and John the Evangelist, and was henceforth known as "St. John on the Lateran" (Pope Sergius III, 904). According to an inscription which Clement XII (1730–40) placed there, this church is "Mother and Head of all the churches of the City and the world." The annual commemoration of its consecration spread beyond Rome, chiefly due to the efforts of the Augustinian Hermits, and in 1570 was included in the Missal of Pius V. In the new General Roman Calendar the old name "Feast of the Dedication of the Archbasilica of the Most Holy Redeemer" has been changed to "Dedication of Saint John Lateran."

The day of the dedication of the two Basilicas of St. Peter and St. Paul (outside the Walls) is an optional memorial in the General Roman Calendar for November 18. Constantine the Great had basilicas built over the tombs of the two Apostles. The dedication of St. Peter's Basilica has been celebrated on November 18 since the twelfth century. The same date was kept for the consecration of the new St. Peter's in 1626.

The Constantinian Basilica of St. Paul outside the Walls, after being rebuilt a number of times, was destroyed by a fire in 1823. The splendid new structure, built with funds collected around the world, was consecrated by Pius IX on December 10, 1854, but the older anniversary day, November 18, was retained.

The Basilica of St. Mary Major on the Esquiline hill was built in the fourth century, but after the Council of Ephesus in 431, at which the divine maternity of Mary was made a dogma, Pope Sixtus III dedicated it as a Marian church on August 5 in one of the ensuing years. A medieval legend that the construction site was covered with snow in midsummer did a good deal, in the miracle-loving fourteenth century, to make the feast known, even outside Rome, as "Our Lady of the Snows." It was accepted into the Roman festal calendar (but did not appear in the 1568 Breviary of Pius V) and has been retained in the new calendar as an optional memorial. The Commentary on the new calendar observes that "the name of today's memorial is changed to 'Dedication of Saint Mary Major' with no mention of the legend attached to the building of the basilica on the Esquiline hill."[44]

Of special significance for each diocese is the anniversary of the dedication of its cathedral church; this is celebrated in all the parishes as a special feast of the diocese, while in the cathedral itself it is celebrated as a solemnity.

The anniversary of the dedication of any individual church, if known, is celebrated there on that date as a solemnity. For churches whose anniversary date is unknown, each diocese celebrates a common annual commemoration in the form of a solemnity. The excesses connected with the various anniversaries of the dedication of churches have caused many provincial synods, ever since the sixteenth century, to call for the celebration of all the dedication feasts within an ecclesiastical province on one and the same day.[45]

The new Missal contains two formularies for the Mass on the anniversary of a church's dedication: one is for use in the church whose anniversary it is, the other for celebrating the anniversary of a different church. In both of the prefaces for a dedication the focus of attention is not simply the stone building in which God gives us his grace in Christ who is the true temple of the new covenant, but also the community of believers that gathers therein. "In the visible building we see shadowed forth the Church, the Bride of Christ" (II, Latin text). This Church is "temple of your Spirit" (II), built "of living stones" (I). In it the faithful who have come together from all places are formed into "the body of Christ": "Here you . . . bring the Church to its full stature . . . to reach its perfection at last in the heavenly city of Jerusalem, which is the vision of your peace" (I).

There is a large selection of scripture readings available for use in both Masses. For the first reading there are two groups: Old

Testament readings, which are used outside the Easter season, and New Testament readings, which are used during the Easter season. Some of the gospel pericopes given are: Mt 5.23-24 (exhortation to reconciliation with one's brothers and sisters before offering one's gift), Lk 19.1-10 (Jesus meets Zacchaeus and enters his house), Jn 2.13-22 (expulsion of the tradesmen from the temple and prediction of the resurrection as the rebuilding of the temple which is the body of Jesus), Jn 4.19-24 (the hour for true worshipers).

The theology of the Christian house of worship and its consecration (along with that of the altar) find excellent expression in the new rite for the *Dedication of a Church and an Altar*. The Congregation for the Sacraments and Divine Worship published this in an *editio typica* on May 29, 1977, as part of the new Roman Ritual; it has since been translated into English.[46]

4 / THE EMBER AND ROGATION DAYS

Ember Days

"Ember days" is the name given to the Wednesday, Friday and Saturday of four weeks of the year; the weeks come at approximately the beginning of the four seasons. Since the eighth century Rome has spoken of these weeks as the *quattuor tempora*, "four seasons."

The question of their origin has not yet been answered with full satisfaction. It is certain, however, that the ember days are an institution of the Roman Church which was unknown in the East and was accepted in other Western countries only when the Roman liturgy made its way into them. The oldest report we have of a fast four times a year is to be found in a fourth-century writer, Pontius Maximus, who commends the practice with an appeal to the prophet Zechariah.[47] The prophetic text in question reads: "Thus says the Lord of hosts: The fast of the fourth month, and the fast of the fifth, and the fast of the seventh, and the fast of the tenth, shall be to the house of Judah seasons of joy and gladness, and cheerful feasts" (8.19).

The next literary witnesses to the practice are the ember week sermons of Pope Leo I († 461). These allow us to conclude that the ember fast was a well-established custom. Leo I connects it with the four seasons of the year. In accordance with the teaching of the Holy Spirit (Leo says) the fasting is spread throughout the year in such a way that "we . . . find (it) in every season. In the spring we fast for forty days before Easter, in summer we fast at Pentecost, in the fall during September, and in winter during December."[48] The reason for this cycle of fasts is that "we may learn from the constantly recurring annual cycle that we are in constant need of purification."[49] Leo sees the December fast as also an expression of gratitude for the harvests of that year: "In our pastoral concern for you we tell you . . . to practice the December fast as a fitting sacrifice of abstinence that is offered to God the giver in gratitude for the now completed harvest of all the fruits of the soil."[50] Leo regards the ember fasts as originating in apostolic tradition, but also in Old Testament regulations which, unlike the ceremonial laws of the former covenant, continue to be binding moral precepts of the new covenant.[51]

This view of the origin and antiquity of the ember fasts lends credibility to the notice in the *Liber pontificalis* (a kind of history of the popes that dates from the first half of the sixth century). Here we are told that Pope Calixtus I (217–22) had ordered a fast on three Saturdays of the year at the seasons "of grain, wine and oil."

The ember fast ended with a vigil celebration during the night between Saturday and Sunday. Leo I mentions this fast no less than fifteen times in his sermons: "On Wednesday and Friday, then, we shall fast, and on Saturday celebrate the vigils at the church of the holy Apostle Peter."[52] Because this nocturnal liturgy was regarded as falling on Sunday, the Sunday had no further liturgy and was denominated a *dominica vacans* (empty or open Sunday). But as the vigil liturgy was moved forward to an increasingly early hour until it was finally celebrated in the morning hours of Saturday (we saw this development in connection with the Easter Vigil), a liturgy of the Mass was provided for these previously "empty" Sundays, with the preceding ember day Masses supplying most of the texts.

Since the end of the fifth century at the latest, the ember days have been the preferred dates for ordinations, with Wednesday and Friday serving as the days for presenting and examining the candidates, and the ordinations taking place during the vigil liturgy prior to Sunday.[53]

Various hypotheses have been suggested for explaining the real origin of the Roman ember days. According to G. Morin they go back to the three pagan Roman harvest festivals that were celebrated in gratitude for the grain harvest, the vintage and (in December) the sowing. In support of this hypothesis is the fact that Rome originally had only three ember weeks.[54] According to L. Duchesne, however, the ember days originated in the Roman custom of fasting in connection with the stations every Wednesday and Friday and, later on, every Saturday as well. Once this weekly three-day fast was dropped, the ember fast was introduced as a kind of substitute.[55]

Recent research has looked for the origin of the ember days in corresponding Old Testament regulations on fasting. Here Zechariah 8.19 and Joel 2.12-19 would have played an important role—a supposition that can find support especially in the sermons of Leo I.[56]

As I mentioned earlier, the custom of ember day fasting spread with the acceptance of the Roman liturgy. Important factors in this diffusion were the sending of Abbot Augustine and his monks to England under Gregory I, the missionary work of Boniface who looked so much to Rome for guidance, and the efforts of Pepin and Charlemagne. For hundreds of years there was some uncertainty about the dates for the individual ember weeks; this perplexity was finally eliminated by Pope Gregory VII at the Roman synod of 1078. Since then, the rule has been that the ember days begin on the Wednesday after the first Sunday of Lent, after Pentecost, after the Exaltation of the Cross (September 14), and after the feast of St. Lucy (December 13).

If we wish to sum up the meaning of the ember days in the light of this short historical survey, we may say that they represented a special ascetical effort at the beginning of each of the four seasons. This effort took the form especially of the triad already recommended in the Old Testament: prayer, fasting and almsgiving. At the same time, the days were days of thanksgiving for the various seasonal harvests; from the fifth century on they also served for the preparation and conferral of holy orders. In our own time they have been revitalized to some extent, and in some countries, as days of prayer for vocations to the priesthood and religious life.

In the reorganization of the liturgical year that followed on the Second Vatican Council, the Church has retained the ember days in principle but has left their date and form to the episcopal conferences so that better account can be taken of "various regions and the different needs of the people."[57] The Roman Commentary on the *General Norms* touches on some important points for making these days meaningful to our contemporaries:

> In our time, when all human beings are fully aware of the serious problems of peace, justice and hunger, the exercises of penance and Christian charity that recur with each of the four seasons need to be given back their original value and power. In each region, therefore, and in the light of local circumstances and customs, a suitable way should be found of celebrating an ember week liturgy and dedicating it especially to the ministry of Christian love.[58]

Ember Days and Thanksgiving for the Harvest

If we survey the thematic content the ember day celebrations have had in the course of history, it is noticeable that especially on the ember days of autumn and December thanksgiving for the various annual harvests played an important part. This suggests that the yearly thanksgiving for the harvest should really be connected with the autumn ember days; the Sunday after the ember days would be the Sunday of thanksgiving for the harvest. In this way the motif of gratitude for the earth's fruits could be organically integrated into the liturgical year as the latter has evolved historically.

It has correctly been pointed out that in the Christian understanding of "feast" there can in fact be no independent feast of thanksgiving for the harvest, since the all-inclusive basis for the Christian celebration is the saving action of Christ and since the latter becomes a festal source of salvation first and foremost in the eucharist. "The real time of festivity for Christians is the celebration of the eucharist. The liturgy is the time and place of communion with Christ in its fullest and closest form. . . . Therefore the primordial feast of the Christian world is the regular communal celebration of the eucharist on Sundays."[59]

On the other hand, Christians too realize that they are dependent on what goes on in our earthly natural world, and subject to the prosperity and dangers this brings. Consequently "the motifs proper to the natural human religious spirit retain their vitality for Christians."[60] For these reasons joy and thanksgiving for the harvest are justified in the life of Christians and have a claim to be recognized in the Christian festal celebration (I have already made the same point in connection with the celebration of the new year, cf. above). Thanksgiving for the harvest should find expression in the celebration of the autumn ember days and, on the part of the entire community, on the following Sunday.

Among its Masses for Various Needs and Occasions the new Missal has one for "After the Harvest." The presidential prayers not only offer thanks for the gifts received but also point out the duty of using these for the good of all (first opening prayer). They ask that "the seeds of charity and justice (may) also bear fruit in our hearts" (second opening prayer) and that in addition to "the fruits of the earth," "the power of this saving mystery (may) bring us even greater gifts." The lectionary has special readings for this Mass, but in many cases the Sunday readings could also be used. The homilist might take as his point of departure the new prayers of praise and thanksgiving (*Berakah*) now used at the preparation of the gifts, since in them we praise God for the gifts of bread and wine, for the produce of soil and vine, and for the fruits of human toil.

Rogation Days

The Easter season saw the development, in Christian antiquity, of two celebrations which by their seriousness contrast to some extent with the joy of the fifty-day period. Amalarius of Metz († ca. 850) was so surprised that he exclaimed: "I am amazed that our Church should have allowed this fast to become customary . . . when the holy Fathers tell us . . . that there is to be no fasting during these fifty days!"[61] He is referring to the rogation processions (and Masses) on April 25, feast of St. Mark the Evangelist, and on the three days before Ascension.

The older procession (*litania maior*, "greater litany") on April 25 has been suppressed in the reorganization of the liturgical year. The Commentary on the *General Norms* justifies the suppression on the grounds that the procession "originated in a purely local custom of the Church of the city of Rome: by instituting such a procession the Roman pontiffs wished to substitute a Christian ritual for an ancient pagan practice."[62] The Commentary on the new calendar observes: "The greater litany is abolished, since it has practically the same object as the lesser litanies or rogations."[63]

The old pagan Roman custom which the procession replaced was the *Robigalia*, celebrated on April 25 in honor of the god *Robigus*, "Mildew" (or the goddess *Robigo*, "Rust") in order to ward off mildew from the grain, a blight widespread in antiquity. It seems that as late as the fourth century the practice of processing around the fields (*Ambarvalia*) still had a strong hold on the people. The Roman Church (in the person of Pope Liberius?) sought to suppress it by means of a Christian counterpart. For not only did the date of the greater litany coincide with that of the *Robigalia* but so, to a great extent, did the route taken by both processions. Pope Gregory I devoted special care to the celebration of this major rogation day.[64]

The lesser litanies (= more recently established intercessory processions) or rogation days originated in Gaul. There, in 469 Bishop Mamertus of Vienne ordered that a fast and special intercessory processions be held on the three days before Ascension Thursday because of the exceptional calamities that had been afflicting the city (earthquake, poor harvests).[65] The practice was quickly adopted by other dioceses and finally prescribed for all of Gaul by the Synod of Orleans in 511. The processions were first introduced into Rome under Pope Leo III († 816), although without the fast that was their obligatory concomitant in Gaul.[66]

The new calendar has kept these lesser rogation days and describes their significance, together with that of the ember days, as follows: "On rogation and ember days the Church publicly thanks the Lord and prays to him for the needs of men, especially for the productivity of the earth and for man's labor."[67] Decisions regarding time and manner are left to the episcopal conferences.[68]

Practice of Ember and Rogation Days

Throughout the world today practice varies widely. Among the English-speaking episcopal conferences some have issued few guidelines while others have made full statements such as the formulation for England and Wales entitled Days of Special Prayer, which was approved by their Episcopal Conference on October 18, 1972.

> In determining such days for England and Wales it seems preferable to abandon all distinction between ember and rogation days, and to speak simply of days of special prayer.
>
> The Episcopal Conference of England and Wales has determined that the intentions for such days in England and Wales shall be as follows:
>   For world peace
>   For Christian unity
>   For the needy and the hungry in the world
>   For God's blessing on human work
>   For vocations to the priesthood and the religious life
>   In thanksgiving for the harvest or for the fruits of human work.
> Days of prayer for several of these intentions have been observed widely throughout England and Wales for some time; it is very suitable that from now onwards they be observed as liturgical days.[69]

Notes

1. Cf. GNLYC, no. 43. The variation in the number of weeks in the year is due to the fact that the average year has one day more than 52 weeks and therefore many years have 53 Sundays.

2. CommALI, cap. I, sect. III. 1 (p. 62).

3. Pascher, pp. 294-95; cf. P. Jounel, "Le dimanche et la semaine," in Martimort, pp. 685-86; Radó 2:1274-75.

4. I cannot agree with G. Kunze, in *Leitourgia* 1:526, that the difference between numbering Sundays after Pentecost (the older Catholic usage) and numbering them after Trinity Sunday (Evangelical usage) may "reflect a profound difference of a dogmatic kind." His reason: the Evangelical Churches advance beyond Pentecost to the feast of the Trinity; Rome, on the contrary "in principle stops at Pentecost and has no great interest in the subsequent period because it is more concerned with developing the Sanctoral."

5. GNLYC, no. 43.

6. P. Jounel, ibid., p. 685.

7. CommALI, cap. I, sect. III. 1 (p. 62).

8. Cf. Lect:Introd, chap. II, sect. V. 1. 3b (p. xxxv).

9. Ibid., chap. I, sect. VI d (p. xxix).

10. Ibid., chap. II, sect. V. 2. 1 (p. xxxvi).

11. Ibid., chap. II, sect. V. 2. 4 (p. xxxvii).

12. Ibid., chap. II, sect. V. 3 2a (p. xxxvii).

13. Ibid., chap. II, sect. V. 3. 1 (p. xxxvii).

14. Ibid., chap. I, sect. VII e (p. xxxi).

15. Cf. A. Bugnini, "Die Reform der Leseordnung für die Messe," Gd 3 (1969), 123-25.

16. Apostolic Constitution *Missale Romanum*, in the *Roman Missal: The Sacramentary*, p. 11; a slightly different English version is cited in Lect:Introd, chap. I, sect. IX (p. xxxii).

17. The first description is used in CommALI, cap. I, sect. III. 2 (p. 62); the second is the title the Lectionary gives to this set of solemnities.

18. Cf. J. A. Jungmann, "The Defeat of Teutonic Arianism and the Revolution in Religious Culture in the Early Middle Ages," in his *Pastoral Liturgy*, p. 35. On the history cf. also A. Klaus, *Ursprung und Verbreitung der Dreifaltigkeitsmesse* (Werl, 1938); and cf. P. Browe, "Zur Geschichte der Dreifaltigkeitsfestes," AL 1 (1950), 65-81.

19. Thus Bernold in his *Micrologus* 60 (PL 151:1020).

20. Thus, e.g., in the Catholic Cathechism of the German Dioceses (the "green catechism"), 1955, no. 78.

21. Cf. P. Browe, *Die Verehrung der Eucharistie im Mittelalter* (Munich, 1933), pp. 26 ff.

22. There is a good survey of the sources in Pascher, pp. 270-72; and cf. Righetti, 2:255-56.

23. Cf. P. Browe, "Die Ausbreitung des Fronleichnamsfestes," JL 8 (1928), 142-43.

24. CommALI, cap. I, sect. III. 2 (p. 62).

25. Browe, *Die Verehrung*, p. 94, says: between 1264 and 1279.

26. R. Berger, *Kleines liturgisches Wörterbuch* (Freiburg, 1969), p. 136.

27. There is a Response of the Congregation of Rites to the Bishop of Graz-Seckau (July 8, 1959): "Since the ceremony is not a liturgical action but 'pious exercise,' the bishop is to make use of his own authority." The exchange of letters is reprinted in LJ 11 (1961), 58. Consequently, during the Easter season of 1960, seventeen German bishops issued a new set of regulations for the Corpus Christi procession (Regensburg, 1960).

28. Cf., e.g., A. Häussling, "Leitideen für Fronleichnam heute," Gd 3 (1969), 78-79.

29. W. Dürig, "Zur Liturgie des Fronleichnamsfeier," in *Am Tisch des Wortes*, Neue Reihe 113 (Stuttgart, 1971), p. 17.

30. Encyclical Letter *Annum sacrum*, in ASS, 1899, pp. 646-51.

31. AAS 48 (1956), 309-53. For the history of the Sacred Heart devotion, cf., among others, J. Stierli (ed.), *Heart of the Saviour: A Symposium on Devotion to the Sacred Heart*, tr. by P. Andrews (New York, 1958); more briefly, Stierli, "Herz-Jesu-Verehrung I u. II," LTK 5 (1960), 289-91. There is also a two-volume standard work: A. Bea and H. Rahner (eds.), *Cor. Jesu. Commentationes in Litteras Encyclicas Pii XII "Haurietis aquas"* (Rome, 1959), which contains a bibliography of 140 pages. On the theology of devotion to the Sacred Heart, cf. K. Rahner, "Some Theses for a Theology of Devotion to the Sacred Heart," in his *Theological Investigations* 3, tr. by K.-H. and B. Kruger (Baltimore, 1967), pp. 331-52.

32. K. Rahner, ibid., p. 145.

33. Reflections on principles in F. Schwendimann, "Herz-Jesu-Verehrung und Seelsorge nach 'Haurietis aquas,'" in Bea-Rahner (eds.), *Cor Jesu*, 2:421-55. New forms for the practice of the devotion are given by, among others, J. Seuffert, *Der Herz-Jesu-Freitag. Modelle für Messfeiern und Andachten* (Munich, 1977).

34. AAS 17 (1925), 593-610.

35. Ibid., p. 603, tr. by J. H. Ryan, *The Encyclicals of Pius XI* (St. Louis, 1927), pp. 142 and 144.

36. Ibid., p. 603 (Ryan, p. 153). This kind of "ulterior purpose" for a feast is not fully consonant with the Christian idea of a feast.

37. *Liturgie*, p. 314.

38. AAS 17 (1925), 608 (Ryan, p. 152).

39. Vatican II, *Pastoral Constitution on the Church in the Modern World*, no. 45 (Flannery, p. 947).

40. Details in Radó 2:1303-4.

41. Historical documentation in, e.g., Righetti 2:261; Pascher, p. 591.

42. Chapters 48–49 (pp. 126-28).

43. Cf. Righetti 4:390; H. Frank, "Anniversarium," LTK 1:577-79.

44. Cap. II (Variationes), for August 5 (p. 133).

45. Cf. Eisenhofer 1:590.

46. In *The Rites of the Catholic Church* 2 (New York, 1980), pp. 185-293.

47. Cf. Radó 2:1099.

48. *Sermo* 19, 2 (PL 54:186).

49. *Sermo* 94, 3 (PL 54:459).

50. *Sermo* 13 (PL 54:172).

51. *Sermo* 12, 4 (PL 54:171); cf. 90, 1 (PL 54:447); 92, 1. 2 (PL 54:453-54); etc.

52. *Sermo* 12, 4 (PL 54:171).

53. Thus Pope Gelasius in a decree attributed to him (PL 59:158).

54. Cf. G. Morin, "L'origine des Quatre-Temps," *Revue bénédictine* 14 (1897), 336 ff.

55. *Christian Worship: Its Origin and Evolution*, pp. 232-33.

56. Cf. J. A. Jungmann, "Altchristliche Gebetsordnung im Lichte des Regelbuches von 'En Fešcha," ZKT 75 (1953), 217-18: "But may not these measures connected with the seasons . . . be a kind of precursor of the Roman ember weeks? Isidore and the entire Middle Ages after him assumed that the ember days are based on Jewish tradition."

57. GNLYC, no. 46.

58. CommALI, cap. I, sect. III. 3 (p. 63).

59. R. Berger, "Erntedank," Gd 6 (1972), 130.

60. Ibid.

61. *Liber officialis* I, 37 (ed. Hanssens 2:178).

62. CommALI, cap. I, sect. III. 3 (p. 63).

63. CommNC, cap. II (Variationes), for April 25 (p. 120).

64. Detailed descriptions of both processions, with documentation, in Eisenhofer 1:556-57; Pascher, pp. 220-21; Radó 2:1256-57.

65. Gregory of Tours, *Historia Francorum* II, 34 (PL 71:231-32).

66. Righetti 2:229.

67. GNLYC, no. 45.

68. Cf. ibid., no. 46, Cf. also the Congregation for Divine Worship, Instruction on Particular Calendars (June 24, 1970), chap. 3, no. 38, in AAS 62 (1970), 660.

69. The formulation, Days of Special Prayer in England and Wales, continues as follows: The Episcopal Conference recommends that, apart from the exceptions noted below, these days of special prayer be observed on Fridays, since these are traditionally days of penance and prayer, and days on which many parishes habitually celebrate a Mass in the evening. On these days any priest may celebrate the occasional Mass suitable to the intention of the day (see below). To ensure the fuller participation of the faithful, however, the appropriate occasional Mass may be celebrated, when this is indicated, once only in any one church or chapel on the appropriate Sunday.

Particular days of special prayer are:

For world peace to be celebrated on the day of prayer for peace (the day appointed) using the Mass for peace and justice.

For Christian unity to be celebrated on Friday between 18 and 25 January (week of prayer for Christian unity). Also, one Mass on the Sunday between 18 and 25 January using the Mass for unity of Christians.

For the needy and hungry of the world to be celebrated on the two family fast days, i.e., Friday of the first week of Lent, and Friday before the first Sunday of October using the Mass in time of famine or for those who suffer from famine.

For God's blessing on human work to be celebrated on either 1 May or (since many priests would like to begin the month of May with a Mass of Our Lady) the Monday before Ascension Thursday using the Mass for St. Joseph the Worker or for productive land or for the blessing of men's labour.

For vocations to the priesthood and to the religious life to be celebrated on the world day of prayer for vocations (4 Sunday of Easter) using the

Mass of the Sunday. Also, a day of prayer for vocations in this country: Friday before the 4 Sunday of Easter using the Mass for priestly vocations or for religious or for religious vocations.

Thanksgiving for the harvest and/or the fruits of human work to be celebrated on Friday between 22 and 28 September. Also, one Mass on a Sunday arranged locally using the Mass after the harvest.

The Saints' Feasts in the Liturgical Year

In speaking earlier of the structure of the liturgical year (Chapter III, 4) I noted that in addition to the temporal cycle there is also a garland, so to speak, of saints' feasts and memorials that is closely interwoven with the temporal cycle. It includes the festal commemoration of the Mother of Jesus, the apostles and martyrs, and the great throng of holy men and women from every walk of life and stratum of society who have taken the following of Christ with full seriousness. Before I describe their feasts and memorials, it is appropriate that I set down a few brief but basic ideas and comments on the theology of veneration of the saints, the history of this veneration, and the guidelines for the reform of the calendar of saints' feasts.

1 / THE VENERATION OF THE SAINTS: SOME PRINCIPLES

a/The Theology of Veneration of the Saints

The veneration of the saints—and this includes above all the cult of Mary Mother of God—has often had to be defended against the suspicion and objection that it denies the sole mediatorship of Christ. It must in fact be admitted that at many times and in many countries there have been exaggerations and erroneous or even improper practices connected with the veneration of Mary and the saints. Yet the official teaching of the Church has never lost sight of the principle enunciated in 1 Timothy 2.5-6: "There is one God, and there is one mediator between God and man, the man Christ Jesus, who gave himself as a ransom for all."

When the Church venerates the saints she is acknowledging and proclaiming the victorious grace of the one Redeemer and Mediator, Christ. She is thanking the Father for the mercy that is bestowed in Christ and that has taken visible, effective form in one of her members and thus in the body of the Church as a whole. There is perhaps no better liturgical expression of this aspect of veneration of the saints than in the two prefaces of holy men and women. In these we read, among other statements: "You are glorified in your saints, for their glory is the crowning of your gifts" (I). "You renew the Church in every age by raising up men and women outstanding in holiness, living witnesses of your unchanging love" (II). The preface of the martyrs formulates the same idea in other terms: "Your holy martyr N. followed the example of Christ and gave his (her) life for the glory of your name. His (her) death reveals your power shining through our human weakness." Elsewhere: "What love you show us as you recall mankind to its first innocence and invite us to taste on earth the gifts of the world to come!" (preface of virgins and religious). The same praise and gratitude find expression in the two prefaces of the Blessed Virgin Mary: "Through the power of the Holy Spirit, she became the virgin mother of your only Son, our Lord Jesus Christ, who is for ever the light of the world" (I); "In celebrating the memory of the Blessed Virgin Mary, it is our special joy to echo her song of thanksgiving. What wonders you have worked throughout the world!'' (II).

The manner in which the saints accepted the grace of God and brought it to fruition is for those still on earth a sign and testimony of faith, a living good news, an example and model that can bring us courage, perseverance and hope as we endeavor to live our own lives as Christians. I do not mean, of course, that we are to copy them in an external way, but rather that we receive from them a wealth of stimuli and helps in our very personal, concrete efforts as individual Christians to follow Christ in our own time and place.

A final but not least important element in veneration of the saints is confidence in approaching them as brothers and sisters of Christ, telling them of our personal cares and needs, and asking them to intercede with God the giver of all good gifts. We have this confidence because we are sure of the fraternal solidarity of all who belong to Christ.

> The "invocation" of the saints is, in the last analysis, simply the courage to love, to say "Thou" despite any death that may threaten, and the faith that no human being lives alone but that in Christ every life has value for all in God's sight. And the "intercession" of the saints does not mean that they form a department of mediators or a series of jurisdictions. It means rather that every life of faith and love possesses an eternal value and significance for all and that those who have been redeemed are happy to accept and live out this value and significance. And because we are dealing here with a spiritual world to which God has communicated himself and in which everything depends on every individual and each can be important to the others, it follows that the explicit or implicit invocation either of an "official" saint or of some departed person who is loved with faith and hope by an individual Christian is always an invocation of *all* the saints; that is, it is a faith-inspired recourse to the full community of all the redeemed.[1]

All these aspects of veneration of the saints have also found authoritative expression in the Second Vatican Council, whose teaching is well adapted to doing away with misunderstanding among both the united and the separated brethren. In the very first document which the Council produced we read: "By celebrating their [the saints'] anniversaries the Church proclaims achievement of the paschal mystery in the saints who have suffered and been glorified with Christ. She proposes them to the faithful as examples who draw all men to the Father through Christ, and through their merits she begs God's favors" (CL, no. 104; Flannery, p. 29). "The feasts of the saints proclaim the wonderful works of Christ in his servants and offer to the faithful fitting examples for their imitation" (CL, no. 111; Flannery, p. 31).

The *Dogmatic Constitution on the Church* speaks at greater length about veneration of the saints, after Pope John XXIII had made known his wish that this subject not be passed over. Chapter 7 of this Constitution describes "the eschatological nature of the pilgrim Church and her union with the heavenly Church."[2] Article 50, after a brief historical survey of the veneration of the saints, sees the significance of these men and women as residing in the fact that they point the way for us by their example and that veneration of them is an expression of the brotherly love which strengthens the unity of the Church in her entirety.

> Exactly as Christian communion between men on their earthly pilgrimage brings us closer to Christ, so our community with the saints joins us to Christ, from whom as from its fountain and head issues all grace and the life of the People of God itself. It is most fitting, therefore, that we love those friends and co-heirs of Jesus Christ who are also our brothers and outstanding benefactors, and that we give due thanks to God for them, "humbly invoking them, and having recourse to their prayers, their aid and help in obtaining from God through his Son, Jesus Christ, Our Lord, our only Redeemer and Savior, the benefits we need" (*Constitution on the Church*, no. 50; Flannery, p. 411).

In Article 51 the Council appeals to "the venerable faith of our ancestors" and "proposes again the decrees of the Second Council of Nicaea, of the Council of Florence, and of the Council of Trent." At the same time, it urges "all concerned" to remove or correct any abuses, excesses of defects which may have crept in here or there. . . . Let us teach the faithful, therefore, that the authentic cult of the saints does not consist so much in a multiplicity of external acts, but rather in a more intense practice of our love, whereby, for our own greater good and that of the Church, we seek from the saints "example in their way of life, fellowship in their communion, and the help of their intercession." On the other hand, let the faithful be taught that our communion with these in heaven, provided that it is understood in the full light of faith, in no way diminishes the worship of adoration given to God the Father, through Christ, in the Spirit; on the contrary, it greatly enriches it (*Constitution on the Church*, no. 51; Flannery, pp. 412-13).

What I have been saying thus far about veneration of the saints generally applies in a special and unique way to Mary the Mother of Jesus Christ. Her election as virginal mother of the Redeemer, the fullness of grace that was given to her in view of her divine maternity, the readiness for service and self-sacrifice that marked her response to God's call: all of these make her superior to all the other saints in holiness and in cooperation with the work of redemption. Here again are some authoritative expressions of Catholic faith from Vatican II:

The *Constitution of the Liturgy* sums up concisely the essential aspects of veneration of Mary: "In celebrating this annual cycle of the mysteries of Christ, Holy Church honors Blessed Mary, Mother of God, with a special love. She is inseparably linked with her Son's saving work. In her the Church admires and exalts the most excellent fruit of redemption, and joyfully contemplates as in a faultless image, that which she herself desires and hopes wholly to be" (CL, no. 103; Flannery, p. 29).

More comprehensive statements on Mariology are to be found in the *Dogmatic Constitution on the Church*, which devotes to her the rather lengthy final chapter entitled: "The Role of the Blessed Virgin Mary, Mother of God, in the Mystery of Christ and the Church" (chapter 8).[3] The very title already brings out the christological and ecclesiological dimensions of Catholic

Mariology; it is these aspects that shape this entire chapter of the conciliar document. The basic statements about Mary are given concisely in the introduction to the chapter:

> The Virgin Mary, who at the message of the angel received the Word of God in her heart and in her body and gave life to the world, is acknowledged and honored as being truly the Mother of God and of the redeemer. Redeemed, in a more exalted fashion, by reason of the merits of her Son and united to him by a close and indissoluble tie, she is endowed with the high office and dignity of the Mother of the Son of God, and therefore she is also the beloved daughter of the Father and the temple of the Holy Spirit. Because of this gift of sublime grace she far surpasses all creatures, both in heaven and on earth. But, being of the race of Adam, she is at the same time also united to all those who are to be saved; indeed, "she is clearly the mother of the members of Christ . . . since she has by her charity joined in bringing about the birth of believers in the Church, who are members of its head" (Augustine). Wherefore she is hailed as pre-eminent and as a wholly unique member of the Church, and as its type and outstanding model in faith and charity. The Catholic Church taught by the Holy Spirit, honors her with filial affection and devotion as a most beloved mother (*Constitution on the Church*, no. 53; Flannery, p. 414).

The divine maternity of Mary also finds expression in cooperation with the work of redemption, so that she becomes, in a transferred sense, the mother of all the redeemed (no. 61).

> Taken up to heaven she did not lay aside this saving office but by her manifold intercession continues to bring us the gifts of eternal salvation. By her maternal charity, she cares for the brethren of her Son. . . . Therefore the Blessed Virgin is invoked in the Church under the titles of Advocate, Helper, Benefactress, and Mediatrix. This, however, is so understood that it neither takes away anything from nor adds anything to the dignity and efficacy of Christ the one Mediator (no. 62; Flannery, p. 419).

Because of Mary's unique role the Council urges veneration of her, especially liturgical veneration; in this context the Council warns theologians and preachers against "all false exaggeration" but also against "too summary an attitude" toward her dignity. "Let the faithful remember moreover that true devotion consists neither in sterile or transitory affection, nor in a certain vain credulity, but proceeds from true faith, by which we are led to recognize the excellence of the Mother of God, and we are moved to a filial love toward our mother and to the imitation of her virtues" (no. 67; Flannery, p. 422).

Among postconciliar declarations on veneration of Mary the Apostolic Exhortation *Marialis cultus* of Pope Paul VI (February 2, 1974) deserves special attention.[4] In the first part of this document the many close connections between the liturgy and veneration of Mary are pointed out (nos. 1–23). The second part offers "Guidelines for Devotion to the Blessed Virgin" (nos. 24–38). Marian devotions would be trinitarian and christological in their focus (no. 25); they must give due place to the person and work of the Holy Spirit (nos. 26–27) and show a clear awareness of the Church (no. 28); they must carefully follow "guidelines from Scripture, liturgy, ecumenism and anthropology" (nos. 29–38). "The ultimate purpose of devotion to the Blessed Virgin is to glorify God and lead Christians to commit themselves to a life which conforms absolutely to His will" (no. 39).

The third part of the Exhortation singles out the Angelus (no. 41) and the rosary (nos. 42–54) as specially recommended forms of Marian devotion. In this context the Pope's warning against exaggeration is worth quoting: "We . . . recommend that this very worthy devotion [the rosary] not be propagated in a way that is too one-sided or exclusive. The rosary is an excellent prayer, but the faithful should feel serenely free toward it. Its intrinsic appeal should draw them to calm recitation" (no. 55).

The Apostolic Exhortation ends by underscoring the theological value of Marian devotion and showing its pastoral value for the renewal of Christian life (nos. 57–58).[5]

b/The History of Veneration of the Saints

The history of the veneration of the saints is so multifaceted and complex and calls for such careful distinctions of time and place that in a book such as this there can be no question of anything but a brief sketch of its important phases.[6]

The second century marks the beginning of veneration of the saints, in the proper sense of the phrase. The first to be venerated were those Christians who gave their lives and thus became witnesses to Christ in a unique way. Bishop Polycarp of Smyrna († ca. 155) was probably the first martyr to be given cultic honors by his community. Initially, the cult of the martyrs was confined to the communities and places which could show possession of the tomb or mortal remains of the martyr in question. Later on, however, many martyrs were taken into the festal calendar of other communities as well. There was an effort to make up for lack of possession of the tomb by relics (including "contact relics") or, still later, by images of the martyr.

With regard to the spiritual origin of this cult of the martyrs Theodor Klauser justly observes: "The Christian cult of the martyrs is rooted in the high esteem and private veneration of the just person and the martyr that had been inherited from Judaism."[7]

At an early stage veneration like that shown to the martyrs was also shown to the apostles as the official witnesses who had been appointed by Christ himself and to whom he had given the promise that they would "sit on twelve thrones judging the twelve tribes of Israel" (Mt 19.28b). Special veneration was also shown to the confessors, that is, those who in time of persecution had not been put to death but did suffer torture, imprisonment and exile. Once the great persecutions of Christians had come to an end, well-known bishops like Gregory Thaumaturgus in the East and Martin of Tours in the West gradually came to be looked on as "martyrs." Finally, the throng of those venerated came to include ascetics and virgins who had been extraordinary in their following of Christ; the entire lives of these individuals was considered to be a kind of bloodless martyrdom.

At a quite early date altars, chapels or even basilicas were built over the tombs of these saints; the acts of the martyrs were read there, and the eucharist was celebrated. Veneration of these men and women did not take the form merely of remembering and honoring their *Natale* ("birthday," i.e., the day of their death) and imitating their virtues, but also meant invoking them and asking their intercession. As in the veneration of holy men and women in late Judaism, so in the Christian veneration of the saints people trusted in the intercession of their martyrs and saints before the throne of God.[8]

The early concentration on the apostles and martyrs may be the reason why there is no clear evidence of a cult of the Mother of God in the first three centuries. However, in addition to the honorable references to Mary in the New Testament we do have the Eve–Mary parallel being developed in the second century (Justin, Irenaeus) and, once the third century begins, praise of her virginal motherhood becomes very frequent. The first expression of a cultic veneration is perhaps a Coptic papyrus from the third century, containing a text that is still used today in the Greek liturgy and is also familiar to the West: "In the shelter of your mercy we take refuge, Mother of God. Despise not our petition in our need, but rescue us from danger, O you who alone are pure and blessed."[9] In section 2 of this chapter I shall speak of the origin and form of the various feasts of Mary.

In order to counteract the uncontrolled extension of veneration of the saints to ever new individuals the Church developed a process of canonization. The first example of such a process was the canonization of Bishop Ulrich of Augsburg († 973) by Pope John XV at a Roman synod in 993. As the number of applications for canonization continually increased, the criteria became stricter; the primary emphasis was on the following of Christ and on proof of miracles that occurred in answer to prayers addressed to the person in question. The rules set down in the present Code of Canon Law, canons 1999–2141, go back, in essentials, to Benedict XIV.

The Middle Ages showed a passionate but theologically undernourished concentration on the saints. It had three characteristics:

These are (a) the specialization of the saints and the assignment of certain roles to them; (b) the parcelling out and distribution of relics as pledges of help from many saints at once; (c) a belief in and obsession with miracles. . . . The Church's teaching was less and less frequently preached to the people in a way they could understand. In religious practice imitation of the saints became less important than invocation of them. In the popular mind the saints developed from intercessors into helpers. The danger of undisciplined religiosity was intensified by the fact that the increasingly passionate cult of the saints was concentrated in places of pilgrimage that possessed large collections of relics, while the practice of seeking indulgences, which was rampant at these shrines, gave still greater encouragement to a quantitative way of thinking.[10]

In view of this widespread eclipse of the Church's authentic veneration of the saints it is not surprising that the Reformers turned against all such veneration, sometimes in a violent manner. It is all the more gratifying, therefore, that in the modern Churches of the Reformation more and more individuals are concerned with developing an authentic veneration of the saints, including Mary.[11]

The exaggerated medieval cult of the saints meant that in the liturgy the temporal cycle was largely obscured by veneration of the saints. In the fifteenth century, it is true, many theologians and bishops issued warnings and called for a reduction in the number of saints' feasts. Many provincial and diocesan synods before and during the Council of Trent (1545–63) took steps in the same direction, but with no lasting success.[12] At the Council itself there were divergent views on the subject, and as a result no reform either of the liturgy or the calendar could be effected. Therefore at the final session of the Council (December 4, 1563) the Fathers entrusted both reforms to the pope.

The reform commission which Pius IV appointed in 1564 saw "the introduction of a uniform and universally binding liturgy as being the most effective solution to the problems of reform."[13] The Breviary (1568) and Missal (1570) which Pius V promulgated saw a sizable reduction in the number of saints' feasts. A general calendar was published for the first time; it was based on the ancient calendar of the city of Rome. Now there were "only" 158 saints' feasts as compared with 156 ferias. According to the principle enunciated in both Breviary and Missal only those exceptional liturgical forms and therefore only those particular calendars could be retained which could prove they had been in use for over two hundred years. But many dioceses and Orders chose not to use their privilege, and the result was a liturgical uniformity which at that time was thought to be healthy and permanent.

But this expectation was not realized as far as the calendar of the saints was concerned. For reasons which I cannot take up here[14] the beginning of our century saw an overloading of the festal calendar once again. The general calendar contained 230 feasts; many diocesan calendars added over 100 special feasts of their own. Thus the praiseworthy intention of Trent, namely, to give greater emphasis to the temporal cycle of the liturgical year, was once again frustrated.

Pope Pius X (1903–14) hoped for an overall reform of the liturgy, but, looking at the situation realistically, he figured it would take thirty years to carry out. For the moment, he endeavored to reduce the excessive number of feasts by means of various rubrical regulations. In addition, he called for a reduction in the number of special feasts in the calendars of the dioceses and religious orders. Only a special connection between such a feast and a particular place could prevent the feast being dropped. This decision did in fact lead to a notable decrease in the number of local feasts, but hardly any change occurred in the general calendar. In fact, despite all these measures the next decade saw the introduction of new feasts into both the general calendar and the particular calendars. In 1950 there were 71 ferias and 262 saints' feasts.

c/Guidelines for the Reform of the Calendar of the Saints

In view of the importance of veneration of the saints, on the one hand, and, on the other, the need of reform in the calendar of the saints, the Second Vatican Council in its *Constitution on the Sacred Liturgy* published important guidelines for a future calendar.

The basic principle is the priority of the temporal cycle over the sanctoral, "so that the entire cycle of the mysteries of salvation may be suitably recalled" (CL, no. 108; Flannery, p. 30); "the feasts of the saints should (not) take precedence over the feasts which commemorate the very mysteries of salvation" (CL, no. 111; Flannery, p. 31).

To attain this goal the Council chose a way that had been very familiar to the early Church: namely, to link the feasts of the saints more closely to the local Churches, or, in other words, to decentralize the calendar of the saints: "Many of them [the feasts of the saints] should be left to be celebrated by a particular Church, or nation, or family of religious. Only those should be extended to the universal Church which commemorate saints who are truly of universal importance" (ibid.). The principle is clear; it is also correct both in what it says and in terms of tradition. At the same time, however, it introduces an element of subjectivity, inasmuch as the criterion of "universal importance" can be applied in varying ways by different persons and groups. "The Roman liturgical commission (*Consilium ad exsequendam Constitutionam de sacra liturgia*) which Paul VI established in his Apostolic Letter *Sacram liturgiam* of January 25, 1964 and entrusted with the implementation of the liturgical reform, was therefore faced with no easy task when it came to reform of the calendar."[15]

The first guideline for its work was that it should reduce the number or at least the importance of the "idea-feasts"; the reference was especially to feasts of the Lord and the Blessed Virgin. The Commentary on the *General Norms* notes that over the last 300 years 16 idea-feasts have been given a place in the general calendar, four of them as first-class feasts and seven as second-class feasts. "Many of these feasts reflect the piety specific to an age or a religious family. . . . It is in the nature of feasts of devotion that few of them should be retained in the general calendar; the rest of them may be left to particular calendars, or their Mass formularies may simply be kept among the votive Masses."[16] The next section of this chapter will take up the Marian feasts in detail. Further guidelines have to do with the choice of saints and the reorganization of their feasts. This will be the subject of section three, below.

All this work on a new calendar bore fruit in the Roman Calendar, revised in accordance with the decree of the Second Vatican Council and promulgated by authority of Pope Paul VI. This new calendar was published by decree of the Congregation of Rites on March 21, 1969, after Paul VI had approved it in his Apostolic Letter *motu proprio Mysterii paschalis* of February 14, 1969. This lengthy document includes (a) the General Norms for the Liturgical Year and the Calendar; (b) the General Roman Calendar with introductory explanations; and (c) the new Litany of the Saints in two basic forms, with some variants. An extensive commentary on these three parts, by the Consilium for Implementing the Constitution on the Sacred Liturgy, completes the document.[17]

In addition to the General Roman Calendar, which forms the basis for the celebration of the liturgical year, the document allows for calendars of individual churches and religious communities and lays down precise rules for these (GNLYC, nos. 49–57). These regulations are supplemented by an Instruction from the Sacred Congregation for Divine Worship, dated June 24, 1970. Especially noteworthy is the provision in the *General Norms* that in addition to the particular calendars of dioceses and religious communities there can also be common calendars for "entire provinces, regions, countries, or even larger areas"; these are to be prepared with the cooperation of all interested parties (no. 51). The same principle applies to calendars for religious communities. In summary, then, the calendar to be followed in a particular parish is a composite document with contributions from the general (= Roman), regional, diocesan and local calendars.

To what extent does the General Roman Calendar meet the expectations cherished in regard to the feasts of the saints? This is a question I shall take up later on. For the moment, let me turn to a more detailed description of the feasts and memorials of Mary Mother of God that are to be found in the general calendar.

2 / FEASTS AND MEMORIALS OF MARY MOTHER OF GOD

Although, as the historical survey showed, the feasts of Mary came into existence after the memorials of the martyrs and the feasts of the apostles, they should be described first. The fact that there are so relatively many Marian feasts and memorials is a sign of the love, gratitude and high esteem the Church has for the Mother of God. However, it is sometimes forgotten that there can be excess when it comes to feasts and that such excess does more harm than good to the authentic veneration of Mary.[18] Although the revision of the calendar has led to the elimination of some needless duplications, there are still a good many Marian feasts and memorials of quite diverse importance and rank.

For clarity's sake, I shall first present the solemnities and feasts in the order of their annual occurrence; then I shall turn to the memorials. But first let me remind the reader that the feasts formerly known as the Purification of Mary and the Annunciation of Mary have already been dealt with among the feasts of the Lord, and the Solemnity of the Mother of God in connection with the octave of Christmas.

Solemnity of the Immaculate Conception (December 8)

The object of this feast is the belief that from the first instant of her existence in the womb of her mother Ann, Mary was "by a singular grace and privilege of almighty God, and in view of the merits of Jesus Christ, Savior of the human race, preserved free from all stain of original sin."[19]

Many factors entered into the establishment of this feast. In the East, around 700, there was already a feast of the "Conception of Mary by St. Ann" on December 9, that is, nine months before the feast of Mary's birth on September 8. The aim of this feast was to celebrate the fact that (according to the apocryphal *Protoevangelium of James*[20]) Ann conceived Mary despite her barrenness and advanced years. This feast soon entered southern Italy, which at that time was Byzantine territory, and passed from there to England and France. In the latter countries, however, the emphasis of the feast shifted to Mary's being conceived immaculately, that is, to the fact that she began her life untouched by original sin.

Even so great a devotee of Mary as Bernard of Clairvaux objected to such a feast in a letter he wrote to the canons of Lyons, since in his view, all human beings, Mary included, required redemption from original sin, even if this deliverance might take place in the womb, as it did in the case of John the Baptist.[21] The theologians gradually ceased objecting only when around 1300, chiefly due to the work of Duns Scotus, the Immaculate Conception was interpreted as a preservative redemption. In 1476 Sixtus IV approved the feast of the Conception of the Immaculate Virgin Mary; in 1708 Clement XI extended it to the entire Church.

The definition of the Immaculate Conception as a dogma by Pius IX had the effect of giving the feast itself a more solid basis. New texts for the Office and Mass appeared in 1863. Leo XIII made the Immaculate Conception a first-class feast with an octave. The Missal of Paul VI has kept the Mass formulary of 1863 for the most part, but has introduced new readings, new intermediate songs, and a special preface.[22]

The entrance antiphon puts words from the Book of Isaiah (61.10) on Mary's lips: "I exult for joy in the Lord, my soul rejoices in my God, for he has clothed me with the garment of salvation and robed me in the cloak of justice like a bride adorned with her jewels." With Mary's privileged grace in mind the presidential prayers ask for deliverance from sin. The special preface locates the festal mystery within the history of salvation and praises Mary as model and first embodiment of the Church, as spotless bride of Christ, and as our pattern of holiness. "Help us by her prayers to live in your presence without sin" (opening prayer).

The gospel is the passage describing the annunciation of the Lord (Lk 1.26-38). The Old Testament reading (Gen 3.9-15) contains not only the judgment passed on the serpent but also the "protoevangelium" (first gospel), according to which there will be enmity between the serpent and the woman and between the progeny of these two: "He shall bruise your head, and you shall bruise his heel." "Although it cannot be claimed that there is a reference here to the Redeemer and his mother as determinate individuals, the text does speak of the tempter being overcome by the posterity of those he has seduced. To this extent the description of this passage as a 'protoevangelium' is justified."[23] Many of the Fathers saw in Genesis 3.15 a promise that Christ (according to the Vulgate, "the woman") would overcome the power of evil.

The responsorial psalm (98.1, 2-4) accepts such an interpretation in terms of salvation history when it urges us: "Sing to the Lord a new song, for he has done marvelous deeds." The second reading (Eph 1.3-6, 11-12) praises the gracious act of redemption; though it is not mentioned explicitly, Mary's cooperation is intended as well.

Feast of the Visitation of Mary (May 31)

The object of this feast is given in the biblical story of Mary's visit to her cousin Elizabeth after the Annunciation of the Lord (Lk 1.39-56). The visit is the occasion for Mary's hymn of praise, the Magnificat. At the same time—so it was thought—the meeting brought about the sanctification of the Precursor in his mother's womb (Lk 1.44 with 1.15). Biblical events like this one had a profound effect on the soul and imagination of medieval men and women. It was chiefly the Franciscans who made the Visitation the object of festal commemoration. Bonaventure, their Minister General, introduced the feast into the Order in 1263. July 2, which until recently was the date of the feast, was chosen because it was the day after the octave of the feast of John the Baptist's birth (June 24).

Urban VI gave official recognition to the feast and, after he died, Boniface IX renewed the approbation in 1389. Only under Pius V, however, did the feast find acceptance in the general calendar and become obligatory for the universal Church. In 1850, after his return from exile, Pius IX made it a double of the second class. The new Roman Calendar has moved the feast to May 31. The reason given is that a date between the solemnities of the Annunciation and the Birth of John the Baptist accords better with the gospel story.[24]

The formulary for the Mass of the feast is much changed from the old formulary. The gospel (Lk 1.39-56) gives the complete text of the Magnificat instead of just the opening verse, and adds v. 56 with its reference to the completion of the three-month visit. The new presidential prayers focus much more sharply than the old ones did on the various aspects of the biblical event, and lead up to corresponding petitions. Thus, Mary, guided by the Spirit, hastened to Elizabeth: "Keep us open to the workings of your Spirit" (opening prayer); "Father, make our sacrifice acceptable and holy, as you accepted the love of Mary" (prayer over the gifts); "May we always recognize with joy the presence of Christ in the eucharist we celebrate, as John the Baptist hailed the presence of our Savior in the womb of Mary" (concluding prayer). The Old Testament reading (Zeph 3.14-18) bids its hearers be joyful, for "the Lord your God is in your midst, a warrior who gives victory." The New Testament reading (Rom 12.9-16b) contains advice on living a Christian life like Mary's.

Solemnity of Mary's Assumption into Heaven (August 15)

There is a quasi-precursor of this feast in the "Day of Mary Mother of God" which is attested for August 15 in a mid-fifth-century lectionary from Jerusalem (extant in an Armenian translation).[25] This ancient feast was rather general in its object and it soon became a commemoration of the *Natale* ("birthday"), i.e., death of Mary (Greek: *koimēsis*; Latin: *dormitio*; = "falling asleep") of Mary. The feast in this form was extended to the entire Byzantine empire by Emperor Maurice (582–602).

The sixth-century Gallic liturgy had a feast of Mary on January 18; in the seventh century this was celebrated as the "Feast of Mary's Assumption" (Bobbio Sacramentary).[26] A feast called *Natale Sanctae Mariae* on August 15 is attested for the middle of the seventh century in Rome (Evangeliary of the Würzburg *Comes*). Under Pope Sergius I (687–701), a Syrian who did much to introduce Eastern feasts of Mary to Rome, the feast in question was celebrated as a feast of her death, and included a procession from the church of St. Adrian to the church of St. Mary. In the Gregorian Sacramentary which Pope Adrian I (772–95) sent to Emperor Charlemagne, the name of the feast is given as "Assumption of Holy Mary." The first prayer, to be read in connection with the procession, says that although the Mother of God died, "she could not be kept in the chains of death."[27]

At an early date this feast was given a vigil and an octave. It acquired special stature when Pope Pius XII, on November 1, 1950, defined Mary's Assumption into heaven to be a dogma. Special heed was given to this dogma of the faith in the new texts (1950–51) assigned for Office and Mass.

According to the new Roman Calendar the vigil can be celebrated with an evening Mass on the 14th; the formulary for this Mass is dominated by the theme of the feast itself. The formulary for the festal Mass is still, for the most part, the 1950 formulary. The two nongospel readings and the special preface are new. The gospel is the same as on the feast of the Visitation; the reason for this is evidently the presence of the Magnificat which on August 15 becomes a hymn of praise sung by the new glorified Mother of God; as such it takes on a special tonality.

The first reading (Rev 11.19a; 12.1, 3-6a, 10ab) recounts the vision of the struggle of the dragon with the woman and her child; this is an apocalyptic description of the conflict between the people of God and the kingdom of Satan, which ends with the power of God winning the victory: "Now the salvation and the power and kingdom of our God and the authority of his Christ have come." Like many of the Fathers, the liturgy sees the woman as also representing Mary (with her child), since Mary is so clearly connected with the mystery and destiny of the Church.

The second reading (1 Cor 15.20-26) speaks of Christ as the first to be raised from the dead and as the pledge of our own resurrection, which has already become a reality in Mary. The mystery of this feast finds expression above all in the special preface: the Mother of God who has been taken into heaven and whose body did not undergo corruption, is "the beginning and the pattern of the Church in its perfection, and a sign of hope and comfort for your people on their pilgrim way." The opening prayer speaks of Mary first as sinless, thus intimating the theological connection between sin and bodily corruption, on the one hand, and sinlessness and assumption into heaven, on the other.

Feast of the Birth of Mary (September 8)

This is another Marian feast that originated in the East. It probably goes back to a feast of the dedication of St. Anne's church in Jerusalem, which was built in the fifth century on the supposed site of the house in which Mary was born. The hymns of the Greek composer Romanos, who worked as a deacon in Constantinople around 500, allow the inference that in his day the feast of Mary's Birth had won fervent acceptance among the people.[28]

There is evidence that the feast was celebrated in Rome in the seventh century and that like the other Marian feasts from the East, such as the Assumption of Mary into heaven, it was, by order of Pope Sergius I, the occasion for a procession. In the thirteenth century the feast acquired an octave, but this was abolished in the rubrical reform of 1955. It is the third feast of an earthly birth in the Roman liturgy, the other two being the births of the Lord and of John the Baptist.

The Mass of the feast sees Mary's birth primarily in the perspective of her divine maternity and the birth of her Son. This is true of the entrance antiphon, the opening prayer and the prayer over the gifts, the alleluia verse and the communion antiphon. Mary has "brought the dawn of hope and salvation to the world" (concluding prayer). The preface (preface of the Blessed Virgin Mary I or II) praises her for being chosen from the human race and being blessed above all other women. The gospel (Mt 1.1-16, 18-23) gives not only the genealogy of Jesus but also an account of the revelation Joseph received regarding Mary's virginal motherhood. The first reading (Micah 5.1-4a) contains the well-known promise to the town of Bethlehem that from it would come a ruler over Israel, a shepherd who would feed his flock in the strength of the Lord, a man who would bring peace. An alternate first reading is Romans 8.28-30 (call and justification of the elect).

I shall now describe briefly, in the order of their occurrence, the obligatory (M) and optional (m) memorials of Mary, but I shall not say anything about the Mass formularies.

a/Memorial (m) of Our Lady of Lourdes (February 11)
This memorial of Mary is based on the 18 apparitions granted to a young girl, Bernadette Soubirous, from February 11 to July 16, 1858. In the course of these apparitions Mary spoke of herself as "the Immaculate Conception." On February 11, 1908, the fiftieth anniversary of the first apparition, Pius X established a feast (double major). In the revision of the calendar it has been reduced to an optional memorial, and its name has been changed from "Feast of the Apparition of the Blessed Virgin Mary" to "Memorial of Our Lady of Lourdes." This title "makes it clearer that the object of the celebration is the Blessed Virgin Mary herself and not the historical fact of her appearances."[29]

In making the change of title for this reason, account had evidently been taken of the generally accepted teaching of the Church that private revelations cannot be an object of obligatory belief, even if they are recognized by the Church. "At the same time, however, such private revelations . . . are not to be condemned or judged valueless. They are a manifestation of the continuing prophetic gift and of the charisms which in particular situations bring the Church decisive stimuli, impulses and aids in her effort to actualize the inexhaustible and, at any given moment, unexhausted revelation of Christ in a way that meets the needs of the age."[30]

b/Memorial (m) of the Immaculate Heart of Mary (Saturday after the Feast of the Sacred Heart of Jesus)
John Eudes († 1680), who did so much to foster devotion to the Heart of Jesus, also promoted devotion to the "most holy heart" of Mary. Beginning in 1646, he and his religious congregation celebrated a feast of the Immaculate Heart which quickly spread throughout France. Ecclesiastical recognition of the feast, but not a universal extension of it, came under Pius VII at the beginning of the nineteenth century. It was Pius XII, himself deeply devoted to Mary, who by decree of the Congregation of

Rites in 1944 made it a feast (double of the second class) for the entire Church; it was to be celebrated on the octave day of Mary's Assumption into heaven.

On December 8, 1942, while the Second World War was raging, Pius XII had already consecrated the human race to the "most gentle heart" (old Breviary, second nocturn, sixth lesson) of the Mother of God. Another event that was not without influence on the acceptance of this feast into the Roman Calendar was the apparitions of the Mother of God at Fatima in Portugal on the thirteenth of the months of May through October, 1917 (apparitions recognized as credible, after careful examination, by the responsible Ordinary, the bishop of Leiria). In the new Roman Calendar the feast remains as an optional memorial, but has been transferred to the Saturday after the feast of the Sacred Heart (Saturday following the second Sunday after Pentecost).[31]

c/Memorial (m) of Our Lady of Mount Carmel (July 16)
This is primarily a feast of the Carmelites, who trace their origins back to a group of hermits on Mount Carmel and whose Rule received ecclesiastical approval at the beginning of the thirteenth century. On July 16, 1251, Simon Stock († 1265), then General of the Order, had a vision of the Mother of God in which she gave him a scapular (a stylized bit of clothing). This date was chosen as the date for a Marian feast of the Order that was introduced between 1376 and 1386 and was extended to the universal Church (as a double major) by Benedict XIII in 1726. In the 1960 Code of Rubrics it was retained only in the form of a commemoration; in the new calendar it is an optional memorial.

d/Memorial (M) of the Queenship of Mary (August 22)
Although during the Middle Ages Mary was regarded and venerated as Queen of the angels and saints, as numerous prayers and hymns attest, it was only in the nineteenth century that local feasts of Mary as Queen came to celebrated. In 1870 Spain and most Latin American dioceses were given the right to celebrate a feast of "Mary Queen of All the Saints" on May 31.[32] On November 1, 1954, at the close of the "Marian Year" Pius XII prescribed the feast (double of the second class) for the univer-

sal Church and kept May 31 as the date. The new Roman Calendar has transferred it to the octave day of the feast of Mary's Assumption into heaven, "in order to bring out more clearly between the Blessed Virgin Mary's Queenship and her Assumption."[33]

e/Memorial (M) of Our Lady of Sorrows

The roots of this popular memorial are in the special devotion to the Sorrowful Mother of God (Mater dolorosa) that became widespread in the Middle Ages, especially in Germany. The Provincial Synod of Cologne in 1423 seems to have ordered such a feast for the first time, assigning it to the third Sunday after Easter.[34] In 1721 Benedict XIII extended it to the entire Church under the name "Feast of the Seven Sorrows of the Blessed Virgin Mary" and assigned it to the Friday before Palm Sunday so as to make clearer the connection with the passion of Mary's Son.

Meanwhile a parallel feast had developed in the Order of Servites on the third Sunday of September (it had been permitted from 1667 on). In thanksgiving for his safe return from exile in France (1814) Pius VII extended this feast to the entire Church. In 1913 Pius X transferred it to September 15, the octave day of Mary's Birth and the day after the feast of the Exaltation of the Cross.

The seven sorrows of Mary were considered to be: the prophecy of Simon, the flight into Egypt, the loss of the twelve-year-old Jesus, the meeting with Jesus on the way of the cross, the hours spent beneath the cross, the resting of the dead Jesus on his mother's lap, and the laying of Jesus in the tomb.

The 1960 Code of Rubrics had already reduced the first of the two feasts just described to a commemoration, allowing it only in places where the old feast had taken deep root. The new calendar has eliminated it completely as being a duplication. In the process the feast on September 15 received a new name. Instead of "Feast of the Seven Sorrows of Mary" it is now called "Memorial of Our Lady of Sorrows."

The ten-stanza sequence that used to be read on the feast, the famous Stabat Mater ("At the cross her station keeping"), may still be said. As regards the authorship of this poem, "it was long thought to be the work of Jacopone da Todi († 1306). But Dreves voiced strong doubts about this, and today scholars prefer to regard Bonaventure († 1274) as the author of this truly Franciscan song."[35]

f/Memorial (M) of Our Lady of the Rosary (October 7)
The prehistory of this "feast of the Rosary" includes the extensive spread of the Rosary itself and of brotherhoods of the Rosary in the fifteenth and sixteenth centuries. There is evidence of a feast of the Rosary on the third Sunday of April as early as 1547 in Spain.[36] When Christians won an important naval battle over the Turks at Lepanto on October 7, 1571, their success was attributed to the praying of the Rosary, and Pius V ordered that on the anniversary of the victory a "feast of Our Lady of Victory" be celebrated. In 1573 his successor, Gregory XIII, allowed churches with a Rosary altar to celebrate a "feast of the Holy Rosary" on the first Sunday of October. When Prince Eugen again defeated the Turks at Peterwardein in 1716, Clement XI extended the feast to the entire Church. Pius X transferred it back to its original date, October 7. The 1960 Code of Rubrics changed its name to "Feast of Our Lady of the Rosary," and this has been retained in the new calendar.

g/Memorial (M) of the Presentation of Mary (November 21)
The impulse for this feast probably came from the feast of the Dedication of the Church of Santa Maria Nova in Jerusalem on November 21, 543. The name "Presentation of Mary" that was given to the Latin feast is based on a legendary account in the apocryphal Gospel of James (chapter 7), according to which at the age of three Mary was brought to the temple in order to be raised there by the (legendary!) "temple virgins." We find the feast being celebrated at Constantinople in the eighth century; under Emperor Manuel Comnenus it was introduced into the list of public holidays in 1166. It appeared in England in the twelfth century and in the fourteenth was introduced into the papal chapel at Avignon (1391). Sixtus IV brought it to Rome and allowed any church to celebrate it. Pius V, however, refused to admit it into the festal calendar for the revised Breviary and Missal because the object of the feast was a legend. Sixtus V had

no such hesitations and prescribed it for the universal Church in 1585. It has surprised many that this "feast" should have been kept in the new Roman calendar. The German regional calendar changes the name to "Memorial of Our Lady of Jerusalem," in an obvious effort to downplay somewhat its legendary content.[37]

Two feasts of Mary have been eliminated from the calendar: the Feast of the Motherhood of the Blessed Virgin Mary on October 11, because the object of the feast has already been celebrated on January 1; and the Feast of Our Lady of Mercy (or Ransom) on September 24, a feast of the Mercedarian Order, so-called because its members labored for the release of Christians living in Saracen captivity and placed their work under the special protection of the Mother of God.

Apart from the above-named feasts and memorials the old Roman Missal contained a further *21 regional feasts of Mary* in the section entitled "Masses for Particular Places."[38] Paul VI evidently had these in mind when he wrote in his Apostolic Exhortation *Marialis cultus* of February 2, 1974: "Nor can one forget that the Roman Calendar does not include all celebrations in honor of the Blessed Virgin. Indeed, individual calendars may, with fidelity to liturgical norms and as an invitation to the piety of the faithful, include Marian feasts proper to the various local Churches."[39]

The pope took this occasion to say that "frequent commemorations of the Blessed Virgin are possible through use of the Saturday Masses of Our Lady. This is an ancient and simple commemoration, one that is made very convenient and varied by the flexibility of the modern calendar and the number of formulas provided by the Missal" (ibid.). In the section of "Commons," the new Missal has seven Marian Masses; the introductory rubric says: "These Masses are also used for the Saturday celebrations of the Blessed Virgin Mary and for votive Masses of the Blessed Virgin Mary." Among these there is one Mass each for Advent (a "Rorate Mass"), the Christmas season and the Easter season.

The "Months of Mary": May and October

Since we are speaking of devotion to Mary in the liturgical year we may also recall briefly that the piety of the Catholic people has devoted two months of the year to special veneration of Mary: May, "Mary's Month," and October, "Rosary Month." Special May devotions are attested as far back as the Middle Ages. Their function at that time was to help in the christianizing of traditional pagan May celebrations of Roman and Germanic origin. However, the practice of "consecrating" the entire month of May to the Mother of God by means of daily or at least frequent prayers is the result of a development that began in the seventeenth century and was completed in the middle of the nineteenth.[40]

In his Encyclical Letter *Mense Maio* (May 1, 1965) Paul VI recommended special devotion to the Mother of God during May and noted: "It has been a favorite custom of Our predecessors to choose this month dedicated to Mary, for urging the Christian people to offer up public prayers whenever the needs of the Church demanded it or some grave crisis threatened the human race."[41]

Leo XIII was the first to speak of a "Rosary Month." He published no less than sixteen Encyclicals and Apostolic Letters on praying the Rosary and ordered that it be said daily in all parish churches during October.

The practical implementation of such Marian months is not without its problems, as P. Lippert showed in a recent essay in which he makes a careful and sensitive analysis of the problem.[42] His concluding judgment is basically a positive one, and one with which we can hardly avoid agreeing:

> Both the month of May devotions and the month of the Rosary provide pastoral points of departure for paraliturgical devotion to Mary; this means: for devotion that is in touch with real life and is full of possibilities. But these devotions should not be offered as a "popular" substitute for a more demanding liturgical prayer. All the concrete

ways of praising and praying to Mary must pass a theological test of their content and their form.[43]

3 / THE FEASTS OF THE SAINTS IN THE ROMAN CALENDAR

a/Guidelines for the Choice

In revising the list of the saints' feast in the general calendar, the
Roman Consilium, which carried out this task, followed certain
guidelines. These are set forth in detail in the Commentary on
the *General Norms*[44] and will be explained and possibly
supplemented in the following discussion.

1/The Critical Historical Examination of the Sanctoral
The principle applied here is that Christians of our day want
"their devotion to the saints to be based on historical truth" and
that this desire "is quite legitimate." The science of hagiog-
raphy has served us with important work along this line, even if
it has not been able to eliminate all obscurities.[45] In this historical examination various categories of saints must be distinguished:

Saints whose lives and cult raise major historical problems are
not to be retained in the new calendar. An exception, however,
has been made for St. Cecilia, of whom we know with historical
certainty only that there was a church of her name in Rome
toward the end of the fifth century and that her feast was being
celebrated there on November 22 by about the middle of the
sixth century.

Regarding the early Roman martyrs the only thing we know in
most instances is the "hagiographical coordinates," namely,
name, place, and date. On the other hand, these martyrs must
be "regarded as the venerable nucleus of the throng of saints
the Roman Church honors." On the other hand, because the
sure historical data are so few, these men and women are for the
most part unknown to twentieth-century men and women.
Consequently, a middle way has been chosen: "In addition to
the solemnity of the holy Apostles Peter and Paul (June 29) and
the feast of St. Lawrence (August 10) the calendar contains
obligatory memorials of the following saints: Agnes (January

21), Justin (June 1), Cornelius and Cyprian (September 16), and Ignatius of Antioch (October 17)."[46] For the other early Roman martyrs only an optional memorial is provided. In addition, a new optional memorial has been introduced (June 30) for the first Roman martyrs who suffered under Nero.

It was thought that by adopting this course justice would be done to the Roman tradition. The supposed founders of the early Roman titular churches, however, have not been retained in the calendar because the accounts we have of them are simple legends.

2/Selection of Saints of Greater Importance
Vatican II had already set down the principle that only those saints should be in the general calendar "who are truly of universal importance" (CL, no. 111; Flannery, p. 31). The Roman Consilium evidently felt that this principle was too demanding: "If the mandate of the Constitution on the Sacred Liturgy had been taken literally and followed to the letter, only a few saints 'of truly universal importance' would have been retained in the general calendar. Such a procedure seemed unsuitable and extreme; it would have caused great astonishment and offense."[47] Understandably, then, the Consilium prefers to speak of "saints of greater importance."

Of the 38 saintly popes celebrated in the calendar of 1960, 23 have been removed or left as optional for particular calendars. The remaining 15 comprise six martyred popes from the period of the persecutions, six from the next four centuries (two of them martyrs), and only three from the second Christian millennium (Gregory VII, Pius V, and Pius X).

The many non-Roman martyrs were divided into three groups: "more famous martyrs of antiquity" with four memorials; especially popular martyrs with eight; and "better known martyrs of the Middle Ages and modern times," also with eight.

In the large group of nonmartyrs heed was given to missionaries of various regions of the world, founders of religious Orders and congregations "who emphasized an important new aspect of religious life in the Church," and all the Doctors of the Church (these being given at least an optional memorial).

Thirty saints, mostly Italian, have been removed from the general calendar "in order to achieve a certain geographical balance in the calendar."[48] Another 33 have been left to particular calendars.

3/Universality of the Calendar of the Saints
The first aim here was to ensure a geographical universality, after a long period in which attention had been given chiefly to saints from the Romance-language countries. And as a matter of fact all five continents are represented in the new calendar, chiefly by martyrs. Thus we find the Japanese Paul Miki and the 25 companions who were crucified with him on February 5, 1597, the first canonized (1882) saints from the Far East; Isaac Jogues and companions, martyrs of Canada and the United States († October 18, 1647); Pierre Chanel, first martyr of Oceania († April 28, 1841); Charles Lwanga and his companions who were martyred in Uganda (June 3, 1886). Rose of Lima († August 24, 1617) was already in the calendar as a representative of South America. Added now are Turibius of Mongrovejo, archbishop of Lima († 1606) and Martin of Porres († 1669), a lay brother highly esteemed among blacks and mulattoes.

In his Apostolic Letter approving the new calendar Paul VI calls attention to this geographical universality when he says:

> These representatives of every group of people are given equal prominence in the lists of saints because they shed their blood for Christ or showed extraordinary signs of virtue. Therefore a new general calendar has been prepared for use in the Latin rite which we feel is more in keeping with modern-day attitudes and approaches to piety and which directs our attention to the universality of the Church.

An effort was also made to do justice to the universality of Christian life by having every state of it represented in the Sanctoral. Similarly, the various expressions and ways of Christian virtue and holiness were meant to be represented, such as commitment to the missions and to caritative work, the lay apostolate, contemplation, asceticism, and so on. The universality of the Church in time was to be brought out by having saints from every century.[49]

Despite a reduction in the calendar of the saints which many found painfully extensive, it must be said that the revision fell short of the goal set by the Council, that is, a significant liberation of the general calendar from saints' feasts in favor of the temporal cycle, with the saints being left primarily to particular calendars. If we prescind from the Marian feasts and memorials we find that there are still four solemnities (Joseph, Birth of John the Baptist, Peter and Paul, All Saints), 17 feasts, 59 obligatory and 88 optional memorials, or 168 saints' days all told. Further subject for criticism is the fact that among these 168 feasts there are 89 memorials of saints from Romance-language countries and 63 from religious Orders and congregations.[50]

It may be worth mentioning that only two twentieth-century saints are in the general calendar: Maria Goretti and Pius X. The dates for the celebration of all these various saints can be seen in the liturgical calendar in section 4, below.

b/Further New Regulations for the Feasts of the Saints

As far as the date of a feast or memorial is concerned, the revised calendar sought to locate it as far as possible on the day of the saint's death, this being regarded as his or her birthday into heaven (natale). The early Church held to this rule for the memorials of the martyrs. As a result, many previous dates have been changed. If the date of a saint's death was already preempted the closest free day before or after was chosen. In many cases the date chosen was "the anniversary of the translation . . . or of the dedication of a church in the saint's honor . . . or of ordination. . . . For many Eastern saints the day chosen is the one on which they are venerated in their homeland."[52]

Some changes are to be explained by application of the basic rule that during the Easter penitential period and the second part of Advent (December 17–24) no feasts or memorials of the saints may be celebrated. Thus, for example, the memorial of Thomas Aquinas was changed from March 7 to January 28, that of Pope Gregory the Great from March 13 to September 3, and that of St. Benedict from March 21 to July 11. The feast of Thomas the Apostle was transferred from December 21 to July 3.

Another change: the old titles "confessor" and "neither virgin nor martyr" have been dropped as unsuitable. And: "it was thought that the title 'widow' should be eliminated since it has lost the religious meaning it once had."[53] The decision was made not to try to assign a title to every saint. The titles retained are: apostle, evangelist, martyr, virgin, pope, bishop, priest, deacon, doctor of the church, abbot, monk, hermit, religious [man] (a nonordained member of a religious Order or congregation) and religious [woman] (if she had been married before entering religious life; otherwise her title is "virgin").[54]

As far as the festal Mass is concerned, the texts of the Proper or Common (a Mass formulary covering a class of persons) are used on solemnities and feasts. On memorials only the opening prayer referring to the saint is obligatory; all the other changeable texts of the Mass may be taken from the ferial Mass. In this restricted form memorials of the saints can be taken into account even on the weekdays of the various festal seasons, with the exception of Ash Wednesday and Good Friday. On the weekdays of Ordinary Time, in addition to any optional memorial provided for that day, the memorial of any saint mentioned in the martyrology for that day may be celebrated.[55]

c/Solemnities of the Saints in the General Calendar

Solemnity of All Saints (November 1)
The origins of this feast are to be found in the East, where a memorial of all the martyrs was being celebrated as early as the fourth century. The day for the celebration differed in the various local churches. According to the Syrian deacon Ephraem it was celebrated on May 13. John Chrysostom knows it as celebrated on the Sunday after Pentecost in the Church of Antioch; it is still celebrated on this day in the Greek Orthodox Church under the name "All Saints' Sunday." The East Syrian liturgy celebrates it on the Friday after Easter.[56]

In Rome there is evidence for all three dates; this is not surprising in view of the close relations between Rome and the East in the fifth and sixth centuries. Under Pope Boniface IV (608–15) May 13 became the established day, inasmuch as the pope accepted a pagan temple, the Pantheon (unused for over 100 years), as a gift from Emperor Phocas and on May 13, 609

(610?) consecrated it as a Christian church in honor of the Virgin Mary and all the martyrs. On this day of consecration the pope had 28 wagonloads of martyrs' bones brought to the church from the catacombs. The antiphons of the old rite for the dedication of a church may refer to that triumphant act of translation; one of them, for example, reads: "Rise up, saints of God, from your dwellings; sanctify this place and bless the people!"[57]

Gregory III (731–41) took a further step toward our present feast of All Saints when he had a chapel built in St. Peter's in honor of all the saints, even those who were not martyrs. This action may have given the impulse to a feast of All Saints for November 1 which is attested in the middle of the eighth century for England and Ireland. At the request of Pope Gregory IV (828–44) and with the agreement of his own bishops, Louis the Pious prescribed this feast for his entire realm. From the beginning it had a vigil; at the end of the fifteenth century it acquired an octave as well. Both vigil and octave were abolished in the reform of 1955.

The festal Mass has taken over the texts of the traditional Mass for the most part, but has been enriched with a second reading and a special preface. The preface sings of the festal mystery in a hymnic fashion: "Today we keep the festival of your holy city, the heavenly Jerusalem, our mother. Around your throne the saints, our brothers and sisters, sing your praise for ever. Their glory fills us with joy, and their communion with us in your Church gives us inspiration and strength as we hasten on our pilgrimage of faith, eager to meet them." Here it is clear that the feast celebrates not only the canonized saints but all the dead who have reached their fulfillment, and therefore surely our dead relatives and friends as well.

The first reading (Rev 7.2-4, 9-14) describes these saints as "a hundred and forty-four thousand . . . out of every tribe of the sons of Israel" and as "a great multitude which no man could number, from every nation, from all tribes and peoples and tongues," who stand before the throne and the Lamb in white robes, with palm branches in their hands. When it is said at the end of the passage that they have come out of great affliction and have washed their robes white in the blood of the Lamb, this is a metaphorical expression of the truth that all the saints are the fruit of the paschal mystery. The second reading (1 Jn 3.1-3) sees the divine sonship already bestowed on us as being the foundation of our glory at the end of time. The road to holiness and fulfillment is signposted by the eight beatitudes of the Sermon on the Mount; these are proclaimed in the gospel (Mt 5.1-12a).

In the presidential prayers the praying Church relies on the intercession of these many saints (opening prayer, prayer over the gifts) and bids us ask: "May we who share at this table be filled with your love and prepared for the joy of your kingdom" (concluding prayer).

Solemnity of Saint Joseph (March 19)
The oldest trace of a cultic veneration of the "Husband of Mary" (to give the feast its official title in the new Missal) is to be found in Coptic calendars of the eighth/ninth century for July 20.[58] Apart from brief notices in various martyrologies of the ninth/tenth century, which give no specific date, we encounter a festal celebration on March 19 for the first time in the twelfth century. This is the period when crusaders built a church in honor of Joseph at Nazareth. It was chiefly the Franciscans, and especially Bernardine of Siena († 1444), who promoted the cult and the feast. There are only guesses as to why March 19 was chosen.

Only at the end of the fifteenth century did Sixtus IV (1471–84) extend the feast to the entire Church (as a simple). Gregory XV made it a holy day of obligation in 1621. In 1870 Pius IX declared Joseph the patron and protector of the universal Church and made the feast a double of the first class.[59] The 1920 edition of the Missal introduced a special preface, which has been retained in the Missal of 1970. Because the feast always falls in Lent, the episcopal conferences may transfer it to another date.[60] It is worth mentioning, too, that in 1962 John XXIII introduced Joseph's name into the Canon of the Mass.

The feast of Joseph was duplicated when a "Patronal Feast" of St. Joseph which the Carmelites of Italy and France had been celebrating since 1860 was extended by Pius IX to the whole Church in 1847 (third Sunday after Easter). Pius X made this a first-class feast with an octave and transferred it to the third

Wednesday after Easter. A decree of the Congregation of Rites abolished it in 1956.[61]

In this context mention must be made of the feast of Joseph which Pius XII introduced into the Roman calendar on May 1, 1955 under the title "Solemnity of St. Joseph the Worker, Husband of the Blessed Virgin Mary, Confessor and Patron of Working People." It was celebrated for the first time on May 1, 1956 (double of the first class). In the secular sphere, workers had long been celebrating May Day as a day in honor of labor and as a symbol of their rights; in the pope's intention, May Day was to be given a Christian dimension by being made the feast day of a worker-saint. In the revised calendar this feast has been retained as an optional memorial. The historical section of the Commentary on the new calendar justifies this reduction in rank by pointing out that in many countries "Labor Day" is celebrated at other times of the year.[62] Then, in its second chapter (changes made in the Roman calendar) the Commentary gives as a reason that "there is question here rather of a secondary commemoration of St. Joseph in connection with 'Labor Day.' "[63] Evidently, the Roman Consilium's aim, mentioned earlier, of eliminating idea-feasts as far as possible prevailed here.[64]

In the festal Mass of March 19 the special preface (the only part of the old Proper that has been retained) paints a picture of the saint. He is the "just man" who was assigned the role of protector during the early phases of the Christ-event: protector of the virgin Mother of God by being her husband, protector of the Son of God "in the place of a natural father." Joseph carried out this mission—so important in the history of salvation—as a "wise and loyal servant," in obedience to God, selflessly, quietly, and with persevering fidelity. The entrance antiphon notes this last-named, essential characteristic of the saint right at the start: "The Lord has put his faithful servant in charge of his household" (cf. Lk 12.42). Such a "good and faithful servant" is rewarded by participation in the festive banquet of his Lord (communion antiphon: Mt 25.21).

The gospel (Mt 1.16, 18-21, 24a) tells of the critical time in Joseph's life when the mystery of Mary's divine maternity was revealed to him and he was instructed to take her as his wife and to give her child the name Jesus. Joseph obeyed and became the legal father of Jesus, to whom he gave the name "God saves." By so doing, Joseph became instrumental in the salvation of the entire race. The story of the twelve-year-old Jesus in the temple can be used as an alternate gospel pericope (Lk 2.41-51a).

The Old Testament reading (2 Sam 7.4-5a, 12-14a, 16) contains the promise that David's house and kingdom will remain for ever; when interpreted typologically, the promise is fulfilled in the messianic rule of Jesus. But "Joseph the husband of Mary" and a descendant of David, was the link between David and Jesus (gospel). The responsorial psalm (Ps 89) is a meditation on this promise. The New Testament reading (Rom 4.13, 16-18, 22) enables us to see an (implicit) parallel between Abraham and Joseph. Abraham is the father of faith, for "in hope he believed against hope, that he should become the father of many nations." Joseph too believed in the "incredible" word of God. The opening prayer and prayer over the gifts refer to the "faithful care" and service that Joseph gave to Jesus and his mother, and ask that God would heed the intercession of Joseph, help the Church to "continue to serve its Lord, Jesus Christ" (opening prayer), and give us the strength to serve Christ faithfully (prayer over the gifts).

Solemnity of the Birth of St. John the Baptist (June 24)
The biblical accounts of the striking events that accompanied John's entrance on the earthly scene and of Jesus' statements about his Precursor make it understandable that the early Church should have esteemed and venerated the Baptist so highly. According to Jesus himself, John is more than a prophet (Lk 7.26); he is the greatest of human beings (Lk 7.28), the one "of whom it is written, 'Behold, I send my messenger before thy face, who shall prepare thy way before thee' (Mal 3.1)" (Lk 7.27). "His seal of canonization is seen in the eulogy addressed to him by the Word of God himself made flesh."[65] In addition, the gospel tells of his martyrdom, which from the beginning won him veneration equal to that shown to the apostles and Stephen.

In both East and West liturgical memorials existed as early as the fourth century, but the dates differ from Church to Church. The Greeks celebrate his feast on January 7, in accordance with the Eastern custom of honoring saints connected with the festal object of a feast of the Lord by celebrating a synaxis in their honor on the day after such a feast. Since Epiphany in the East focuses primarily on the baptism of Jesus, the Baptist may not pass unnoticed.

The feast of John on June 24 arose in the West, where in accordance with Luke 1.36a it was celebrated six months before the feast of the Lord's birth. Both of these feasts come on the eighth day before the first of the following month (*dies VIII ante Kalendas*—counting the day at both ends). In speaking of the date of Christmas, I pointed out that in the third century great significance was attached to the solstices in connection with the history of salvation. Since the days grow longer after the summer solstice and shorter after the winter solstice, Augustine sees in the two dates a cosmic confirmation of John's own words: "He must increase, but I must decrease" (Jn 3.30).[66]

In Rome there were no less than 20 churches built in honor of the Baptist. In the sixth century the feast already has a vigil. On the feast day itself as many as three Masses are mentioned, one of them being celebrated *ad fontem* ("at the font"), i.e., in a baptistery.[67]

The great esteem for the saint in the East led to two other feasts there: the commemoration of his beheading and a feast of his conception. Only the first of these gained a place in the West, and via the Gallo-Frankish liturgy even entered the Roman calendar, in which it is listed for August 29. This date is probably that of the dedication of the church of St. John at Sebaste (Samaria), where his disciples supposedly buried him. The most recent revision of the calendar has retained this feast as an obligatory memorial. The second of the two feasts named—the conception of the Baptist—was celebrated in the East nine months before the feast of his birth (September 24); it is still celebrated in the Byzantine Church.[68]

The liturgical celebration of the feast of John's birth has a vigil Mass, celebrated on the previous evening (before or after first vespers of the solemnity). It retains most of the texts from the old vigil Mass, but adds a second reading, an alleluia verse, and the special preface of the feast itself.

In the Mass of the feast the gospel (Lk 1.57-66, 80) tells of the birth, circumcision and naming of John. The marvelous circumstances of these events caused great bewilderment throughout the region and made people ask: "What then will this child be?" The final verse of the pericope bridges the gap between John's childhood and his appearance on the public stage as an adult.

What is said about the "Servant of God" in the Old Testament reading (Is 49.1-6) is largely applicable to the Precursor as well: "The Lord called me from the womb. . . . He made my mouth like a sharp sword. . . . to bring Jacob back to him and that Israel might be gathered to him. . . . He says: . . . 'I will give you as a light to the nations.'" John's importance in the history of salvation is also brought out by Paul when preaching in Pisidia (second reading: Acts 13.22-26): John preached a baptism of repentance and gave witness to the Lord, "the sandals of whose feet I am not worthy to untie." The alleluia verse praises the saint with a sentence from the Benedictus (Lk 1.76): "You, child, will be called the prophet of the Most High; you will go before the Lord to prepare his ways."

In a splendid synthesis the special preface proclaims the favor shown to the Baptist and the vocation bestowed on him: "You set John the Baptist apart from other men, marking him out with special favor. His birth brought great rejoicing: even in the womb he leapt for joy, so near was man's salvation. You chose John the Baptist from all the prophets to show the world its redeemer, the Lamb of sacrifice. He baptized Christ, the giver of baptism, in waters made holy by the one who was baptized. You found John worthy of a martyr's death, his last and greatest act of witness to your Son." With pregnant brevity the entrance antiphon describes John's mission: "There was a man sent from God whose name was John. He came to bear witness to the light, to prepare an upright people for the Lord" (Jn 1.6-7; Lk 1.17).

Inspired by the festal mystery the Church prays: "Give your Church joy in spirit and guide those who believe in you into the way of salvation and peace" (opening prayer); "You have renewed us with this eucharist, as we celebrate the feast of John the Baptist, who foretold the coming of the Lamb of God. May we welcome your Son as our Savior, for he gives us new life" (concluding prayer).

Solemnity of Peter and Paul, Apostles (June 29)
The high esteem in which all the apostles were held because of their importance for the Church as a whole is already reflected in the New Testament writings, where it is said that the community of "the saints and members of the household of God" is "built upon the foundation of the apostles and prophets" (Eph 2.19-20) and that the wall of the new Jerusalem has twelve foundations on which are written the names of the twelve apostles of the Lamb (Rev 21.14). These men were eyewitnesses of the Christ-event; they were the messengers and shepherds appointed by Christ himself to carry the message of salvation to the entire world as his representatives and to build the community of the Lord as men on whom full authority to bind and loose had been bestowed (Mt 18.18). All this holds especially for Peter whom Christ himself had made the rock of foundation for his Church and to whom as an individual he gave "the keys of the kingdom of heaven" (Mt 16.18-19).

Emperor Constantine is reported to have built at Constantinople a magnificent church in honor of all the apostles, in which he wanted to be buried; he is also said to have placed twelve richly ornamented pillars around the tomb of the Lord in the church of the Anastasis. These actions were not simply a reflection of Constantine's personal devotion; they expressed the veneration of the entire community.[69]

In the East there seems originally to have been a feast of all the apostles; traces of this may also be found in the Roman liturgy. The individual apostles were venerated chiefly in the places in which their tombs were located or which had special memories of the apostles connected with them. This is true most especially of the two "princes of the apostles," Peter and Paul. These two apostles suffered martyrdom at Rome under Nero (54–68), Peter by crucifixion, Paul by beheading. Although there is no historical proof that the two martyrdoms occurred in the same year and on the same day, the two have nonetheless been commemorated together on June 29 since the middle of the third century.[70]

Various documents show that on this day three different liturgies were celebrated in various places: a liturgy of Peter in the church named for him on the Vatican Hill along the Via Aurelia; one of Paul on the road to Ostia (St. Paul outside the Walls); and finally a commemoration of both together on the Appian Way "at the catacombs," near the present-day church of St. Sebastian, where their bodies or at least their heads were kept, probably temporarily, during the Valerian persecution.[71] Since three celebrations on the same day at sanctuaries so far apart caused difficulties, the commemoration of St. Paul was shifted to the following day at the beginning of the eighth century, although Paul continued to be included in the Masses of June 29.

The double Roman feast spread to Italy and North Africa in the third century, and to the other Western countries and most Churches of the East in the fifth/sixth century. Ambrose († 397) already speaks of a vigil being celebrated.[72]

In the revised Roman calendar the vigil is kept in the form of a Mass on the evening before the feast. In this Mass the entrance antiphon, second reading (Gal 1.11-20), presidential prayers and special preface are new. The Commemoration of St. Paul on June 30 has been removed from the general calendar and "left in the calendar of the Roman Basilica of St. Paul. . . . There is no reason for this double solemnity anywhere but in the city of Rome."[73] This change caused greater attention to be paid to Paul the Apostle in the liturgy of the solemnity on June 29.

The leitmotiv of the festal Mass is given in the new entrance antiphon: "These men, conquering all human frailty, shed their blood and helped the Church to grow. By sharing the cup of the Lord's suffering, they became the friends of God." The first reading (Acts 12.1-11) tells of the persecution which the young Christian community of Jerusalem suffered under King Herod Agrippa. Peter was arrested but was delivered during the night before the trial. The well-chosen responsorial psalm (from Ps 34) with its refrain: "The angel of the Lord will rescue those who fear him," becomes a hymn of praise to the helping hand

236

of God. The second reading (2 Tim 4.6-7, 17-18) shows the Apostle Paul full of confidence in the face of his coming martyrdom: "I have fought the good fight, I have finished the race, I have kept the faith. Henceforth there is laid up for me the crown of righteousness. . . . The Lord will rescue me from every evil and save me for his heavenly kingdom."

In the gospel (Mt 16.13-19) we hear Peter's confession of faith: "You are the Christ, the Son of the living God." The Lord makes him the rock of foundation for his Church and gives him full authority to bind and loose. This theme is taken up in the alleluia verse and communion antiphon. On this solemnity the special preface once again brings real enrichment to the formulary, as it describes with masterful concision the ecclesiological importance of the two Apostles: "We honor your great apostle Peter, our leader in the faith, and Paul, its fearless preacher. Peter raised up the Church from the faithful flock of Israel. Paul brought your call to the nations and became teacher of the world. Each in his chosen way gathered into unity the one Church of Christ. Both shared a martyr's death and are praised throughout the world."

The presidential prayers have been partially revised: "Through them your Church first received the faith. Keep us true to their teaching" (opening prayer); "May the breaking of bread and the teaching of the apostles keep us united in your love" (concluding prayer).

Commemoration of All the Faithful Departed (All Souls, November 2)
This day is a memorial of a unique kind. It cannot be called a solemnity or a feast, yet in rank it belongs with "solemnities of the Lord, the Blessed Virgin Mary, and the saints listed in the general calendar."[74]

The pagans of antiquity kept fixed memorial days for their dead; for example, the Roman *Parentalia* (festival in honor of dead relatives), February 13–22 (see below, "Feast of the Chair of Peter, Apostle"). Christians initially retained such customs insofar as these did not seem incompatible with their faith. There is evidence from as early as the second century that such commemorations included prayers for the dead and were soon accompanied by the celebration of Mass.[75] In the beginning, the third day after burial and the yearly anniversary of death were the preferred days for commemoration; later, the seventh and thirtieth days were added and, in many places, the fortieth. "All of these fixed days for the memorial of the dead, along with the ritual solemnization of the day of burial, derive from pre-Christian tradition, with the celebration of the eucharist taking the place of ancient sacrifice for the dead and sometimes perhaps of the *refrigerium* too."[76]

The idea of dedicating one day a year to a commemoration of all the faithful departed is one we meet first in Bishop Isidore of Seville († 636) who ordered his monks to offer Mass for the souls of the departed on the day after Pentecost.[77] At the beginning of the ninth century Abbot Eigil of Fulda prescribed that on December 17, the anniversary of St. Sturmius, founder of the monastery at Fulda, commemoration should be made of all the deceased "in Mass, psalmody and holy prayer."[78] There were similar commemorations in the Eastern Churches. Amalarius of Metz was accustomed to add the Office of the Dead to the Liturgy of the Hours on the feast of All Saints.[79]

The year 998 saw the inauguration of All Souls' Day, for that was the year in which Abbot Odo of Cluny (994–1048) ordered all the monasteries under his authority to celebrate a festal memorial of all the faithful departed; he added: "If anyone else follows the example of our faith-inspired innovation, may he share in the good prayers of all."[80] This commemoration quickly spread through France, England and Germany. It was accepted in Italy, and especially at Rome, only in the thirteenth century.[81]

At the end of the fifteenth century the Dominicans of Valencia in Spain made it a custom for all their priests to celebrate three Masses on this day (as on Christmas). Benedict XIV approved this practice in 1748 and extended the privilege to all priests of Spain, Portugal and Latin America. Benedict XV extended it still further in 1915 to all priests of the Church, with the proviso that each priest might offer only one Mass for a stipend and must celebrate a second as compensation for all the Mass foundations that for various reasons had not been fulfilled in the course of the centuries or had been forgotten.[82] This rule still holds today, although a priest need not use the privilege of celebrating three Masses.

Although the *General Norms* had prescribed that if All Souls' Day fell on a Sunday, the Sunday was to be given precedence, the new Missal of 1970 gives precedence to All Souls' Day (rubric in the Missal). As in all Masses of the dead purple vestments may be worn on this day instead of black.[83] The liturgy of the Mass for the dead has been especially enriched by the addition of four prefaces of Christian death to the ancient preface of the dead. The new liturgy is determined to "express more clearly the paschal character of Christian death" (CL, no. 81; Flannery, p. 24) and, instead of grieving "as others do who have no hope" (1 Thess 4.13), to proclaim the paschal mystery of Christ as the foundation of our hope. For this reason the ancient sequence *Dies irae* has been eliminated, along with other texts in which fear at the thought of a grim judgment by God obscures the radiant light of faith in the resurrection.[84]

All the readings, prayers and songs of the three Masses on All Souls' Day are marked by faith in the Easter mystery and by prayer that the deceased may share in this mystery. Let me show this by using the first Mass as an example.

The entrance antiphon (1 Thess 4.14; 1 Cor 15.22) speaks of participation in the mystery of Christ in lapidary sentences: "Just as Jesus died and rose again, so will the Father bring with him all those who have died in Jesus. Just as in Adam all men die, so in Christ all will be made alive." Our faith in the resurrection of Jesus leads us to ask: "Strengthen our hope that all our departed brothers and sisters will share in his resurrection" (opening prayer). The first reading (2 Mac 12.43-45) gives an Old Testament testimony to faith in the resurrection and in the possibility of expiatory sacrifice in behalf of the deceased. The responsorial psalm is the psalm about the Good Shepherd (Ps 23); it expresses the trust and confidence of believers. This confidence is based on "the love of God in Christ Jesus our Lord" who after death and resurrection sits now at God's right hand and intercedes for us (second reading: Rom 8.31b-35, 37-39).

This love of God for the human race reaches its climax in the gift of his only Son, in order that "those who believe in him might have eternal life" (alleluia verse: Jn 3.16).

The gospel (Jn 14.1-6) is a consoling message that tells the sorrowing: "Let not your hearts be troubled. . . . In my Father's house are many rooms. . . . I go and prepare a place for you." The communion antiphon repeats this promise of eternal life, using John 11.25-26: "I am the resurrection and the life, says the Lord. If anyone believes in me, even though he dies, he will live. Anyone who lives and believes in me, will not die." Relying on these promises we ask that our departed brothers and sisters may be received "into the glory of your Son" (prayer over the gifts) and, with our gaze fixed on the death and resurrection of Christ, we cry: "May the death and resurrection of Christ . . . bring the departed faithful to the peace of your eternal home" (concluding prayer).

d/The Feasts of the Saints

In addition to the four solemnities of saints the new general Roman calendar still has a good number of saints' feasts and a feast of the angels. Foremost among the feasts of the saints are the feasts of the individual apostles, some of which were admitted into the calendar only at a late period and after hesitation. This series of feasts of the apostles contains a secondary feast of Peter and another of Paul. My description will follow the order of the liturgical year. I remind the reader that I have already discussed the feasts of the saints that occur during the Christmas season.

Feast of the Conversion of Paul, Apostle (January 25)
Although the *Martyrologium Hieronymianum* [85] speaks of a Roman commemoration entitled *Translatio S. Pauli* ("translation" = transferral of relics) and celebrated on January 25, the Roman sources of the fourth to ninth centuries know nothing of such a feast. Because the term *translatio* is sometimes used in the sense of *conversio* ("conversion"), it is thought that perhaps a feast of the Conversion of Paul is meant, but this appears first in the Gallo-Frankish liturgy.

The date was probably chosen because it was the octave day of a Gallic commemoration of Peter on January 18 (celebrating the giving of the primacy to Peter).[86]

According to the German Missal, "the reason for the feast is that because of the manner of his calling and the scope of his work Paul has a unique place among the apostles." The first reading (Acts 22.3-16 or 9.1-22) tells of the extraordinary event before the gates of Damascus.

Feast of the Chair of Peter, Apostle (February 22)
Recent research has brought to light for the first time the meaning and history of this feast.[87] It appears that this Roman memorial, which is attested as early as the mid-fourth century (in the *Depositio martyrum*), goes back to a custom of prechristian antiquity. In ancient Rome a commemoration of dead relatives and friends *(Parentalia)* was celebrated at the end of the year (which at that time began on March 1), from February 13 to February 22. At this commemoration a chair *(cathedra)* was left empty for particular deceased persons. Now, since the actual date of Peter's death was not known to the Roman community, it was commemorated on February 22. Only later on did the community interpret the term *cathedra* as referring to the chair which the bishop occupied when teaching his community, and see in the feast a commemoration of Peter's taking charge of the Church of Rome.

In addition to this "Chair of Peter," there was a commemoration in Gaul, on January 18, of the giving of the primacy to Peter (see above, under "Feast of the Conversion of Paul"). As a result of liturgical exchanges between Rome and Gaul, Rome accepted this second feast and, around 600, interpreted it as referring to Peter's see of Rome, while the feast on February 22 was thought of as referring to his tenure of the see of Antioch. The two commemorations were extended to the entire Church only in 1558 by Paul IV. The Code of Rubrics issued under John XXIII in 1960 eliminated the feast on January 18 in favor of the original feast on February 22. The Roman calendar retained the latter as a feast entitled "Chair of Peter," with no commemoration of St. Paul.

Feast of Mark, Evangelist (April 25)

Mark is the John Mark whose mother Mary put her home at the disposal of the first community for its assemblies (Acts 12.12). With his cousin Barnabas Mark took part in Paul's first missionary journey (Acts 13.2-5) but not in the second (Acts 15.36-39). The estrangement that occurred between him and Paul at that time was later overcome. Subsequently we find him acting as Paul's highly esteemed fellow worker (e.g., 2 Tim 4.11). Tradition also has him as a coworker of Peter and author of the second gospel (in which connection he is symbolized by a lion). In the sixth century his relics were transferred to Venice from Alexandria, where he had supposedly been the first bishop and had suffered martyrdom; as a result, he became the famous patron of the Italian city. The first evidence of a feast of Mark at Rome comes only in the tenth/eleventh century. The feast coincided there with the "greater litany"; as a result, Mark was venerated as one of the "masters of the weather."[88]

Feast of Philip and James, Apostles (May 3)

Philip of Bethsaida was one of the first men Jesus called to be apostles (Jn 1.43-44). He always comes fifth in the lists of the apostles and is mentioned several times in the gospel of John. We have little reliable information regarding his later life and activities.

James the Lesser, son of Alphaeus (Mt 10.3), is not named in the New Testament outside the lists of the apostles. The older view, that he is to be identified with James, the brother of Jesus (Mk 6.3), who later governed the community of Jerusalem and died a martyr in about 42, is held by few today. The same is true of his supposed authorship of the Letter of James.[89] We have no certain knowledge of his later life and activities.

The two apostles have never been celebrated together in the Eastern Churches. At Rome, on the contrary, the joint celebration of the two began when their relics were deposited in the Church of the Twelve Apostles. This church had been built in the fourth century under Popes Pelagius I (556–61) and John III (561–74), but was later completely rebuilt. Its date of consecration, May 1 (in the year 570), then became the feast of the two apostles.[90] When Pius XII in 1955 made May 1 the feast of

"Joseph the Worker," the feast of the apostles had to be transferred to May 11. In the new calendar it has been moved back closer to its original date.

Feast of Matthias, Apostle (May 14)
According to Acts 1.15-26 Matthias was selected to take the place of Judas the betrayer; Matthias was one who had been an eyewitness of the entire public life of Jesus (vv. 21-22). There is no historical evidence for his later life. Empress Helena supposedly had some of his relics brought to Rome, others to Trier (Abbey Church of St. Matthias). The early Gelasian Sacramentary has his name in the Canon of the Mass, but his feast seems to have been introduced only around the year 1000. In the new Roman calendar the feast has been transferred to May 14 because the old date, February 24, usually falls in Lent.

Feast of Thomas, Apostle (July 3)
Thomas, whom the gospel of John speaks of several times as "the twin," is famous chiefly for his initial scepticism toward the news of the resurrection (Jn 20.24-29). According to Eusebius, a historian of the Church, he preached the gospel in Persia and India and suffered martyrdom in those regions. [91] Part of his relics were supposedly brought to Edessa on July 3, 384; some of them passed from Edessa to Ortona in Apulia in the thirteenth century. According to the *Liber pontificalis* Pope Symmachus (498–514) built a small chapel in the saint's honor in St. Peter's Basilica. The Gregorian Sacramentary has December 21 as the date of his feast. [92] Because the Advent liturgies of December 17–24 are so important, his feast was moved in 1969 back to the traditional date (that of the transferral of his relics to Edessa).

Feast of James the Greater, Apostle (July 25)
This James was a brother of John the Apostle and, with Peter and John, was one of the special inner circle of disciples (cf. Mk 5.37; 9.2; 14.33). He was put to death by the sword in the persecution of Herod Agrippa in about 42. A church in his honor was later built over his tomb in Jerusalem. His supposed preaching in Spain and the transferral of his relics there are simply legends. For this reason it is likewise very difficult to accept

the story that the bishop of Iria rediscovered the relics at Compostela in 830. In the tenth century, pilgrimage to his supposed tomb became an important religious custom and brought countless throngs to Santiago de Compostela; as a result James became an immensely popular saint. According to several sacramentaries of the eighth century his feast was being celebrated at that time on July 25. His feast has been celebrated in Rome since the ninth century.[93]

Feast of Lawrence, Deacon and Martyr (August 10)
Lawrence was a deacon of Pope Sixtus II and suffered martyrdom during the persecution of Emperor Valerian, along with four others of the seven deacons, on August 6, 258.[94] According to the *Liber pontificalis* Lawrence died on August 10 of that year, along with four other clerics. The *Depositio martyrum* of 354 already shows a liturgical commemoration of Lawrence being celebrated in the "Cemetery on the Road to Tibur" *(Via Tiburtina)*. The early *Passio*, or account of his martyrdom, already has a detailed account of his being put to death on a white-hot grill; it claims that amid his suffering and as death approached the martyr still had the strength to jest with his tormentors.[95]

Constantine built a basilica in Lawrence's honor near the site of his tomb, which was surrounded by other tombs; there was a special passage linking the basilica to the tomb. (Tombs at that time were regarded as inviolable.) This church was several times rebuilt and enlarged and, as the Basilica of San Lorenzo, is today one of the seven principal churches of Rome. "About twenty other churches and the introduction of his name into the Canon show how greatly he was esteemed."[96] This veneration spread quickly throughout the entire West. It received an important stimulus when the West defeated the Hungarians at the Lech River on the feast of St. Lawrence in 955, since the victory was attributed to the saint's prayers. At an early date the feast was given a vigil, which was suppressed only in the revision of 1969. The liturgy of the Mass emphasizes not only the martyr's courage but also his concern for the poor (cf. entrance antiphon, opening prayer, first reading, and responsorial psalm).

Feast of Bartholomew, Apostle (August 24)
Bartholomew's name occurs in the New Testament only in the

lists of apostles. He is probably to be identified with Nathanael of Cana, whom Philip brings to the Lord, "an Israelite indeed, in whom is no guile" (Jn 1.47). We have no certain historical information about him. According to Armenian traditions he preached the gospel and suffered martyrdom in that country. The Byzantine liturgy for August 25 speaks of his bones being transferred to the island of Lipari and to Benevento. Some of these bones may have brought from Benevento to Rome around the year 1000 due to the intervention of Emperor Otto III[97]; at Rome they were entombed in a church on Tiber Island. The cathedral of Frankfurt claims to possess the skull of the apostle, who on this account is regarded as patron of the cathedral and the city. The gospel of the Mass for the feast tells the story of his calling (Jn 1.45-51).

Feast of Matthew, Apostle and Evangelist (September 21)
Matthew, who is called "the tax collector" in the list of apostles in Matthew's gospel (10.3), is identical not only with the tax collector Matthew who is named in Matthew 9.9 but possibly also with Levi, son of Alphaeus, who is called from his tax booth in Mark 2.13-15. Reports regarding his later life are certainly mingled with legend. He is said to have been a missionary in Ethiopia and Persia. The Greek and Latin Churches venerate him as a martyr. His relics were supposedly brought from Ethiopia to Salerno. The cathedral built over his tomb in Salerno was dedicated in 1084 by Pope Gregory VII, who had been driven from Rome and who died the next year and is likewise buried at Salerno.[98]

Feast of Luke, Evangelist (October 18)
According to Colossians 4.4 Luke was a physician and came from a gentile Christian milieu. He accompanied St. Paul during part of the latter's second missionary journey and also was present to help the Apostle during his later two periods of imprisonment at Rome. A number of testimonies from as early as the second century make him the author of the third gospel and the Acts of the Apostles. After Paul's death Luke supposedly worked in Greece and died a natural death. His bones were brought to Constantinople in 357 and interred in the Church of the Apostles. The Eastern Churches, like the Western, celebrate

his feast on October 18. He has been venerated at Rome since the ninth century.[99]

Feast of Simon and Jude, Apostles (October 28)
Simon, who is also called the Cananaean (from Cana: Mk 3.19; Mt 10.4) and the Zealot (Lk 6.15; Acts 1.13), is mentioned in the New Testament only in the lists of apostles. The name "Zealot" indicates that he had previously belonged to the Zealot party. We know nothing of his later life.

Jude (New Testament: Judas), who is also called Thaddaeus (Mt 10.3; Mk 3.18) and described as "the brother of James" (Lk 6.16) or "the son of James" (Acts 1.13), is hardly to be identified with "Judas, brother of the Lord" (Mk 6.3). Elsewhere in the New Testament he is mentioned only briefly in Jn 14.22. Once again, we have no further historical information about him.

The Eastern Churches honor these two apostles separately. The *Martyrologium Hieronymianum*, however, already speaks of a common commemoration of the two on October 28. The feast came from Gaul to Rome at a relatively late period. The *Calendar of Charlemagne* still makes no mention of it.[100]

Feast of Andrew, Apostle (November 30)
Andrew, brother of Peter, was from Bethsaida and later lived with his brother at Capernaum, where the two worked as fishermen. Andrew was a disciple of John the Baptist at the time when Jesus called him; he in turn brought his brother Peter to Jesus (Jn 1.35-42). With Peter, James and John he belongs to a smaller circle of more favored disciples; he was, for example, a witness of the transfiguration of Jesus. According to later accounts, he preached the gospel in the countries south of the Black Sea, in the lower Danubian area, and finally in Greece. He is said to have suffered martyrdom on November 30, 60, by crucifixion on an X-shaped cross (the St. Andrew's Cross).

In the fourth century his bones, or some of them, were interred in the Church of the Apostles at Constantinople. From here they were transferred to Amalfi in 1208, while the head was brought to Rome. Veneration of Andrew at Rome began at a relatively early date, after Pope Simplicius (468–83) had dedicated a church to him (near St. Mary Major). His feast has been listed in all calendars since the beginning of the sixth century and was given a vigil at an early period.[101] This vigil, along with many others, was suppressed in the rubrical reform of 1955.[102]

Feast of Michael, Gabriel and Raphael, Archangels (September 29)

According to Catholic teaching, angels are "personal beings created by God, spirits not embodied after human fashion."[103] The title archangel refers to a higher class of angels. In the New Testament this title is given to Michael (Jude 9; perhaps also 1 Thess 4.16). The apocryphal Greek Book of Enoch mentions seven archangels; "later Christian tradition lists Gabriel and Uriel (from the Fourth Book of Esdras) among the archangels, along with Michael and Gabriel."[104]

While Gabriel and Raphael were included in the Roman festal calendar only in 1921 (on March 24 and October 24, respectively), Michael has been venerated in the Roman liturgy since early times. At the beginning of the fifth century there were many churches and chapels already dedicated to him in Italy.[105] In Rome the principal church of Michael was the one on the Via Salaria, the dedication of which was commemorated on September 30 or 29 in the oldest sacramentaries. His cult received a special impetus from his appearance on Mount Gargano in southern Italy on May 8, 492; a famous sanctuary was built there in his honor. This event was commemorated, until 1960, by a "Feast of the Apparition of St. Michael the Archangel." Just as he was considered to be the protector of the Old Testament people of God (cf. Dan 10.13), so the Roman Church and, later, the Holy Roman Empire regarded him as a powerful patron and protector.[106]

The revised Roman calendar combines the feasts of Gabriel and Raphael with that of Michael on September 29. The new preface sees veneration of the angels and archangels as a tribute to their creator and goes on to say: "Their splendor shows us your greatness, which surpasses in goodness the whole of creation. Through Christ our Lord the great army of angels rejoices in your glory."

A commemoration of all the other angels, including the guardian angels, was originally included in the feast of Michael the Archangel. A special feast of the guardian angels appears first in the sixteenth century, in Spain and France. In 1667, at the request of Emperor Ferdinand II, Clement IX prescribed this feast for the emperor's realm and assigned it to the first Sunday in September. Clement X extended it to the rest of the Church, but to be celebrated on October 2. Pius X later made October 2 the univeral day for the feast. [107] The new calendar retains this feast as an obligatory memorial.

4 / THE LITURGICAL CALENDAR

In its section on the particular calendars of local Churches and religious communities the new *General Norms for the Liturgical Year and the Calendar* allows "entire provinces, regions, countries, or even larger areas" to have a common calendar (no. 51; see this chapter, section 1c). The Instruction on particular calendars which the Congregation for Divine Worship issued on June 24, 1970 gives as a reason for this provision, that in this way "fitting honor may be given to saints who have played an especially important role in the religious history of particular nations or regions, chiefly because of their teaching of their apostolic zeal" (no. 14).

The following pages give the Roman liturgical calendar with the additional celebrations which are peculiar to the major English-speaking nations. In the calendar celebrations without any designation after them are optional memorials.

JANUARY

solemnity	1	MARY, MOTHER OF GOD
memorial	2	Basil the Great and Gregory Nazianzen/ bishops and doctors
	3	
memorial	4	Elizabeth Ann Seton (United States)
memorial	5	John Neumann/bishop (United States)
solemnity	6	EPIPHANY[1]
	7	Raymond of Penyafort/priest
	8	
	9	
	10	
	11	
	12	Marguerite Bourgeoys/virgin (Canada)
	13	Hilary/bishop and doctor
memorial		Kentigern/bishop (Scotland)
	14	
	15	
	16	
memorial	17	Anthony/abbot
	18	
	19	
	20	Fabian/pope and martyr Sebastian/martyr
memorial	21	Agnes/virgin and martyr
	22	Vincent/deacon and martyr
	23	
memorial	24	Francis de Sales/bishop and doctor
feast	25	CONVERSION OF PAUL/apostle
memorial	26	Timothy and Titus/bishops
	27	Angela Merici/virgin
memorial	28	Thomas Aquinas/priest and doctor
	29	
	30	
memorial	31	John Bosco/priest
feast		BAPTISM OF THE LORD[2] Sunday after January 6
feast		SANTO NIÑO (Philippines) Third Sunday of January

[1]Epiphany is the Sunday between January 2 and 8 in Australia, New Zealand and the Philippines.
[2]If Epiphany falls on January 7 or 8, the Baptism of the Lord is the Monday after Epiphany in Australia.

FEBRUARY

feast	1	BRIGID/virgin (Ireland)
feast	2	PRESENTATION OF THE LORD
	3	Blase/bishop and martyr
		Ansgar/bishop
feast	4	JOHN DE BRITTO/martyr (India)
memorial	5	Agatha/virgin and martyr
memorial	6	Paul Miki and companions/martyrs[1]
	7	
	8	Jerome Emiliani
	9	Teilo/bishop (Wales)
memorial	10	Scholastica/virgin
	11	Our Lady of Lourdes
	12	
	13	
memorial	14	Cyril/monk, and Methodius/bishop
	15	
	16	
	17	Seven Founders of the Order of Servites
	18	
	19	
	20	
	21	Peter Damian/bishop and doctor
feast	22	CHAIR OF PETER/apostle
memorial	23	Polycarp/bishop and martyr
	24	
	25	
	26	
	27	
	28	

[1]February 6 is the memorial of Gonsalo Garcia, Paul Miki and companions in India; of Paul Miki, Pedro Bautista and companions in the Philippines.

MARCH

feast	1	DAVID (England)[1]
	2	
	3	
	4	Casimir
	5	
	6	
memorial	7	Perpetua and Felicity/martyrs
	8	John of God/religious
	9	Frances of Rome/religious
feast	10	JOHN OGILVIE/priest and martyr (Scotland)
	11	
	12	
	13	
	14	
	15	
	16	
	17	Patrick/bishop[2]
	18	Cyril of Jerusalem/bishop and doctor
solemnity	19	JOSEPH, HUSBAND OF MARY
	20	
	21	
	22	
	23	Turibius of Mongrovejo/bishop
	24	
solemnity	25	ANNUNCIATION
	26	
	27	
	28	
	29	
	30	
	31	

[1]March 1, David, is celebrated as a solemnity in Wales.
[2]March 17, Patrick, is celebrated as a solemnity in Ireland and New Zealand and as a feast in England, Wales, and Scotland.

APRIL

	1	
	2	Francis of Paola/hermit
	3	
	4	Isidore/bishop and doctor
	5	Vincent Ferrer/priest
	6	
memorial	7	John Baptist de la Salle/priest
	8	
	9	
	10	
	11	Stanislaus/bishop and martyr
	12	
	13	Martin I/pope and martyr
	14	
	15	
	16	
	17	Kateri Tekakwitha/virgin (Canada)[1]
	18	
	19	
	20	Beuno/abbott (Wales)
	21	Anselm/bishop and doctor[2]
	22	
	23	George/martyr[3]
	24	Fidelis of Sigmaringen/priest and martyr
feast	25	MARK/evangelist
	26	
	27	
	28	Peter Chanel/priest and martry[4]
memorial	29	Catherine of Siena/virgin and doctor
	30	Pius V/pope
		Marie de l'Incarnation/religious (Canada)

[1]April 17, Kateri, Tekakwitha, is celebrated as a memorial in the United States.
[2]April 21, Anselm, is celebrated as a memorial in England.
[3]April 23, George, is celebrated as a feast in England and Wales.
[4]April 28, Peter Chanel, is celebrated as a memorial in Australia and New Zealand.

MAY

	1	Joseph the Worker
memorial	2	Athanasius/bishop and doctor
feast	3	PHILIP AND JAMES/apostles
	4	Beatified Martyrs of England and Wales (Wales)[1]
	5	Asaph/bishop (Wales)
	6	François de Montmorency Laval/bishop (Canada)
	7	
	8	
	9	
	10	
	11	
	12	Nereus and Achilleus/martyrs
		Pancras/martyr
	13	
feast	14	MATTHIAS/apostle
	15	Isidore (United States)
	16	
	17	
	18	John I/pope and martyr
	19	
	20	Bernardine of Siena/priest
	21	
	22	
	23	
	24	
	25	Venerable Bede/priest and doctor[2]
		Gregory VII/pope
		Mary Magdalene de Pazzi/virgin
memorial	26	Philip Neri/priest
	27	Augustine of Canterbury/bishop[3]
	28	
	29	

[1]May 4, the Beatified Martyrs of England and Wales, is celebrated as a feast in England.
[2]May 25, Venerable Bede, is celebrated as a memorial in England.
[3]May 27, Augustine of Canterbury, is celebrated as a feast in England.

	30	
feast	31	VISITATION

solemnity   HOLY TRINITY
First Sunday after Pentecost

solemnity   CORPUS CHRISTI[4]
Thursday after Holy Trinity

solemnity   SACRED HEART
Friday following second Sunday after Pentecost
Immaculate Heart of Mary
Saturday following second Sunday
after Pentecost

solemnity   OUR LADY HELP OF CHRISTIANS
(Australia and New Zealand)
First Sunday on or after May 24

[4]Corpus Christi, is celebrated on the Sunday after Holy Trinity in Australia, New Zealand, and the Philippines.

JUNE

memorial	1	Justin/martyr
	2	Marcellinus and Peter/martyrs
memorial	3	Charles Lwanga and companions/martyrs
	4	
memorial	5	Boniface/bishop and martyr
	6	Norbert/bishop
	7	
	8	
	9	Ephrem/deacon and doctor
		Columba (Colum Cille) (Scotland)[1]
	10	
memorial	11	Barnabas/apostle
	12	
memorial	13	Anthony of Padua/priest and doctor
	14	
	15	
	16	
	17	
	18	
memorial	19	Romuald/abbott
memorial	20	Alban (England)
		Alban, Julius and Aaron (Wales)
memorial	21	Aloysius Gonzaga/religious
	22	Paulinus of Nola/bishop
		John Fisher/bishop and martyr and
		Thomas More/martyr[2]
	23	
solemnity	24	BIRTH OF JOHN THE BAPTIST
	25	
	26	
	27	Cyril of Alexandria/bishop and martyr
memorial	28	Irenaeus/bishop and martyr
solemnity	29	PETER AND PAUL/apostles[3]
	30	First Martyrs of the Church of Rome

June 9, Columba, is celebrated as a feast in Ireland.

[2]June 22, John Fisher and Thomas More, is celebrated as a feast in England and a memorial in Wales.

[3]The Solemnity of Peter and Paul is celebrated on the first Sunday on or after June 29 in Australia and New Zealand.

JULY

feast 1   OLIVER PLUNKETT/bishop and martyr
           (Ireland)

      2

feast 3   THOMAS/apostle[1]

      4   Elizabeth of Portugal
           Independence Day (United States)

      5   Anthony Zaccaria/priest

      6   Maria Goretti/virgin and martyr

      7

      8

      9

      10

memorial 11   Benedict/abbot

      12   John Jones/priest and martyr (Wales)

      13   Henry

      14   Camillus de Lellis/priest

memorial 15   Bonaventure/bishop and doctor

      16   Our Lady of Mount Carmel

      17

      18

      19

      20

      21   Lawrence of Brindisi/priest and doctor

memorial 22   Mary Magdalene

      23   Bridget/religious
           Philip Evans and John Lloyd/priests and
           martyrs (Wales)

      24

feast 25   JAMES/apostle

memorial 26   Joachim and Anne/parents of Mary

      27

      28

memorial 29   Martha

      30   Peter Chrysologus/bishop and doctor

memorial 31   Ignatius of Loyola/priest

[1]July 3, Thomas, is celebrated as a solemnity in India.

AUGUST

memorial	1	Alphonsus Liguori/bishop and doctor
	2	Eusebius of Vercelli/bishop
	3	Germanus of Auxerre/bishop (Wales)
memorial	4	John Vianney/priest
	5	Dedication of Saint Mary Major
feast	6	TRANSFIGURATION
	7	Sixtus II/pope and martyr, and companions/martyrs Cajetan/priest
memorial	8	Dominic/priest
	9	
feast	10	LAWRENCE/deacon and martyr
memorial	11	Clare/virgin
	12	
	13	Pontian/pope and martyr, and Hippolytus/priest and martyr
	14	
solemnity	15	ASSUMPTION
	16	Stephen of Hungary
	17	
	18	
	19	John Eudes/priest
memorial	20	Bernard/abbot and doctor
memorial	21	Pius X/pope
memorial	22	Queenship of Mary
	23	Rose of Lima/virgin
feast	24	BARTHOLOMEW/apostle
	25	Louis Joseph Calasanz/priest
	26	Dominic of the Mother of God/priest (England) David Lewis/priest and martyr (Wales)
memorial		Ninian/bishop (Scotland)
memorial	27	Monica
memorial	28	Augustine/bishop and doctor
memorial	29	Beheading of John the Baptist/martyr
	30	
	31	

SEPTEMBER

	1	
	2	
memorial	3	Gregory the Great/pope and doctor[1]
	4	
	5	
	6	
	7	
feast	8	BIRTH OF MARY
memorial	9	Peter Claver/priest (United States)
	10	
	11	Deiniol/bishop (Wales)
	12	
memorial	13	John Chrysostom/bishop and doctor
feast	14	TRIUMPH OF THE CROSS
memorial	15	Our Lady of Sorrows
memorial	16	Cornelius/pope and martyr, and Cyprian/bishop and martyr
	17	Robert Bellarmine/bishop and doctor
	18	
	19	Januarius/bishop and martyr
	20	
feast	21	MATTHEW/apostle and evangelist
	22	
	23	
memorial	24	Our Lady of Ransom (England)
	25	
	26	Cosmas and Damian/martyrs
memorial	27	Vincent de Paul/priest
	28	Wenceslaus/martyr[2]
feast	29	MICHAEL, GABRIEL, AND RAPHAEL/archangels
memorial	30	Jerome/priest and doctor

[1]September 3, Gregory, is celebrated as a feast in England.
[2]September 28 or 29 is pending in the Philippines as a memorial of Domingo Ibañez, Lorenzo Ruiz and companions, martyrs.

OCTOBER

memorial	1	Theresa of the Child Jesus/virgin[1]
memorial	2	Guardian Angels
	3	
memorial	4	Francis of Assisi
	5	
	6	Bruno/priest
memorial	7	Our Lady of the Rosary
	8	
	9	Denis/bishop and martyr, and companions/martyrs John Leonardi/priest
	10	
	11	
	12	
memorial	13	Edward the Confessor/king (England)
	14	Callistus I/pope and martyr
memorial	15	Teresa of Avila/virgin and doctor
	16	Hedwig/religious Margaret Mary Alacoque/virgin Marguerite d'Youville/religious (Canada) Richard Gwyn/schoolmaster (Wales)
memorial	17	Ignatius of Antioch/bishop and martyr
feast	18	LUKE/evangelist
memorial	19	Isaac Jogues and John de Brebeuf/priest, and companions/martyrs (United States and Canada)
	20	
	21	
	22	
	23	John of Capistrano/priest
	24	Anthony Claret/bishop
feast	25	CUTHBERT MAYNE, JOHN HOUGHTON, EDMUND CAMPION, RICHARD GWYNN, AND 36 COMPANIONS/martyrs (England) THE SIX WELSH MARTYRS AND COMPANIONS/martyrs (Wales)
	26	
	27	
feast	28	SIMON AND JUDE/apostles
	29	
	30	
	31	

[1]October 1, Theresa of the Child Jesus, is celebrated as feast in India and New Zealand.

NOVEMBER

solemnity	1	ALL SAINTS
	2	ALL SOULS
	3	Martin de Porres/religious
		Winefride/virgin (Wales)
memorial	4	Charles Borromeo/bishop
	5	
feast	6	ALL SAINTS OF IRELAND (Ireland)
		Illtud/abbot (Wales)
	7	
feast	8	ALL SAINTS OF WALES (Wales)
feast	9	DEDICATION OF SAINT JOHN LATERAN
memorial	10	Leo the Great/pope and doctor
memorial	11	Martin of Tours/bishop
memorial	12	Josaphat/bishop and martyr
memorial	13	Frances Xavier Cabrini/virgin (United States)
	14	Dyfrig/bishop (Wales)
	15	Albert the Great/bishop and doctor
	16	Margaret of Scotland[1]
		Gertrude/virgin
memorial	17	Elizabeth of Hungary/religious
	18	Dedication of the churches of Peter and Paul/apostles
	19	
	20	
memorial	21	Presentation of Mary
memorial	22	Cecilia/virgin and martyr
	23	Clement I/pope and martyr
		Columban/abbot[2]
	24	
	25	
	26	
	27	
	28	
	29	
feast	30	ANDREW/apostle[3]
		Thanksgiving Day (United States)
		Fourth Thursday
solemnity		CHRIST THE KING
		Last Sunday in Ordinary Time

[1]November 16, Margaret of Scotland, is celebrated as a feast in Scotland.
[2]November 23, Columbanus, is celebrated as a feast in Ireland.
[3]November 30, Andrew, is celebrated as a solemnity in Scotland.

DECEMBER

	1	
	2	
memorial	3	Francis Xavier/priest[1]
	4	John Damascene/priest and doctor
	5	
	6	Nicholas/bishop
memorial	7	Ambrose/bishop and doctor
solemnity	8	IMMACULATE CONCEPTION
	9	
	10	John Roberts/priest and martyr (Wales)
	11	Damasus I/pope
memorial	12	Our Lady of Guadalupe (United States)
		Jane Frances de Chantal/religious
memorial	13	Lucy/virgin and martyr
memorial	14	John of the Cross/priest and doctor
	15	
	16	
	17	
	18	
	19	
	20	
	21	Peter Canisius/priest and doctor
	22	
	23	John of Kanty/priest
	24	
solemnity	25	CHRISTMAS
feast	26	STEPHEN/first martyr
feast	27	JOHN/apostle and evangelist
feast	28	HOLY INNOCENTS/martyrs
	29	Thomas Becket/bishop and martyr[2]
	30	
	31	Sylvester I/pope
feast		HOLY FAMILY
		Sunday within the octave of Christmas or
		if there is no Sunday within the octave,
		December 30

[1]December 3, Francis Xavier, is celebrated as a solemnity in India and
as a feast in New Zealand.
[2]December 29, Thomas Becket, is celebrated as a feast in England.

5 / THE CALENDARS OF DIOCESES AND RELIGIOUS COMMUNITIES

Since the early days of Christianity it has been the custom and right of local Churches (dioceses) to have their own special liturgical celebrations. This is true especially of the veneration of the martyrs and saints, since the veneration of a given martyr or saint was originally a local phenomenon. The tendency to centralization of the liturgical calendar arose only with the promulgation of the posttridentine liturgical books. At the same time, however, the right of the dioceses to have their own calendars has never been suppressed. Vatican II explicitly defends this right when it says regarding the feasts of the saints: "Many of them should be left to be celebrated by a particular Church, or nation, or family of religious" (CL, no. 111; Flannery, p. 31).

The Roman documents which I cited at the beginning of the previous section contain more precise statements on the calendars of dioceses and religious communities. The *General Norms*, for example, says in its no. 52:

> A diocesan calendar, in addition to celebrations of its patrons and the dedication of the cathedral, contains those saints and blessed who bear some special connection with that diocese, e.g., birthplace, domicile over a long period, or place of death. . . . A calendar for individual churches, in addition to celebrations proper to the diocese or religious community, contains those celebrations proper to that church which are found in the table of liturgical days and also of a saint who is buried in that church.

The Instruction issued by the Congregation of Rites on June 24, 1970 repeats in large measure what is said in the *General Norms* but is a bit more specific: "A diocesan calendar is formed by inserting into the general calendar celebrations either proper or allowed by indult to an entire nation or region or even a larger area; celebrations proper or allowed by indult to an entire diocese. On the basis of this diocesan calendar the calendars of individual places, churches or chapels are then constructed."[108]

Special regulations in both documents are meant to keep the calendar of the diocese as a whole or the religious community as

262

a whole from becoming unduly inclusive."[109] Before saints or blesseds are accepted into a particular calendar, there must be a careful examination in order that "their life and deeds and the origin and spread of their cult may be shown to be historically credible."[110] Saints whose history (not: whose legend!) contains little or almost nothing that is historically certain are not to be given a place in the calendar. "The names of those saints, too, are to be removed who at an earlier time were inserted into the calendar due to special circumstances but who now have little or no connection with the diocese or religious family."[111]

The two Roman documents also have specific instructions for the calendars of religious Orders and congregations; in part, these regulations are the same as for the diocesan calendars. The right to a special calendar belongs to "Orders of men whose calendar is also to be used by the nuns and sisters, if any, of that same Order and by tertiaries of the Order who live a common life and take simple vows" and to "religious congregations, societies and institutes of pontifical law that are in any way obliged to the divine Office."[112]

"A religious calendar, in addition to celebrations of the titular saint, founder, or patron, contains those saints and blessed who were members of that community or had some special relationship with it."[113]

"The calendar of religious is formed by inserting into the general calendar celebrations proper to the Order or congregation or allowed to them by indult."[114] In order to confirm and strengthen the links of religious communities with the local Church, the former are to celebrate, with the diocese, the anniversary of the dedication of the cathedral, the chief patron of the diocese and of the province, nation, region or larger area, in which the religious community lives.[115]

6 / THE CALENDAR OF SAINTS' DAYS

When the General Roman Calendar was published in 1969, many names familiar to the people were no longer to be found in it. The result was unexpectedly severe criticism. It was said that some saints had been abolished or demoted, that others had been turned into "lesser" saints and had been disdained;

these saints nad been the victims of liturgical reform. People reacted as though the highest authorities in the Church were personally responsible for driving some saints from heaven.

Clearly, there was a good deal of misunderstanding, which had not been allowed for in the reform of the calendar. The critics were mistakenly identifying the liturgical calendar with the list of the saints whose names occur on a Catholic wall calendar or pocket calendar in the course of the year. They overlooked the fact that at no point in the entire history of the Church had all the saints ever appeared in any calendar listing the liturgical celebrations of the saints. A year of 365 days is simply too short for that to be possible.

On the other hand, the Church has indeed made an effort to include all the saints in the book entitled the *Martyrology*. It too is a liturgical book; from it the names of the saints whose anniversaries occur on a given day are read out during the Liturgy of the Hours or at some other appointed time.[116] The revision of the Roman liturgical calendar has not involved the deletion or erasure of even a single saint's name from the martyrology.

In Christian antiquity efforts were made in the Eastern Churches to have saints' names given to children at baptism. Thus John Chrysostom († 407), patriarch of Constantinople and a Father of the Church, advises the faithful: "We do not give children just any names, nor simply the names of their parents and forebears, nor the names of men and women famous for their lineage; we give them, instead, the names of the saints, men and women who have won renown for their virtues and whose trusting faith made them most powerful before God."[117]

Since the thirteenth century the West too has seen the practice spread of choosing saints' names, even those of saints from other lands. Only in the sixteenth century, however, did the Roman Church begin to issue similar exhortations.[118] At the same period there was a revival of the late medieval custom of celebrating in a special way the feast of the saint whose name one bore. The patron saint was seen to be a model one must follow, but also an intercessor with God.

Many Christians, of course, pay no heed to the fact that they bear a saint's name, but the enemies of Christianity see the custom as a bulwark which they attack with fierce determination. Thus in 1977 we read in the newspapers that President Mobutu of the African Republic of Zaire forbade the giving of Christian names to children. A similar prohibition was reported in the Central African Republic of Chad.[119] Similar efforts have been made in other totalitarian states.

Notes

1. K. Rahner, "Vom Geheimnis der Heiligkeit, der Heiligen und ihrer Verehrung," in P. Manns (ed.), *Reformer der Kirche* (Mainz, 1970), p. 26.

2. [This is the full title in Latin and in the English translation in W. M. Abbott (ed.), *The Documents of Vatican II* (New York, 1966), p. 78. Flannery, p. 407, has simply "The Pilgrim Church."—*Tr.*]

3. [Again, the title here is as in the Latin text and the Abbott translation, p. 85. Flannery, p. 413, has simply "Our Lady."—*Tr*]

4. Tr. in *The Pope Speaks* 19 (1974), 49-87.

5. W. Beinert provides a more modern "Short Introduction to Mariology" in his book *Heute von Maria reden?* (Freiburg, 1975³). The same author has edited a collective work, *Maria heute ehren. Eine theologisch-pastorale Handreichung* (Freiburg, 1977). There is a valuable survey of "Mariologie im 20. Jahrhundert" by H.-M. Köster in H. Vorgrimler and R. V. Gucht (eds.), *Bilanz der Theologie im 20. Jahrhundert* 3 (Freiburg–Basel–Vienna, 1970), pp. 126-47. Köster lists the most important literature.

6. This necessary sketchiness can be helpful in dealing with the extensive literature on the veneration of the saints. I shall mention but a few of the many books and articles: P. Molinari, *Saints and Their Place in the Church*, tr. by D. Maruca (New York, 1965); M. Lackmann (an Evangelical), *Verehrung der Heiligen* (Stuttgart, 1958); Th. Klauser, *Christlicher Märtyrerkult, heidnischer Heroenkult and spätjüdische Heiligenverehrung* (Cologne–Opladen, 1960); B. Kötting, "Heiligenverehrung," in H. Fries (ed.), *Handbuch theologischer Grundbegriffe* 1 (Munich, 1962), 633-41; idem, "Entwicklung der Heiligenverehrung und Geschichte der Heiligsprechung," in P. Manns (ed.), *Reformer der Kirche* (Mainz, 1970), pp. 27-39.

7. Klauser, ibid., p. 37.

8. Ibid., p. 31.

9. Text and references in Radó 2:1320.

10. Kötting, "Heiligenverehrung," pp. 638-39.

11. Mention may be made, among others, of W. Stählin, *Maria, die Mutter des Herrn, ihr biblisches Bild* (Düsseldorf, 1951); M. Lackmann (n. 329, above); M. Thurian, *Mary, Mother of All Christians*, tr. by N. B. Cryer (New York, 1963).

12. Harnoncourt, pp. 71-72.

13. Ibid., p. 74.

14. Ibid., pp. 78-84.

15. Ibid., pp. 117-18.

16. CommALI, cap. II, sect. I (pp. 66-67).

17. The Apostolic Letter of Paul VI, the *General Norms* and the General Roman Calendar are all translated at the beginning of the new Missal. The Commentary on the Revised Liturgical Year and the Commentary on the New Calendar are given in *The Roman Calendar: Text and Commentary* (Washington, D.C., United States Catholic Conference, 1975).

18. A "period of Marian 'overheating' " that occurred around the middle of the present century may "have proved a hindrance to the faith of young people and thoughtful adults," according to P. Lippert in Beinert (ed.), *Maria heute ehren*, pp. 249-50.

19. This is the dogmatic definition given by Pius IX in his Bull *Ineffabilis Deus* of December 8, 1854 (DS 2803).

20. For an English translation cf. M. R. James, *The Apocryphal New Testament* (London, 1924), pp. 38-49, or, more recently, E. Hennecke and W. Schneemelcher, *New Testament Apocrypha*, translation edited by R. McL. Wilson, 1 (Philadelphia, 1963), pp. 374-88.

21. *Epist.* 174 (PL 182:332-36).

22. Extensive references in, e.g., Righetti 2:291-97; Radó 2:1332-36.

23. H. Junker, "Genesis," in F. Nötscher (ed.), *Das Alte Testament* (Würzburg, 1953), p. 19.

24. Thus in the CommNC, cap. II (Variationes), for July 2 (p. 128).

25. Radó 2:1343; cf. O. Heiming, "Literaturbericht," AL 3/2 (1954), 409-11.

26. Righetti 2:285.

27. Ibid. 2:286.

28. Radó 2:1349-50; Righetti 2:299-300.

29. CommNC, cap. II (Variationes), for February 11 (p. 116).

30. L. Scheffczyk, in Beinert (ed.), *Maria heute ehren*, p. 171, referring to K. Rahner, *Visionen und Prophezeiungen* (Freiburg, 1958²), pp. 18 and 41 ff. [In English: K. Rahner, *Visions and Prophecies*, tr. by C. Henkey and R. Strachan (Quaestiones Disputatae 10; New York, 1963), pp. 16-17 and 28-30.]

31. For the theology of devotion to the Heart of Mary cf., among others, J. Storck, *Unser liebe Frau vom heiligsten Herzen Jesu* (Münster, 1954); F. Lakner, "Das Rundschreiben Pius' XII 'Haurietis aquas' und der Kult des unbefleckten Herzens Marias," in Bea-Rahner (eds.), *Cor Jesu* p. 723-80.

32. Detailed references in Radó 2:1352.

33. CommNC, cap. II (Variationes), for May 31 (p. 125). Cf. E. Sauser, "Kritische Überlegungen zum Gedenktag 'Mariä Königin,'" HD 32 (1978), 82-84.

34. Righetti 2:303.

35. Pascher, p. 657, gives an extensive appreciation of the Office and Mass for this memorial (pp. 649-59).

36. Radó 2:1335. References are also given here for the following survey.

37. On the problem cf. F. Mussner and B. Fischer, "Was wird bei einer Kalenderreform aus dem Fest Praesentatio B. V. M. (21.11)?" TTZ 70 (1961), 170-81. The two authors, one as a New Testament exegete, the other as a liturgiologist, agree in rejecting the feast.

38. A survey of their history and geographical extent is given in Radó 2:1357-60, who refers to F. G. Holweck, *Fasti mariani* (Freiburg, 1892). According to Holweck in the course of time and in various countries there have been over 1000 local Marian feasts.

39. No. 9, in *The Pope Speaks* 19 (1974), 56.

40. Cf. J. Metzler, "Die Marien-Maiandacht. Ihre Entstehung, Entwicklung und Ausbreitung," ZAM 3 (1928), 89-101.

41. Translated in *The Pope Speaks* 19 (1964-65), 221.

42. "Die 'Marienmonate,'" in Beinert (ed.), *Maria heute ehren*, pp. 249-58.

43. Ibid., p. 258.

44. CommALI, cap. II, sect. I (pp. 65-75); see above, this chapter, section 1c.

45. The commentary explicitly mentions the works of H. Delahaye and the Bollandists (p. 68).

46. Ibid., p. 70.

47. Ibid., p. 68.

48. Ibid., p. 73.

49. Cf. A. Bugnini, "Der neue Kalender," Gd 3 (1969), 73-74.

50. Thus, e.g., Harnoncourt, pp. 127-28.

51. In the circular letter sent out by the Church of Smyrna on the martyrdom of St. Polycarp the anniversary of his death is already spoken of as the anniversary of his birthday into heaven (PG 51:1043). Bishop Cyprian of Carthage urged that a record be kept of the martyrs' deaths "so that we can include commemoration of them among the memorial days of the martyrs" (Epist. 37; PL 4:337). Cf. CommALI, cap. II, sect. I. 4 (pp. 73-74).

52. CommALI, cap. II, sect. I. 4 (p. 74).

53. Ibid., cap. II, sect. II. 3 (p. 82).

54. Ibid. (pp. 82-83).

55. GIRM, no. 316.

56. Details in Radó 2:1391; Schmidt, Introductio, p. 653; Pascher, pp. 708-9.

57. Radó 2:1391-92.

58. Kellner, p. 205.

59. Cf. Righetti 2:339-40; Radó 2:1378-79.

60. CommNC, cap. I, for March 19 (p. 89).

61. Cf. n. 59.

62. CommNC, cap. I, for May 1 (p. 92).

63. Ibid., cap. II (Variationes), for May 1 (p. 121).

64. For criticism of the style of recent devotion to Joseph and of the two additional feasts cf. E. Sauser, "Stillschweigende Korrekturen," Gd 10 (1976), 63-64; but. cf. J. Mechelen, "Josefsverehrung nicht zu 'nüchtern,'" Gd 11 (1977), 31.

65. Schuster 4:265.

66. Cited in Radó 2:1381; cf. also Sermo 287, 3 (PL 38:1302), in Pascher, p. 559.

67. Righetti 2:336.

68. Ibid., 2:338; Radó 2:1382.

69. Radó 2:1370.

70. Ibid., 2:1370-71; W. Dürig, "Apostelfeste," LTK 1 (1957), 742-43.

71. This translation on June 29, 258 "under the Consuls Tuscus and Bassus" is disputed. Dürig (ibid.) rejects it; Radó (2:1371) accepts it; Pascher (pp. 475-77) defends it with several considerable arguments.

72. *De virginitate* 19, 124-25 (PL 16:299).

73. CommNC, cap. II (Variationes) for June 30 (p. 128).

74. GNLYC, chap. III, "Table of Liturgical Days according to their order of precedence," I, 3.

75. Righetti 2:368-69, 375-77; Jungmann, 1:217-19.

76. Jungmann 1:218. [The *refrigerium* was the memorial meal for the dead: Jungmann 1:218, n. 43.—*Tr.*]

77. *Regula* 24, 2 (PL 83:294).

78. *Vita S. Eigilii* 25 (PL 105:400).

79. *De ordine Antiphonum* 65 (Hanssens 3:98).

80. *Statutum Odilonis* (PL 142:1037).

81. In the Church of Milan the memorial was celebrated on the day after the feast of the dedication of the cathedral (October 16), until Charles Borromeo transferred it to November 2 in 1582 (Righetti 2:398).

82. H. Kneller, "Geschichtliches über die drei Messen am Allerseelentag," ZKT 42 (1918), 74-113.

83. GIRM, no. 306d-e; cf. the Instruction on the Implementation of the Constitution on the Liturgy, of May 4, 1967, nos. 23–24.

84. A detailed description of the older All Souls liturgy in Mass and Office is given in Pascher, pp. 718-31. Despite all efforts to give a positive interpretation of it Pascher concludes: "Nonetheless it is the wish of many that a future Office of the Dead should be characterized to a greater degree by confidence in the paschal mystery of death and resurrection with Christ" (p. 731).

85. [A mid-fifth-century martyrology from Italy, wrongly attributed to St. Jerome.—*Tr.*]

86. Detailed references in Paschar, p. 505; Radó 2:1376.

87. See especially J. P. Kirsch, "Die beiden Apostelfeste Petri Stuhlfeier und Pauli Bekehrung im Januar," JL 5 (1925), 48-67; Th. Klauser, *Die Kathedra im Totenkult der Heidnischen und christlichen Antike* (Münster, 1927); D. Baldoni, "Natale Petri de cathedra," EL 68 (1954), 97-126.

88. Cf. Radó 2:1377; Pascher, 538-39.

89. J. Blinzler, "Jakobus der Jüngere," LTK 5 (1960), 837; idem, "Jakobus, der Bruder Jesu," ibid., 837-38; idem, "Jakobusbrief," ibid., 861-63.

90. Schmidt, *Introductio*, p. 621; Pascher, pp. 521-22; Radó 2:1372-73.

91. *Historia ecclesiastica* III, 1, 1 (ed. E. Schwarz [Berlin, 1952], p. 77).

92. Radó, 2:1374; Pascher, pp. 734-35.

93. Pascher, pp. 526-27; Radó 2:1373.

94. Cyprian, *Epist*. 80 (CSEL 3/2:840) provides historical attestation of the martyrdom of Xystus and his four deacons.

95. Ambrose gives a detailed account in his *De officiis* I, 41 (PL 16:84-85).

96. B. Kötting, "Laurentius," LTK 6 (1961), 831.

97. The "may have" allows for the not ungrounded suspicion that the Church of Benevento might have given Emperor Otto III (983–1002) the bones of some other saint and not those of the apostle. Cf. Schuster 5:69-70.

98. Schuster 5:126-27.

99. Cf. J. Schmid and W. Dürig, "Lukas I u. II," LTK 6 (1961), 1203-4; Radó 2:1073.

100. Kellner, pp. 224-25.

101. Ibid., p. 218; Radó 2:1374.

102. Congregation of Rites, General Decree *Cum hac nostra aetate* on the Simplification of the Rubrics (March 23, 1955), Tit. II.9, in AAS 47 (1955), 226.

103. R. Haubst, "Engel, III: Systematisch," LTK 3 (1959), 870. The existence of angels was defined by the Fourth Lateran Council (DS 800) and the First Vatican Council (DS 3002).

104. "Erzengel," in H. Haag (ed.), *Bibellexikon* (Einsiedeln, 1956), p. 432.

105. H. Leclercq, "Anges," DACL 1/2:2148.

106. Righetti 2:329-34; Radó 2:1386-89.

107. Cf. Radó 2:1390.

108. *Instruction*, no. 13, in AAS 62 (1970), 655.

109. *Instruction*, no. 17 (p. 655).

110. *Instruction*, no. 18 (p. 656).

111. *Instruction*, no. 19 (p. 656).

112. *Instruction*, no. 16 (p. 655).

113. GNLYC, no. 52b.

114. *Instruction*, no. 16b (p. 655).

115. *Instruction*, no. 16d (p. 655).

116. The Roman Martyrology was radically revised in 1583 (Cardinal Sirleto) and since then has been frequently reprinted and translated. The most recent English edition was published in 1962 (ed. J. B. O'Connell); the most recent Latin edition (the 4th after the typical edition of 1913–14) in 1956.

117. *Homilia 21 in Genesim* 3 (PG 53:179).

118. Cf., e.g., the *Roman Catechism* of 1566 (Part II, chap. 2, question 73) and the *Roman Ritual* (Title II, chap. 1, no. 30). In these documents it was even prescribed that if parents insisted on a nonchristian name, the priest was to add a Christian name and enter both in the register of baptisms.

119. Cf. HK 29 (1975), 50.

The Liturgical Year and the Liturgy of the Hours

The liturgical year, with the paschal mystery of Christ as its basic inspiration, shapes not only the eucharistic liturgy, which is the center, source and summit of Christian liturgy, but also the Church's liturgy of the hours. This too is an important part of the total liturgy and, as such, embodies the common action of Christ and the Church for the sanctification of human beings and the glorification of the heavenly Father. For here too the Lord is present and active, inasmuch as he himself speaks to us in the reading of scripture and unites with the praying Church and her members. As I made clear in the introduction to the present book, there can be no question here of interpreting all the texts of the Office for the various seasons and feasts. I can only sketch its historical development and explain its importance and present structure.

1 / ORIGIN AND DEVELOPMENT OF THE LITURGY OF THE HOURS

The entire life of Jesus was a hymn glorifying the heavenly Father. His preaching, his hours of public and solitary prayer, his ministry of healing and helping his fellow human beings and, finally, his expiatory suffering and death: all these served both the salvation of the human race and the glorification of his Father. As Jesus himself expresses it in his high priestly prayer: "I glorified thee on earth, having accomplished the work which thou gavest me to do" (Jn 17.4). The gospels frequently tell us that Jesus was a great man of prayer and that he taught his disciples to pray (cf. the "Lord's Prayer") and urged them "always to pray and not lose heart" (Lk 18.1).

The community of disciples was faithful to the example and instruction of its Lord, as the Acts of the Apostles and the various apostolic letters frequently attest.[1]

At a very early period special daily times of prayer were established, partly in imitation of the fixed hours for prayer and sacrifice in Judaism. The most important of these were Morning and Evening prayer, but there was also prayer at the third, sixth and ninth hours (as calculated according to the "twelve hours of light" which, in the Greek and Roman division of the day, began at 6 AM).

> According to a great many witnesses there was, from as early as the beginning of the second century, a horarium of prayer for all the faithful. In this horarium nearly all of our present liturgical hours were included: prayer at around midnight, prayer on rising, prayer at the third, sixth and ninth hours, and prayer in the evening; almost certainly these periods of prayer went back to apostolic times. But the prayer in question was the private prayer of individuals; as they prayed they were to reflect on the phase of Christ's passion that corresponded to the time of day.[2]

This private form of prayer seems soon to have given way to an official prayer on the part of the community. This is especially true of Morning Prayer and Evening Prayer. Tertullian speaks of these two as *orationes legitimae* ("appointed prayers"), i.e., in all probability times of prayer that were prescribed by law and custom.[3] According to Hippolytus of Rome deacons and priests were to assemble each morning at a place appointed by the bishop and, together with the people, celebrate a liturgy of the word (instruction and prayer).[4] As far as evening prayer was concerned, the principal quasi-model was the *lucernarium* ("lamplighting ceremony"), a religious rite that accompanied the lighting of the lamps in the evening and was to be found, in varying forms, among Jews, Greeks and Romans. In the *Apostolic Constitutions* (later fourth century) this evening prayer already has a form resembling that of Evening Prayer of the present Liturgy of the Hours.[5]

After the Peace of Constantine a widespread pattern began to appear. The focal points remained Morning Prayer (lauds) and vespers (Latin: *vesper* or *vespera*, "evening"); in these the community took part.[6] The monastic communities were the primary influence in determining the further development of the Office. Thus St. Benedict, who adapted the monastic usage he found at Rome, left a profound mark on the later Roman prayer of the hours. The hours included matins (which originated in the celebration of nocturnal vigils), lauds (also called *laudes matutinae*, "morning lauds" or "morning prayer"), prime, terce, sext, none, vespers and compline. The Office kept this form down through the centuries until the reform of 1970

The entire collection of hours has several *names*. The names "Prayer of the Hours" and "Canonical Hours" call attention to the fact that prayer is offered at appointed times and is intended to sanctify the entire day.

The term "Breviary" is a medieval one, derived from the Latin word *breviaria*. *Breviaria* were short lists in which the texts for the prayer of the hours were indicated by means of key words and concise references. At that time, monks in choir used several books for their communal prayer, taking the prescribed texts from each. Only in the eleventh century did the practice arise of including all the needed texts in a single book, to which the name of the previous lists of texts (also called *tabellaria*) was given. Such a book made it significantly easier for individuals to pray the Office privately and for people to pray it while traveling. According to other authors, however, the word "Breviary" is derived "from the curtailment that occurred when the various types of books (Psaltery, Antiphonary, Collectary, Lectionary) were combined into one for recitation by individuals . . . It refers to the length of the readings."[7]

Another frequently used name is "Office," often accompanied by the adjective "divine" or "canonical." Originally, *officium* meant "duty" and "assigned function" and referred to the entirety of the liturgy; gradually, its range of use narrowed and it referred only to the prayer of the hours. Finally, in the consciousness that the hours are indeed part of the liturgy, the term *liturgia horarum*, "liturgy of the hours," has come into use recently.[8]

As the Roman liturgy spread to most countries of the West, the Roman prayer of the hours was also adopted. In the early Middle Ages there was a growing tendency to increase the number and length of the prayers; so far did this trend go that there was great dissatisfaction with the Office and a consequent neglect of it. The call for radical reform grew louder and louder, especially at the beginning of the sixteenth century. The much shorter reformed breviary which Cardinal Quiñones published in 1535 for private recitation of the Office was greeted with enthusiasm and went through about a hundred printings within a few years, but it was replaced by the uniform breviary of Pius V in 1568.

This book in its turn was the object of many authorized and unauthorized attempts at reform.[9] Especially deserving of mention are the steps taken under Pius X which led to, among other things, a reduction in the number of psalms at matins from 18 or 12 to 9.[10] Pius XII revived the unimplemented plans of Pius X for breviary reform and in 1948 appointed a commission to prepare for a radical reform of the entire liturgy. The commission published five volumes of studies between 1950 and 1957. The work bore its first fruits in the rubrical reforms of 1955 and 1960.[11]

Vatican II dealt in detail with the reform of the Office and devoted a special chapter to the subject in its *Constitution on the Liturgy* (chapter IV, with 19 articles, 83–101).[12] The Council makes important statements here about the theology and spirituality of the Office, stresses the fact that it is a communal prayer, and lays a great deal of emphasis on the *veritas temporis* ("truthfulness in relation to the time of day"), that is, on praying the various hours at the proper times, "so that, as far as possible, they may again become also in fact what they have been in name" (CL, no. 88; Flannery, p. 25). The Council also sets down some very important guidelines for a concrete reform:

> Therefore, in the revision of the office these norms are to be observed:
>
> (a) By the venerable tradition of the universal Church, Lauds as morning prayer, and Vespers as evening prayer, are the two hinges on which the daily office turns. They must be considered as the chief hours and are to be celebrated as such.
>
> (b) Compline is to be drawn up so as suitably to mark the close of the day.
>
> (c) The hour called Matins, although it should retain the character of nocturnal prayer when recited in choir, shall be so adapted that it may be recited at any hour of the day, and it shall be made up of fewer psalms and longer readings.
>
> (d) The hour of Prime is to be suppressed.
>
> (e) In choir the minor hours of Terce, Sext, and None are to be observed. Outside of choir it will be lawful to select any one of three most suited to the time of the day (CL, no. 89; Flannery, pp. 25-26).

These and other directives which I cannot cite in detail started a period of intense work on a new breviary. The Roman Consilium appointed a commission, with several subcommissions, that worked for seven years and finally produced the new Office which Paul VI approved in his Apostolic Constitution *Laudis canticum* (feast of All Saints, 1970). The Congregation for Divine Worship published the first volume on Easter Sunday 1971. This volume also contains the *General Instruction of the Liturgy of the Hours* (GILH). This introduction is 74 pages long (with 284 numbers or articles) and, like the corresponding introduction to the Missal, contains material that is not simply rubrical but also, and primarily, explanatory of meaning and content. Three further volumes of the Office appeared in the following year.

The first volume of the English *Liturgy of the Hours* (comprising the Advent and Christmas seasons) appeared in 1975. Volumes 3 (Ordinary Time, Weeks 1–17) and 4 (Ordinary Time, Weeks 18–34) appeared in the same year, while volume 2 (Lent and Easter) appeared in the next year.

2 / MEANING AND IMPORTANCE OF THE LITURGY OF THE HOURS

Both the *Constitution on the Liturgy* and the *General Instruction* see the meaning and importance of the Liturgy of the Hours as residing in the fact that the Church, which is the body of Christ and the holy people of God, offers this prayer as one who participates in the priesthood of Christ and raises its voice with him in glorification of the Father and intercession for the entire human race.

> In the Holy Spirit Christ carries out through the Church "the work of man's redemption and God's perfect glorification" [CL, no. 5], not only when the Eucharist is celebrated and the sacraments administered but also in other ways, and especially when the Liturgy of the Hours is celebrated. In it Christ himself is present, in the assembled community, in the proclamation of God's word, "in the prayer and song of the Church" [ibid.] (GILH, no. 29).

Augustine was familiar with this view of the Church's prayer, for he wrote in his commentary on Psalm 85, 1: "Our Lord Jesus Christ, Son of God, is the sole Savior of his body. He prays for us, he prays in us, and we pray to him. He prays for us as our priest; he prays in us as our head; we pray to him as our God. Therefore let us recognize not only that we speak in him but also that he speaks in us."[13]

All who take part in the Liturgy of the Hours "are not only performing a duty for the Church, they are also sharing in what is the greatest honor for Christ's Bride; for by offering these praises to God they are standing before God's throne in the name of the Church, their Mother" (CL, no. 85; Flannery, pp. 24–25). But when the Church raises her voice in prayer she does so by the power of the Holy Spirit who fills and guides both

Christ and his Church. For "there can be no Christian prayer without the action of the Holy Spirit who unites the whole Church and leads it through the Son to the Father" (GILH, no. 8).

As liturgy, the Prayer of the Hours is dialogical. For in every liturgical action God comes, in his Son, to human beings and sanctifies them by the power of his word that is spoken to us in the Prayer of the Hours (psalms, readings, etc.) no less than in the Mass, but also by the power of the paschal mystery that produces its fruitful effects in encounter and communion with Christ. At the same time, Christ leads the Church in prayer and prays with her, thus giving human praise and petition a new quality and effectiveness. The result is a mutual giving and receiving in which the initiative comes from God who wills our salvation. "Man's sanctification is accomplished, and worship is given to God, in the Liturgy of the Hours in an exchange or dialogue between God and man" (GILH, no. 14). Because the salvation and sanctification of human beings is at the same time the supreme form of glorification of God, the intercessory prayer of the Church in the Liturgy of the Hours is not only a service of love to human beings but also a glorification of God.

In this dialogue the important thing is that the participants should not act in a merely outward and quasimechanical way (like a record or a prayer wheel), but consciously and with personal devotion, so as "to attune their minds to their voices" (CL, no. 90; Flannery, p. 26). "Mind and voice must be in harmony . . . if this prayer is to be made their own by those taking part in it, and be a service of devotion, a means of gaining God's manifold grace, a deepening of personal prayer, and an incentive to the work of the apostolate" (GILH, no. 19). In order the better to achieve this harmony the *Constitution on the Liturgy* recommends a more extensive biblical and liturgical formation, especially in regard to the psalms (CL, no. 90).

Vatican II and the *General Instruction* both attribute special value to the fact that the Liturgy of the Hours is communal in character. Because the Office is not simply a private prayer but is the official prayer of the Church, its communal celebration is to be preferred to recitation in private; the same holds for other liturgical actions (cf. CL, nos. 26–27, 99). The *General Instruction* directs an appeal on this point not only to such priests and religious as may not be obliged to the communal recitation of the Office; it also issues an invitation to the laity and the parishes: "Where possible, the principal Hours should be celebrated communally in church by other groups of the faithful" (GILH, no. 21). By so doing, "they show forth the Church in its celebration of the mystery of Christ" (ibid., no. 22). The family, too, "the domestic sanctuary of the Church," is exhorted not only to pray together but, as far as possible, to celebrate some part of the Liturgy of the Hours and thus to enter more deeply into their life of the Church (ibid., no. 27).

A further concern of the *General Instruction* is the recitation of the individual Hours at the proper time, a point already emphasized by the *Constitution on the Liturgy* (cf. nos. 88 and 94). Because the prayer of the hours is meant to sanctify the day and in many passages refers explicitly to certain times of the day, it would be absurd, for example, to pray the morning hour of lauds in the afternoon and the evening hour of vespers in the morning. Yet until a couple of decades ago it had become the custom of many priests to "anticipate" matins and lauds on the afternoon of the previous day and to pray vespers and compline in the early morning, because they feared that pastoral obligations in the evening would not leave them time for the Office then. [14] In order to facilitate the praying of the hours at the right time under the conditions of contemporary life and work, Vatican II set down some more detailed guidelines for the reform of the breviary (CL, no. 89). I shall speak of these below when describing the individual hours.

The Liturgy of the Hours is obligatory for all bishops, priests, deacons (preparing for priesthood), and religious (GILH, no. 17). It is regarded as desirable that "permanent" deacons recite at least part of the prayer of the hours; the competent episcopal conference is to determine which part (ibid., no. 30). As for the kind or degree of obligation, the relevant passages in the *General Instruction* seem to suggest some relaxation of the previous strict obligation, as well as a differentiation between the various hours. In the past it was considered a serious sin to omit, even once, a little hour or an equally lengthy part of some other hour.[15]

Vatican II, on the other hand, allowed the substitution of other liturgical actions and gave bishops and higher religious superiors authority "in particular cases, and for adequate reasons," to "dispense their subjects, wholly or in part, from the obligation of reciting the divine office" or to "change it to another obligation" (CL, no. 97; Flannery, p. 27). The Fathers of Vatican II expressly refused to require "serious" reasons for such a dispensation or commutation.

The language of the *General Instruction*, for its part, amounts to an exhortation to the Church that it faithfully carry out its mission. Only in connection with the two principal hours, Morning Prayer and Evening Prayer, is this exhortation reinforced by saying that "the hinge of the Liturgy of the Hours, that is, Morning and Evening Prayer . . . should not be omitted except for a serious reason" (GILH, no. 29). This moderation in imposing serious obligations should help priests and others to put aside certain anxieties and to pray the Office in accordance with the limitations of time and health and thus with greater joy.

3 / REVISION AND ADAPTATION TO THE LITURGICAL YEAR

In order that the laity, who have had no close contact with the Church's prayer of the hours, may gain some idea of its structure, I shall here describe each part of it and call attention to the most important changes that have been made. I shall then go on to indicate the components of the Liturgy of the Hours that reflect the seasons and feasts of the liturgical year, so that, together with the celebration of the eucharist, the Office becomes a comprehensive memorial of the saving acts of Christ.

a/Revision of the Prayer of the Hours

The new Liturgy of the Hours has the following overall structure: (1) an introduction (the invitatory); (2) the Office of Readings; (3) Morning Prayer (lauds); (4) Terce, Sext and None (little hours); (5) Evening Prayer (vespers); (6) Night Prayer (compline).

1) The Invitatory introduces the Liturgy of the Hours. It consists of the verse, "Lord, open my lips. And my mouth shall declare your praise," followed by a variable antiphon and Psalm 95. But Psalms 100, 67 or 24 may be used instead. When the Liturgy of the Hours begins with Morning Prayer, the psalm with its antiphon may be omitted (GILH, no. 35).

2) As successor to the old matins the Office of Readings is to be kept as a night office of praise when celebrated in choir, but it is so constructed that it is suitable for recitation at any time of the day (GILH, no. 57), "even during the night hours of the previous day" (GILH, no. 59). It is meant to help open to Christians the treasures of sacred scripture and the ecclesiastical writers, especially the Fathers of the Church. It consists of an opening verse, a hymn, three psalms (or parts of psalms), a verse, reading from scripture and another from the ecclesiastical writers or one dealing with the saint of the day, a responsory after each reading, and the prayer of the day. On certain days the responsory after the second reading is followed by the Te Deum.

The new Latin (and English) breviary contains only one annual cycle of readings[16] but a two-year cycle is provided for optional use in a supplement (cf. GILH, nos. 145, 161). It is worth noting that some modern writers are included. On Sundays, solemnities and feasts the Office of Readings can be expanded into a vigil service; the *General Instruction* gives further regulations for this (nos. 70–73).

3) Morning Prayer and Evening Prayer are "the two hinges on which the daily office turns" (CL, no. 89a; Flannery, p. 25) and "are therefore to be considered the principal Hours and celebrated as such" (GILH, no. 37). The older name, "morning lauds," shows that it was the Church's real morning prayer; therefore, to avoid duplication the old hour of prime, which had originated in monastic circles, was abolished.

Morning Prayer comprises an introductory verse, a hymn, psalms (including one morning psalm, an Old Testament canticle, and another psalm of praise), a short reading with a responsory, the Canticle of Zechariah (Lk 1.68-79) with an antiphon, invocations for the consecration of the day and its work, a concluding prayer and a blessing. According to an ancient tradition, Morning Prayer also recalls the resurrection of Christ (cf. GILH, no. 38).

4) According to the *General Instruction*, the minor hours of terce, sext and none have been observed principally "because these Hours were linked to a commemoration of the events of the Lord's Passion and of the first preaching of the Gospel" (no. 75). Outside of choir only one of the three need be prayed, whichever one best corresponds to the time of day. The structure of all three is the same: introductory verse, hymn, three psalms, short reading and responsory, and concluding prayer.

5) Evening Prayer is a prayer of thanksgiving for the day now ending but also for the saving acts of Christ on Holy Thursday evening and for his sacrifice of the cross on Good Friday afternoon (GILH, no. 39). In structure, Evening Prayer is the same as Morning Prayer: introductory verse, hymn, psalmody (two psalms and a New Testament canticle from the Letters or Revelation), short reading (in community vespers this may be replaced by a longer reading and a homily), responsory (which, again, may be replaced by an appropriate authorized song), the Magnificat with an antiphon, intercessions, Our Father, and concluding prayer. In community vespers the priest or deacon speaks (sings) the concluding rite as at Mass. In his Apostolic Constitution *Laudis canticum* Paul VI explicitly adverts to the introduction of the Our Father into Morning and Evening Prayer and sees this as a return to the early Christian practice of reciting the Lord's Prayer three times each day (the third time now is at Mass).[17]

6) Night Prayer or compline (Latin: *completorium*, "completion") is to be prayed just before retiring for the night, even if this be after midnight (GILH, no. 84). If possible, the introductory verse should be followed by an examination of conscience. The hymn is followed by psalms, usually two of them but on Sunday Psalm 91 alone. In order to make it easier to pray compline from memory, the Sunday psalm or the two Sunday evening psalms, 4 and 134, may be used on weekdays as well.

After the short reading and the responsory comes the Canticle of Simeon (Lk 2.29-32) with an antiphon, then the concluding prayer and blessing. The Office ends with one of the Marian antiphons. Except for the *Regina caeli* during the Easter season, these antiphons are no longer assigned to specific periods of the year (GILH, no. 92). The Hail Mary and the prayer "We fly to your protection" may also be used.

In order to foster inwardness in the praying of the Office, a reasonable time should be allowed for "reverent silence" (CL, no. 30; Flannery, p. 11) at each of the hours, especially after the psalms and readings (GILH, nos. 201-3).[18]

b/Adaptation to the Liturgical Year

Not only is the prayer of the hours characterized by a relationship to the various times of the day; in many of its texts it also proclaims the mystery proper to the seasons and feasts of the liturgical year. Because of its greater length it can develop and meditate on the message of God's saving deeds more fully than is possible in the celebration of the eucharist. As a result, the Office has over the centuries become a unique reflection of the liturgical year and a highly expressive means of prayer. It has also become a literary work of art that gives voice both to festive joy at the redemptive work of Christ and to the suppliant prayers of God's pilgrim people in their manifold concerns and tribulations.

At the very beginning of the Office the variable antiphon for the invitatory psalm already serves as a leitmotif. However, it is chiefly the hymns of the individual hours that celebrate the special object of the feast; these hymns are often marvelously beautiful poems. According to the *General Instruction*, "they also provide participation for the people. Indeed, they generally have an immediate effect in creating the particular quality of the Hour or individual feast, more so than the other parts of the Office, and are able to move mind and heart to devotion, a power frequently enhanced by their beauty of style" (GILH, no. 173). For regional breviaries the episcopal conferences may adapt the Latin hymns to suit the character of their own language and may use suitable new compositions (ibid., no. 178).

In choosing psalms (which are distributed over a four-week period) attention is paid to the mystery of the feast or special season, so that the psalmody and accompanying antiphons may take on a special tonality and give insight into the mystery being celebrated.[19] Following the example of Christ (cf., e.g., Lk 24.44; Mt 22.42-45), the Fathers of the Church

> saw the whole psalter as a prophecy of Christ and the
> Church and explained it in this sense; for the same reason
> the psalms have been chosen for use in the sacred liturgy.
> Though somewhat tortuous interpretations were at times
> proposed, yet, in general, the Fathers, and the liturgy itself,
> could legitimately hear in the singing of the psalms the
> voice of Christ crying out to the Father, or of the Father
> conversing with the Son; indeed, they also recognized in
> the psalms the voice of the Church, the apostles, and the
> martyrs (GILH, no. 109).[20]

The new Liturgy of the Hours facilitates such a christological interpretation of the psalms by giving each psalm a title which is meant "to explain its meaning and its human value for the life of faith" (GILH, no. 111) and by adding "a sentence from the New Testament or the Fathers of the Church" which "invites one to pray the psalms in their christological meaning" (ibid.).

It is chiefly the antiphons that give the psalms and canticles an "individual quality" that varies with occasion and feast and contributes much to an understanding of the feast being celebrated (GILH, no. 113). This is because the antiphons are chosen or composed with the festal mystery in mind. During the Easter season alleluia is regularly added to the antiphons.

The readings from scripture and the Fathers also pay special heed to the character of the individual feasts and special seasons.[21] In particular, the short readings in the individual hours present in a striking way important thoughts of the feasts and seasons of the liturgical year (GILH, nos. 156–58; cf. also no. 451).

The responsories after the readings and short readings, as well as the verses in the little hours, reflect on and penetrate more deeply into the message of the reading. They too, therefore, bear the stamp of the festal mystery being celebrated.

The invocations at Morning Prayer and the intercessions at Evening Prayer (both are called *preces*, "prayers") are likewise inspired by the festal mystery and are constantly changing. The same holds for the concluding prayer which asks in ever new ways that we may participate in the fruits of redemption and may embody the festal message in our Christian lives.

The Liturgy of the Hours thus has its fixed place in the cosmos that is the liturgical year, and nothing can substitute for it. It opens up the treasures of Christ's saving work to us. If we approach it with the eyes of faith and pray it in the love and joy of the Holy Spirit, it will accompany us through the liturgical year, bringing happiness, consolation and strength.

Notes

1. Cf. Rom 12.12; Eph 5.19-20; 6.18; Col 3.16-17; 4.2; 1 Thess 5.17; Heb 13.15.

2. J. A. Jungmann, "Die vormonastische Morgenhore," in idem (ed.), *Brevierstudien. Referate auf der Studientagung von Assisi 14.-17. September 1956* (Trier, 1958), p. 22.

3. *De oratione* 25, 5 (CCL 1:272-73).

4. *Traditio apostolica* 39; 41 (ed. Botte, pp. 86 ff.).

5. VIII, 35, 2–37, 7 (ed. Funk 1:544-46). Cf. P. Salmon, "La prière des heures," in Martimort, p. 795.

6. A. Raes, an expert on the Eastern liturgies, reports that even in our time the Chaldaeans in the villages of Iraq assemble daily, morning and evening, in the church to pray matins and vespers with the priest: "The old idea has survived here in its original form": "Streiflichter auf das Brevier in den orientalischen Riten," in Jungmann (ed.), *Brevierstudien*, p. 122.

7. E. J. Lengeling, "Liturgia horarum. Zur Neuordung des kirchlichen Stundengebetes," LJ 20 (1970), 146, n. 22; S. Bäumer, *Geschichte des Breviers* (Freiburg, 1895), pp. 579–602, allows validity to both interpretations.

8. The *Constitution on the Liturgy* speaks only of the "divine office," but the documents which introduce the new Latin breviary (Decree of the Sacred Congregation for Divine Worship, Apostolic Constitution *Laudis canticum* of Paul VI, and the General Instruction of the Liturgy of the Hours) prefer to speak of "the Liturgy of the Hours."

9. Cf. Bäumer, op. cit., pp. 592-95.

10. Righetti 2:552.

11. Details in Lengeling, art. cit., pp. 142-43.

12. There is a good introduction to the comprehensive preparatory work in Lengeling, art. cit., pp. 143-44.

13. *Enarrationes in Psalmos* 85, 1 (CCL 39:1176).

14. Even the Code of Rubrics of 1960 said it was better "to pray each canonical hour at its proper time, as far as possible" (no. 142). But the rubrics also held to the principle that the obligation to pray all the hours extends to the entire twenty-four hour period; this meant that if a man did not have time to pray the morning hours in the morning he must get them in before the day was over (no. 143). The Code also allowed matins, but not lauds, to be anticipated on the previous afternoon (no. 144).

15. Thus, e.g., H. Noldin, *Summa theologiae moralis* 2 (Innsbruck, 1911⁹), p. 792.

16. Contrary to the original plan, which was to provide two cycles of readings in the breviary itself. Cf. Lengeling, art. cit., pp. 238-40, for an explanation of why the plan was changed.

17. Cf. *Didache* 8, 3 (Bihlmeyer, p. 5).

18. Valuable helps for praying the new Office are given in *Beten mit der Kirche*, published by the Secretariat of the German Episcopal Conference (Regensburg, 1978).

19. In his little book *Sinngerechtes Brevierbeten* (Munich, 1962), pp. 45-65, J. Pascher shows how this is true of the psalms for Christmas.

20. GILH, no. 109; cf. B. Fischer, *Die Psalmenfrömmigkeit der Märtyrerkirche* (Freiburg, 1949).

21. GILH, nos. 143–55 has further details on the cycle of readings for the Office of Readings.

Excursus: The Problem of a Perpetual Calendar

Our present annual calendar (also known as the Gregorian calendar ever since its reform under Pope Gregory XIII [1572–85] in 1582) has been under criticism for some time, and the criticism has led to many plans for reform. The fact that the League of Nations, the United Nations and the Second Vatican Council, among others, have dealt with the question is enough to underscore the importance of the problem.

The chief complaints about the present calendar have to do with the unequal length of the months, the mobility of many feasts, and annual shift of the dates of the month to new days of the week. The reason for these various phenomena, as everyone knows, is that a normal year has one day more than fifty-two weeks. What is desired is an annual calendar that has symmetrical divisions, is clearly structured, and is less changeable, so that we may more easily survey the year ahead and plan for the future. The question of the movable date of Easter may be left out of consideration here since I have already dealt with it in an earlier chapter (Chapter V, 1).

Before I explain and comment on the various proposals for reform, let me first sketch briefly the history of our present calendar.

1 / THE HISTORY OF OUR ANNUAL CALENDAR

The Gregorian calendar is based, in the last analysis, on the calendar reform which Gaius Julius Caesar instituted in 46 BC and which went into effect on January 1 of the year 45. The old calendar familiar to Caesar can be described as lunisolar. It had twelve months of varying lengths that yielded 355 days in all. In order to adjust this year, which was much too short, intercalary months were provided, but because these were employed in a confused manner, they could not prevent the year from varying significantly in length from the solar year. Thus at the beginning of the Gallic War (56 BC) and again in the following year "the new calendar suddenly went into effect a month ahead of time. The year 54 began in November, the year 53 probably in December. It is clear that an orderly administration of the state could not be satisfied with such an uncertain calendar as this."[1]

Caesar decided that a radical reform was needed. A new calendar was produced for him by Sosigenes, an astronomer from Alexandria, who was able to make use of the ancient calendar of the Pharaohs. In 46 BC (= 708 *ab Urbe condita*, "from the foundation of the City" of Rome in 753 BC = Varronian Era), in addition to the regular intercalary month two further months were added; as a result the year was 445 days long and later became known as the *Annus confusionis*, "Year of Confusion." From 45 on, every year was to have 365 days, which is to say that it was to be a solar year. Every fourth year would have one extra day, which would be introduced after February 28, the day after which the old intercalary month had previously been inserted. In the Roman method of calculation, February 24 was the "sixth day before the kalends of March" (= *dies sextilis*, "sixth day");

the intercalated day therefore became known as *dies bissextilis* (a "double sixer") and the year with the extra day became known as *annus bissextilis*, a description that has survived in French, where a leap year is an *année bissextile*.

In this new system the average length of a year was 365.25 days. This is an approximation to the exact length of the tropical year, which is 365.2422 days; the calendar year is thus 11.25 minutes too long and falls behind the solar year. For the sake of completeness let me note that Caesar's rule for intercalation was misunderstood and misapplied until Emperor Augustus introduced the needed correction in 9 BC.[2]

As part of the Julian calendar reform the beginning of the year was shifted from March 1 to January 1. There is evidence that the consular term of office had begun on this latter day ever since 153 BC. The old start of the year in March explains the names we still give today to certain months, such as September (seventh), October (eighth), November (ninth) and December (tenth). The old names for July and August were Quintilis (fifth) and Sextilis (sixth), until they were renamed to honor the two reformers of the calendar, Julius Caesar and Augustus Caesar. In regard to the length of the months, Caesar followed the older system, but only partially; in that system March, May, July and October had 31 days, February 28, and the other months 29.

In the early Middle Ages it was already becoming clear that the calendar year and the solar year were not in harmony. Yet the Council of Trent was the first body to call for the formation of a commission to deal with the calendar; Pope Gregory XIII appointed such a commission in 1576. With the help of a large gnomon (a shaft that casts a shadow) in a church at Bologna it was determined that the spring equinox had already occurred on March 11. It was therefore decided to skip ten days and so bring the calendar year into step with the solar year. The Bull *Inter gravissimas* of February 24, 1582, accordingly ordered that October 4, 1582 should be immediately followed by October 15.

In order then to maintain the accord of calendar year and solar year it was decided that only those centurial years which are divisible by 400 should be leap years. The difference between calendar year and solar year that still remains will increase to a full day only around the year 4500. In order to lessen the discrepancy still further, the astronomers have developed increasingly precise rules. As a result, the Panorthodox Congress of Istanbul in 1923 decided that while accepting the Gregorian calendar it would also adopt the rule for intercalation that was developed by the Jugoslav Milankovich; according to this rule there would be two centurial leap years every 900 years (e.g., 2000, 2400, 2900). The Belgian astronomer Warzée achieves even greater precision by making only every fifth centurial year a leap year; if this is done, it will take 30,000 years for calendar year and solar year to differ by a day.[3]

The Gregorian calendar, although it is basically the Julian calendar, was accepted only hesitantly by non-Catholic countries. The last to accept it were Russia in 1918 and the Panorthodox Congress of Istanbul in 1923; even then, the last-named rejected the rule for intercalation as applied to centurial years and also made an exception for the date of Easter, which is to be calculated according to the Julian calendar. It is worth noting that even despite these reservations the action of the Congress led to division within the Greek Orthodox Church. The *Palaioemerologitai* (Old Calendarists), chiefly monks of Mount Athos, still reject the Gregorian calendar and follow the Julian. The same is true of some autocephalous Orthodox Churches and Eastern rites, although the Gregorian calendar is observed in civic life.

2 / EXPERIMENTS AND PLANS FOR CALENDAR REFORM

If we consider that between 1923 and 1937 about 200 plans for reform were presented to the League of Nations' calendar commission, we will immediately see that in this excursus I cannot explain every plan. I shall look only at the most important and, where possible, group them.

a/The Calendar of the French Revolution

The first attempt at a reform goes back to the French Revolution. With the intention of breaking radically from all tradition, Romme, a mathematician, devised a calendar which divided the year into four equal quarters, each having three months of

30 days, or 360 days in all. The remaining five days of a normal year were to be *jours complémentaires* (extra days), while the added extra day in leap year would be the *jour de la Révolution* (Revolution Day). These extra days were to be holidays.

The twelve months were given new names which reflected the special character or activities of each season. The seven-day week was replaced by three decades in each month, and the names of these new days were taken from the corresponding ordinal number (Primedi, Duodi, Triadi . . . Décadi). Décadi was to be a day of rest. Even the traditional divisions of each day were abolished: from midnight to midnight a day now had ten hours, and each hour was in turn subdivided into ten parts. The new calendar

> was put into effect by laws of October 5 and November 24, 1793, but was retroactive to September 22, 1792. Previously, with the taking of the Bastille on July 14, 1789, as the starting point, the years had been numbered as Years of Liberty; thus January 1, 1792, began Year IV of Liberty. As early as April 8, 1802 (= Germinal 18, Year X [of Equality or of the Republic]) the revolutionary calendar was partially abrogated by the reinstitution of the old division of the week. Finally, an edict of Napoleon effective January 1, 1806 (= Nivôse 11, Year XIV) restored the Gregorian calendar.[4]

b/The "Perpetual Gregorian Calendar" and the "World Calendar"

One of the most remarkable and, at the same time, one of the oldest plans for calendar reform was the work of an Italian priest, Marco Mastrofini. In 1834, at Rome, he published a book, with an Imprimatur, in which he proposed that the year should continue to have 52 weeks but that the 365th day should be a nonhebdomadal day after the end of December. In a leap year the 366th day would likewise become a day outside any week or month and would be inserted before January 1.[5]

In this plan every year would begin on the same day of the week, and each saint's feast would fall on the same day of the week every year. If Easter were assigned to a set Sunday at the end of March or the beginning of April, the often bemoaned movability of the feasts and seasons that depend on Easter would be eliminated. The chief justification Mastrofini offered for his reform plan was that from both the religious and the secular standpoints the year would become a much more manageable entity.[6]

Later on, Mastrofini's proposals were further developed so that the year would have four equal quarters, each having three months of 31, 30 and 30 days respectively; in other words, each quarter would have 91 days or 13 weeks. Each quarter would begin on a Sunday and end on a Saturday. The corresponding days of each quarter would therefore always occur on the same day of the week; e.g., the first day of January, April, July and October would always be a Sunday, the first of February, May, August and November always a Wednesday. The first month of each quarter being 31 days long, that month would have five Sundays, the other months four, and the number of weekdays in each month would be the same. The 365th day of a normal year would be outside the weeks and months and placed after December 30, while the 366th day in a leap year would be intercalated after June 30. It has been suggested that these intercalary days —also called "white days" or "null days"—be declared worldwide holidays.

Since 1930 the World Calendar Association, founded in New York, has been promoting Mastrofini's plan (in the developed form which I have just described) as a "World Calendar."[7] It has found many supporters, both in religious circles and among politicians and scientists. In 1953 India petitioned the Economic and Social Council of the United Nations for the introduction of this calendar. However, statements from various nations, religious communities, and organizations made it clear that the "white days" would meet with strong resistance, especially from Jews, Mohammedans and some Christian communities. As a result, the question of calendar reform was indefinitely tabled in 1956.

The Old Testament contains a kind of precursor of the World Calendar. After the exile many groups followed a perpetual calendar of 52 weeks (364 days; the months of each quarter of the year had 30, 30 and 31 days respectively; the weekdays fell on the same dates in each quarter.[8]

In connection with the World Calendar I may mention the work of W. Dietze and W. A. Kral who have introduced some variations into this calendar and have sought approval of it among the general public.[9]

c/The Thirteen-Month Calendar

Back in 1849 Auguste Comte, the French philosopher and sociologist, proposed to divide the year into 13 months of four weeks each, with the first day of each month being a Monday and the last a Sunday. The 365th day, and the 366th in leap year, would not belong to any week or month. Comte's plan was endorsed by the International Positivist Association in 1913 and found many supporters, especially in the United States (George Eastman, for example). In 1937 the League of Nations became interested in the plan, but it found little acceptance from the states and religious communities that were approached. It was rightly pointed out that at present the two solstices and the two equinoxes divide the year into four natural parts, i.e., the four seasons, but that if there were thirteen months this natural division would be obscured and obstructed.

d/A Calendar with Intercalary Weeks

Because "white days" met with the objection that they destroyed the uninterrupted rhythm of the seven-day week, it was proposed at the beginning of the present century that the 365th day of the year, and the 366th in leap year, be simply omitted until they added up to a week, which would then be added to a year. All years would then consist of complete weeks; a normal year would have 364 days, and a year with an intercalary week would have 371 days.

Various proponents added many variations to the basic plan. In one such variant each quarter of the year would have one month of 35 days and two of 28, so that like the year each month would also consist of only complete weeks. Other proponents were ready to accept the monthly system of the World Calendar (31, 30 and 30 days respectively in the three months of each quarter). Various rules were elaborated for the recurrence of the year with the extra week; some suggested a 28-year cycle, with the 6th, 12th, 17th, 23rd and 28th years having an extra week;

others recommended making every year divisible by 7 or 25 a onger year, with the exception of any year divisible by both 7 and 25 (i.e., every 175th year).[10]

Such a system would certainly avoid "white days," but it gives rise to other difficulties. The year would vary from 364 to 371 days, and yet the revolution of the earth around the sun is the natural, pregiven measure of time. Nor would there any longer be fixed dates for the equinoxes and solstices.

e/Calendar Reform in Small Stages

In view of the reservations and protests with which all reform plans meet, many authors believe we should be satisfied to advance in small stages so as not to disrupt unduly the unity thus far achieved. Thus L. Meesen, a Benedictine, suggests making the months more equal in length by taking a day each from January and March and adding them to February. The extra day every fourth year should be put at midyear and observed as June 31, so that it would not continue to complicate still further the calculation of the date of Easter. Finally, he accepts the rules for intercalation with regard to centurial years that have been proposed by J. Warzée.[11]

Such moderate proposals certainly have more hope of proximate success than do the others I have described which are more far-reaching.

3 / A COMMENT ON THE EFFORTS AT REFORM

Although the movements of the earth and the moon, which are the astronomical basis of our measurement of time, take place with clockwork precision, human beings have not yet succeeded in discovering a temporal division of the year that matches these movements perfectly. This is true of lunar systems as well as of lunisolar systems. The tropical solar year can be divided into seven-day weeks only if one nonhebdomadal day is added, or, in leap year, two. This is the price that must be paid for the perpetual calendar which would certainly be advantageous in many areas of life and is therefore regarded as a necessity by many.

Nonhebdomadal days represent, however, a break with the Christian, Jewish and Islamic traditions and are therefore regarded as a scandalous novelty. Not a few people see them as an attack on traditional faith and a capitulation to the commercial and materialistic spirit of the age. In their view, the perpetual calendar (World Calendar) is "the calendar of a robot, of depersonalized, manipulable, calculable mass-man."[12]

> There can be no doubt that the outlook behind most plans for a perpetual calendar derives from a one-sided or intellectualist utilitarian approach to reality. The proponents of these plans may have the best of intentions. In my opinion, however, I have shown that a perpetual calendar can do incalculable harm, since it is not consonant with the reality of the human person as a spiritual being or with the overall pattern of laws governing the universe. It does not in any way reflect the irrational element in human life or the incommensurable element in the working of the universe.[13]

Peter Brunner, an Evangelical theologian, sees nonhebdomadal days as bringing not only "a certain stereotyped monotony" but also "the destruction of the week, which plans for calendar reform necessarily entail," because "I have radically destroyed the week itself when I abandon it as a unit at even a single point in the course of a year." Brunner sees nonhebdomadal days as a departure that militates against Sunday. "We are in a position today to appreciate better than earlier generations did the importance of the weekly anamnesis of the resurrection of Christ. Have we any right, then, to agree to the destruction of this living memorial of the basic fact of salvation in which we believe?"[14]

Others think that at the present time the human race has more urgent problems to solve and should not get itself involved in a cosmetic operation on a calendar that is thousands of years old. Even with the traditional calendar undreamt-of economic advances and material prosperity have been achieved in many countries. A perpetual calendar will not feed a single starving person nor bring any international conflict even a step nearer to a peaceful solution.

Given these and similar objections and emotional reactions, there is need to weigh the arguments calmly and objectively. First of all, I must point out that in a perpetual calendar of the World Calendar type the seven-day week is not destroyed but on the contrary protected, in its substance, against the dangers that threaten from achristian divisions of time. A nonhebdomadal day introduced at the end of the year in order to bring the year into full harmony with the naturally determined unit of time that is a revolution of the earth around the sun, does not in principle affect the structure of the week and its value for a meaningful alternation of work, rest and worship. All that a nonhebdomadal day does is make it clear that as a unit for measuring time the year is of higher rank than the week; that the year is already determined by the order of creation itself, while the week as a temporal unit is of historical origin and must be subordinate to the year.[15]

The early Christian community did not hesitate to abandon the sabbath and, while retaining the seven-day cycle, to make Sunday, as the day of the resurrection, the sacred day of assembly for worship. Much less was there any hesitation about abandoning the Old Testament laws regarding the sabbatical year or year of redemption (every seventh year) and the jubilee year (every fiftieth year), even though these prescriptions, like those regarding the sabbath and the week, were regarded as given by God himself. Finally, I must mention the abandonment of the Old Testament month (the synodic month). In our present solar time-order the phases of the moon no longer play any role, even though we continue to use the word "month" (which is derived from "moon"). Much less does any Christian Church feel bound any longer by the law of sacrifice at the new moon, though this precept again was regarded as originating in God himself.[16]

In view of these facts and relationships we cannot say that people are violating a still valid divine command when they suggest observing the 365th day of the year as a nonhebdomadal day, in order that the new solar year may begin on the first day of the week. The removal of this one day of the year from any weekly cycle is fully in accord with the subordinate role of the week as a means of subdividing a preexisting unity of time (the year). To seek the best possible division of time is certainly not to go beyond the competence of human beings; it is rather an exercise of that right of domination which the Bible tells us God has given to the human race (Gen 1.28).

Anyone who says we should not unnecessarily tackle a delicate problem or risk burning our fingers without reason is over-looking a serious danger. The human race is developing into, and increasingly experiencing itself as, a single great family of peoples, whose members are indeed not homogeneous nor intimate with one another but, from an organizational standpoint, are at least living under the single roof that is provided by the United Nations Organization. Yet, as far as religion and vision of life are concerned, this human race will be, in the future as in the past, a pluralistic and in large measure secularized society. The peoples of the world will be increasingly thrown together in life and work, and this state of affairs will require some minimum of common approaches to reality. Among the latter must be a shared method of reckoning time, one which all peoples, including those who are not Christian, can accept because it is rationally structured and economically useful.

In order to achieve this common approach to time, the Christians Churches (and the same holds for the Jewish and Islamic religious communities) must make concessions which, on the one hand, are not a violation of a valid divine commandment and, on the other, are required for the sake of an optimal calculation of time. A nonhebdomadal holiday after the last day of December seems one such concession. Those who remain inflexible on this point run the risk of seeing (perhaps quite soon) the majority of nations adopting a calendar which is utterly alien to tradition and inimical to Christianity and in which no heed at all will be given to the seven-day week.

The Second Vatican Council was not blind to this danger. It certainly recognized its obligation to tradition and therefore wished to retain unbroken the sequence of seven-day weeks. Nonetheless it expressed a readiness to change its position if great difficulties should arise. As Archbishop Corrado Bafile put it at the 17th general meeting of the first session, the Council would not shut the door in principle to the adoption of a world calendar.[17] This is why the Council, in an Appendix to the *Constitution on the Liturgy*, makes the following statement on the question of a perpetual calendar:

> The sacred Council likewise declares that it does not oppose efforts designed to introduce a perpetual calendar into civil society. But among the various systems which are being devised with a view to establishing a perpetual calendar and introducing it into civil life, those and only those are unopposed by the Church which retain and safeguard a seven-day week, with Sunday, without the introduction of any days outside the week, so that the succession of weeks is left intact, unless in the judgment of the Apostolic See there are extremely weighty reasons to the contrary (CL, Appendix; Flannery, p. 37).

As the Catholic Church of today—unlike the Church at the time of the calendar reform of 1582—is well aware, no single Church has the right to take any cavalier step that will only lead to new divisions within Christianity and new tensions with other theistic groups. The end result must be an improvement; any new division or tension can only be an evil.

The need today is for ongoing dialogue with the various religious and national groups in an effort to reach the best possible solution. The goal must be a calendar which all communities can accept, with full freedom, as better for the common good of the entire race. And while committees of leaders do their work, a readiness for calendar reform must be cultivated in the masses. Only if this last-named condition is met will calendar reform be accomplished in an effective and lasting way. We can only hope that these various needs are recognized and that there is still time enough for the task. Otherwise historians of Christianity will once again have to rewrite their chapter on lost opportunities.

Notes

1. H. Schneller, "Wie unser Kalender entstand," in *Kalender für Sternfreunde 1952*, p. 113.

2. Ibid., pp. 113-14.

3. Cf. L. Meesen, "Oecuménisme et réforme du calendrier," MD, no. 81 (1965), 115 ff. M. Lang has also adopted this suggestion, especially in view of the steady shortening of the year (Newcomb's Theory); cf. the notice in *Anzeiger der Österreichischen Akademie der Wissenschaften, Mathematischwissenschaftlichen Klasse*, 1964, no. 4, pp. 104-5.

4. H. Litzmann, *Zeitrechnung der römischen Kaiserzeit, des Mittelalters und der Neuzeit für die Jahre 1-2000 nach Christus*, 3rd ed., revised by K. Aland (Sammlung Göschen 1885; Berlin, 1956), p. 83.

5. *Amplissimi frutti da recogersi ancora sul calendario Gregoriano perpetuo.*

6. In his preface, p. vi; cf. I. Pizzoni, "De reformatione calendarii," EL 65 (1950), 368 ff.

7. A cofounder and, for a time, president of the World Calendar Association was Elizabeth Achelis, a German-American born in Bremen. One of her last publications was *The Calendar for the Modern Age* (New York, 1959).

8. Details in, e.g., A. Jaubert, *La date de la Cène* (Paris, 1957); some details also in Maertens, op. cit., pp. 115-21.

9. W. Dietze, *Kalenderreform. Dringende Forderung der Gegenwart* (Barmke, n.d.); W. A. Kral, *Memorandum "Kalenderreform." Denkschrift für die Arbeiten zu einer Reformierung des gegenwärtig benützten Kalendersystems nach dem Reformvorschlag von W. Dietze* (Heidelberg–Barmke, 1969).

10. Since this excursus is meant only as a concise introductory guide to the subject, I do not intend to give references for all the variant proposals. The reader may consult, among others, Abbé Chauve-Bertrand, *La question des Pâques et du calendrier* (Paris, 1936); W. Röhrig, "Der Kalender als kosmische Einheit," *Stimmen der Zeit* 143 (1948–49), 433–41; A. Veys, "La question du calendrier. Son état actuel," *Questions liturgigues et paroissiales* 36 (1955), 245-49; O. Stevens, "Gedanken zur Kalenderreform," EL 76 (1962), 418-22.

11. Meesen, art. cit., pp. 107-26.

12. W. Bühler, *Der bewegliche Osterfest. Kalenderreform und Osterdatum als Problem des Rhythmus* (Tübingen, 1965), p. 131.

13. Ibid., p. 137. For a comment on the question, cf. A. Adam, "Fragen der Kalenderreform," TTZ 75 (1966), 167-68.

14. "Adiaphoron–Symbolon," *Lutherische Rundschau* 5 (1956), 434-41, at pp. 435, 436, and 441.

15. On the origin of the week cf. pp. 7-8.

16. Num 28.11-15. In v. 1 this command is expressly said to be a command of God to Moses. The author of sacred scripture regards God as

in principle the "first cause" of all reality and therefore as source of Israel's social order and ceremonial laws, although in these areas human and historical factors were also at work, so that these precepts seem conditioned by culture and historical period, as is clear from, e.g., the regulations governing sacrifice.

17. *Acta synodalia Concilii Vaticani Secundi*, vol. I, Periodus I, pars 2 (Vatican City, 1970), p. 596.

INDEX

Bernard of Clairvaux, 174, 213
Bernardine of Siena, 140, 230
Bernold, 193
Bertsch, L., 55
Berulle, P. de, 174
Bihlmeyer, K., 54, 56
Blankenberg, W., 32
Blinzler, J., 114, 269
Bollandists, 267
Bonaventure, 174, 221
Boniface IV, 228
Botte, B., 33, 119
Breviary. See Hours, Book of
Browe, P., 193, 194
Brunner, P., 297
Bühler, W., 301
Bugnini, A., 193, 267

Caesar, 28, 139, 290f.
Caesarius of Arles, 146
Calendar, 2, 290ff.
Calixtus I, 187
Calixtus III, 181
Candles, blessing of, 150f.
Candles, procession with, 150f.
Canonization of saints, 207
Carmel, Our Lady of, 219
Casel, O., 21-22, 63, 89, 114, 115,
   116
Cassian, 117
Cathedral church, 185
Cavalieri, P. F. de, 54
Cecilia, 224
Chair of Peter, 241
Charlemagne, 132
Charles Borromeo, 269
Chauve-Bertrand, A., 301
Chavasse, A., 118
Chrismal Mass, 112
Christ the King, 147, 177ff.
Christmas, 121ff.
Church history, 26
Circumcision of the Lord, 140
Clement V, 170
Clement IX, 248
Clement X, 248
Clement XI, 213, 221

Clement XII, 184
Clement XIII, 50, 175
Clement of Alexandria, 144
Code of Canon Law, 45
Code of Rubrics, 27
Comes of Würzburg, 160, 215
Comites Christi, 141
Comte, A., 295
Confirmation, 82
Constantine, 44, 235
Corpus Christi, 169ff.
Corpus Christi procession, 172f.
Cox, H., 32
Croce, W., 133, 155
Cross, Exaltation of, 181f.
Cross, Veneration of, 71, 74
Cyprian, 97, 268
Cyril of Jerusalem, 85, 117

Daniel-Rops, H., 17
Day, 1
Dedication of a church, 183ff.
Delahaye, H., 267
Devotio moderna, 174
Devotion feasts. See Idea-Feasts
Didache, 38, 52
Didascalia, 38, 52
Dietze, W., 295, 301
Diocesan calendar, 262f.
Dionysius of Alexandria, 91
Dölger, F., 54, 55, 116
Dominica vacans, 187
Dominicum, 38
Duchesne, L., 154, 157, 188
Dürig, W., 32, 156, 194, 268
Dumaine, H., 54
Duns Scotus, 213
Durandus, William, 106, 115

Easter, 24, 57ff.
Easter candle, 78f., 85f.
Easter, date of, 57ff., 293-294
Easter fire, 77-78
Easter octave, 85
Easter penitential period. See
   Lent
Easter season, 84

303

307